Published by Black Sparrow Press:

CHARLES OLSON & ROBERT CREELEY

Charles Olson & Robert Creeley: The Complete Correspondence
Volume 1 & 2 (1980)
Charles Olson & Robert Creeley: The Complete Correspondence
Volume 3 (1981)
Charles Olson & Robert Creeley: The Complete Correspondence
Volume 4 (1982)
Charles Olson & Robert Creeley: The Complete Correspondence
Volume 5 (1983)
Charles Olson & Robert Creeley: The Complete Correspondence
Volume 6 (1985)
Charles Olson & Robert Creeley: The Complete Correspondence
Volume 7 & 8 (1987)
Charles Olson & Robert Creeley: The Complete Correspondence
Volume 9 (1990)
Charles Olson & Robert Creeley: The Complete Correspondence
Volume 10 (1996)

CHARLES OLSON

A Nation of Nothing But Poetry: Supplementary Poems (1989)

CHARLES OLSON & ROBERT CREELEY:

THE COMPLETE CORRESPONDENCE

VOLUME 10

EDITED BY RICHARD BLEVINS

❧

BLACK SPARROW PRESS
SANTA ROSA ᔧ **1996**

ACKNOWLEDGMENTS

The originals of these letters, housed in the collections of the University of Connecticut Library, Storrs and Stanford University, are printed here with those libraries' kind cooperation. The passage quoted from George F. Butterick's unpublished essay appears by permission of the Poetry/Rare Books Collection, SUNY-Buffalo. Grateful acknowledgment must continue to be made to Donald Allen, who, at the start of this project, provided George F. Butterick with transcripts of many of Charles Olson's letters. The editor also extends his thanks to Kevin Ray, curator of manuscripts at Washington University, St. Louis, who made me welcome and provided copies of letters and photographs from Robert Creeley's papers before they found a permanent home at Stanford University; to Richard H. Schimmelpfeng, retired director of special collections, and Richard C. Fyffe, curator of literary and cultural archives, and the staff at the Special Collections Library, University of Connecticut at Storrs; to Robert J. Bertholf, curator at SUNY-Buffalo; to the University of Pittsburgh for the travel grant that helped to fund the research for this volume and to Colette Levin for her translations from French; to James R. Lowell, proprietor of Asphodel Book Shop, Burton, Ohio; to Robert Creeley, Gerrit Lansing, the late Joel Oppenheimer, Ralph Maud; to the late Sherman Paul, for his criticism of a draft of the introduction, and for his example; to Willard "Skip" Fox, who tracked down maverick correspondence in the archives at Storrs and St. Louis; to my research assistant Beth Shabel; to Bonnie Chambers and Douglas Blevins, who helped read the proofs; to Michele Filshie, who ably coordinated this book at Black Sparrow; to John Martin, for his continued faith in monumental projects; but especially to my editor, Seamus Cooney, for his clear-headed close readings of the manuscript and all his continued support.

Black Sparrow Press books are printed on acid-free paper.

LIBRARY OF CONGRESS CATALOGING-IN-PUBLICATION DATA
(Revised for volume 10)

Olson, Charles, 1910–1970.
    Charles Olson & Robert Creeley : the complete correspondence.
    Vol. 10 — edited by Richard Blevins.
    Includes bibliographical references and indexes.
    1. Olson, Charles, 1910–1970 — Correspondence.
    2. Creeley, Robert, 1926–   — Correspondence.
    3. Poets, American — 20th century — Correspondence.
    I. Creeley, Robert, 1926–   .   II. Butterick, George F.   III. Blevins, Richard.
    IV. Title: Charles Olson and Robert Creeley.
    PS3529.L655Z544   811'.54   80-12222
    ISBN 0-87685-400-5 (cloth trade: v. 1)
    ISBN 0-87685-399-8 (pbk.: v. 1)
    ISBN 1-57423-005-0 (cloth trade: v. 10)
    ISBN 1-57423-006-9 (signed: v. 10)
    ISBN 1-57423-004-2 (pbk.: v. 10)

TABLE OF CONTENTS

Editor's Introduction

This volume, its letters beginning the third year of the correspondence, opens *allegretto scherzando*. Both poets are on the move, their lives still in flux. The Creeleys, Ann pregnant, move household and two children from Fontrousse to Lambesc. Amidst his new surroundings, he writes for the first time to Martin Seymour-Smith—as if already anticipating his next move, to Mallorca, and the life in letters he will begin to fashion for himself there as editor of Roebuck and Divers presses. Creeley's June 20th letter to Olson is especially rich in portent: we read there of the beginnings of the still unnamed *Black Mountain Review*, and of *Le Fou*, Creeley's first book of poems. For now, Mallorca and the publications that will begin to bring the names of Olson and Creeley to a wider reading public exist only in the undreamed of future and, despite his relocation, Creeley at 27 remains isolated in Provence. By June 17, 1952, he would write Olson: "One sees a lot of funerals here."

The profound changes in the 42-year-old Olson's life, revealed only begrudgingly over the course of his letters to Creeley in this and the next volume, seem even more fateful, less willed. Indeed, in his May 20th letter, Olson is moved to declare a Melvillean sense of the tragedy of individual freedom: "... we are *separate* from all things ... *except* in our acts / and ... this is freedom," while "fixed fate itself is no single pattern but is the pattern any man imposes ... and ... the limits of his freedom are only the limits of his willingness to acknowledge force...." Nevertheless, Olson swears, in his best Ahab manner: "... i will not be intimidated by any assumptive pattern, even the most pressing dream, let alone any agent or expression of force outside myself...." Years later, in 1967, Creeley would recall that "it is really Charles Olson I must thank for whatever *freedom* I have as a poet.... *Freedom* has always been for me a difficult experience in that, when younger, I felt it had to propose senses of experience and of the world I was necessarily *not* in possession of—something in that way one might escape to ... I ... was slow in realizing the nature of Olson's proposal, that 'Limits / are what any of us / are inside of' ..." (*The Collected Essays of Robert Creeley*, Berkeley and Los Angeles, 1989, p. 503).

And still Olson drifts, during the period, on busses and trains between Black Mountain and Washington, D.C. Even the award of money from the Wenner-Gren Foundation for Anthropological Research unsettles Olson. The $2,500 grant can be spent exclusively for the field study of Mayan glyphs in Mexico and Guatemala, but Olson tells Creeley that he wishes only the kind of isolation which nurtures the creative mind, presumably within the Washington apartment on Randolph Place NE he has kept over the years. George Butterick has noted that it is during these weeks that Olson, "for the first time … begins to see Black Mountain as his fate, his role and responsibility, talking of it (in a [May 22nd] letter to Creeley) as 'Olson's University.' Nevertheless, he spends the fall of 1952 in Washington, still preferring that as his 'base,' from which he could return [to the college] periodically in 'Chinese' fashion"* ("Charles Olson and the Black Mountain Poets," unpbd. MS.). A reader today may find himself urging the correspondents to switch identities: exchange Robert Creeley, who is all too alone in Europe and longing to act on Olson's offer of a teaching job at Black Mountain College (he actually sends Olson a reading list for a dream course in narrative prose, though he has never taught a course), for Charles Olson, who continues to teach at the college but dreams alternately of a leave of absence and a new curriculum. Olson has yet to confide to his correspondent the most immediate source of his unrest. In October, he and Constance end their common-law marriage.** She stays on at Black Mountain as its registrar and he resumes residence in Washington, on leave from teaching. The couple had met in May 1940.

The sometimes conflicting private moods of the two literary collaborators are dramatically played out in a flare-up in the letters, beginning in this volume with Creeley's May 27th response, over a forgettable four-line poem, "For Us," which Olson had included in his May 22nd letter. The poem would be difficult to identify as Olson's effort, if we did not know the authorship; the quatrain is determinedly sentimental, divided as it is into two homely couplets, the first expressing the poet's gratitude toward his parents and the second asking aloud that his seven-month-old daughter Katherine Mary "be able one day to feel

---

*Olson, after Robert Payne, on "the base of instruction in China for 3000 years": "the scholar lives in the imperial city, does his work, and, once a month, tells the children what he has found out" (I.28).
**Olson breaks this bad news to Creeley in a November 9, 1952 letter to be printed in the next volume of the correspondence.

likewise." In the context of the present volume, Olson's angry defense of his failed poem seems incongruous. However, if the letters are read backward, starting from November 1952, Olson's mood and manner make better sense. For, in retrospect, it becomes clear how some of Creeley's statements, while they may read to us as sage insights into the condition of his own emerging poetry, would have read to a sensitized Olson in the throes of an estrangement from his wife and infant daughter. "... I think that no one can be open," Creeley writes in his letter of May 27th, "... unless there is singleness in him.... It is very close to Lawrence's, his emphasis here, the *non-isolate singleness*, what must be.... In that sense I have no children, and want none." In another mood, on July 4th, he tells Olson: "I don't think I could write 'unmarried.'..." And Creeley's June 29th commentary on what he calls the "dead end" possibilities for a man to sustain "a multiple love" must have read to Olson, in his relationship with Frances Boldereff, as a portent.

As revealing as such documents are, especially since the poets' biographies have only begun to be written, the letters are never without their literary interest as well. Olson writes on May 29th—now from the calm center of the swirl of his marital vortex, an Ishmael who universalizes his plight in a "Grand Armada"—on the treatment of women in the writings of Homer, Rimbaud, D. H. Lawrence, William Carlos Williams, and especially Dostoyevsky. Even when the message gets delayed, both poets *are* communicating lifelong concerns that, in turn, are central preoccupations of their work. Olson's speculations on the limits of freedom demonstrate the maturation of his thought since his essay "Dostoyevsky and the Possessed" appeared in *Twice a Year* (nos. 5/6, 1940–41). And Creeley's understanding of individual experience as art anticipates the credo of selfhood he will write as the Preface to *For Love* (1962): "... we live life as we can, each day another—there is no use in counting. Nor more, say, to live than what there is, to live. I want the poem as close to this fact as I can bring it; or it, me."

Even after nine volumes of the letters, there are discoveries to be made in this installment. The first is announced, appropriately enough, in Olson's reference to the great excavator of Homeric cities, Heinrich Schliemann (letter of May [10th], 1952). Olson's practice, through the earlier volumes, has been to road-test his ideas, often whole essays, in the form of letters to Creeley. But it is a surprise to learn, in the May 10th letter, that Olson's original notes on The Institute in the New

Sciences of Man date from months before what had been long considered his "1st [sic] Draft of Possibilities for THE INSTITUTE OF THE SCIENCES OF MAN" (*OLSON*, 10, Fall 1978, pp. 3–5).

Thanks to Olson's May 29th letter, his interest in dance-drama—a pursuit leading to the early work "Wagadu," which he adapted from Frobenius and staged at Black Mountain, as well as to the better-known plays collected in *The Fiery Hunt*—can now be dated as early as 1936, when Olson attended Asadata Dafora's production of "Kykunkor" in New York City. Olson's reminiscences of the city's music scene of the late 1930s, also recounted in the same letter to Creeley, may be read now in the context of the younger poet's continued references to, and uses of, contemporary jazz.

In my search in the archives, I have often marveled at Creeley's ability, present even so near the beginning of the practice of his craft, to realize his poems (and later a novel, *The Island*) whole—to almost inevitably produce, without rewriting, first drafts that stood as final drafts. When he did "make a mistake" in typing a manuscript, it was his habit to "take the paper out and copy it down to that point, correct the mistake, and then throw the paper away" (*Collected Essays*, pp. 530–31). Creeley's genius, unfortunately for the scholar and student, precludes insight into his methods of composition and the circumstances under which he came to write the poems. However, in two letters, Creeley carefully glosses the creative process of how he arrived at two of his best early poems, "The Festival" (letter of June 17th) and "After Lorca" (June 23rd).

The intense run of poetry writing during the weeks of Volume 9, which brought Creeley to his maturity as a poet, continues into these months. During a sustained period beginning on May 19, 1952, the day he wrote "The Rites," and lasting through the writing of "After Lorca" on June 23rd, Creeley produced four notable poems ("The Question" has not been mentioned), in addition to four poems published here for the first time. This installment also features a review of the Jung and Kerényi *Introduction To A Science of Mythology*, a formative book for the poet.

Olson, for his part, produces no important poetry at this time. (He realizes in his June 4th apology to Creeley: "… i am not making poems of any importance, and it always leaves me weak and irascible.") His work on *The Maximus Poems* has been suspended since 1951, and the next poem, "Letter 3," will not be written until late July. The poems "The Leader" and "The Thing Was Moving," as well as Olson's revision of the earlier "There Are Sounds ... ," are easily the most distinguished; but the slight "For Us" is more representative of his work during these weeks, when he tended to write poetic fragments—the merest phosphenes of his vision—and speculate in prose.

But what stunning prose Olson makes in these letters! His May 5th letter (written to Creeley, but sent first to Cid Corman) is an impassioned attack on the poetry of Wallace Stevens—what Olson calls "the Poetry of Dis-Course"—and a repudiation of Samuel French Morse's essay on Stevens which Corman had printed in *Origin* 5. The letter stands on its own as an early Postmodernist declaration of independence from the Moderns. His letter of May 24th is writ large: in the middle of pages of on-going speculation, continued from earlier letters and essays, concerning the origin of language from Sumerian pictograms to Peruvian quipus and Dakota Indian drawings, Olson writes an essay ("The Attack, Now, In Painting & Writing," previously unpublished) in which he declares that "Cezanne was the last huge painter," and then makes his call, like Emerson for a Whitman, for the still unnamed "men around who, by the nature of a wish for vision and by the care they devote to paint, are ready to push beyond that old perspective confinement and the newer false freedom of the visual surface   who—placed there at that point, that one-dimensional stand that a painter or sculptor or architect is as he stands before any surface as he is also, a man—stands where his audience also will stand—works from that point not for perspective ... but to inform it by the only three-dimension which ever properly mattered, that cultural one ... : that man is round, two eyes, a nose, and a mouth, like any pumpkin or like any man who ever lived and sought—light."

Much of Olson's later thinking on methodology and sequence also dates from his June 15th letter to Creeley. Here he trances the etymology of "methodology" (an act that prefigures "The Methodology Is The Form," an essay written circa July-August 1952 in the style of M. Elath), and acknowledges Boulez's theories of serial composition. The letter is badly water-damaged and survives only in a carbon copy, but its import is clear: "... *methodos*, which turns out to be meta hodos," Olson writes in the letter, "better ... the principle of—PATH   What could be more exactly what we are: method is not the path but it is the way the path is known.... METHODOLOGY is the discipline to express [TOTALITY.]" Olson writes here, as was his habit, directly out of *Webster's Collegiate Dictionary*, 5th edition, and the concept of "meta hodos" he located on page 629 will show up again, in two prose pieces he wrote in 1952. "The methodological question is the primary one, now," he declares in "The Necessary Propositions." "And it can be answered swiftly & concisely. The methodology is the form" (*OLSON*, 8, Fall 1977, p. 44). Elsewhere, Olson uses the etymology of the word to distinguish "methodology" as a projective act. In a manuscript which Olson probably wrote during this period for Mary Fitton, a student at Black Mountain, he explains that the Greek roots for "methodology," *meta* and *hodos*, make "the Traveller ... distinct from what he travels on ... that is, the methodological is an insistence that this distinction is an authoritative one: one travels, but there is something on which one travels distinct from sd Traveller!" ("Note on Methodology," in *OLSON*, 8, p. 43). The new poetics that Olson and Creeley are exploring in these letters reopens the word to experimentation in open forms. Furthermore, in the same June 15th letter to Creeley, Olson is calling for a science of methodology to replace the outmoded myths in the postmodern age: "... when der weg stirbt, long live the methodology ... the science of (-logy, the principal of—PATH[.]" Olson had, after Pound's teaching, adapted the phrase "Der Weg stirbt" from Frobenius' African folktales, and it appears three times in the "Human Universe" essay. Years later, in *The Special View of History* (1970), Olson will explain methodology "as the correct application of the old Western conception of *The Way* and the Eastern conception of *the Tao* (the Way is the path, follow me etc. of Christianity, the 'Law' literally in Judaism, etc.—the 'light,' say. Or, more excitingly for me, the African 'Der Weg,' as in the folk tale in which Der Weg stirbt—dies" (p. 54). It was Creeley who had described the movement in poetry "beyond the achievement of Pound, Williams, et al." in terms of a dilemma of methodology when he wrote, in his 1951 review of Olson's first book of poems, *Y & X*, that "[u]nless we also can find for ourselves a *method* equal to our content, show some comprehension of the difficulties involved, we stay where we are" (*Collected Essays*, p. [97]).

Finally, this installment gives the reader many striking and memorable snapshots of Olson and Creeley. Here is a Creeley who, living in penury in a forgotten village deep inside a culture and a tradition of language that remain alien to him, keeps so in touch with what is new and provocative in the little magazines of the day—*Intro, Points, The Window, trans/formation*, Raymond Souster's *Contact*—that he keeps Olson, who maintains an apartment in the city of The Library of Congress, current. Both writers subscribe to *Contemporary Issues*, and they passionately debate the significance of the authors and ideas they find in its pages. (Olson, in his June letters to Creeley—inspired by new European journals and deeply frustrated by Cid Corman's floundering *Origin*, which remained his chief outlet for poems and essays—begins to dream of a Creeley-edited *Black Mountain Review*.) We find Creeley, before he has published his first book, a tireless champion for the new poems of Larry Eigner, Paul Blackburn, and Seymour-Smith. And we are afforded glimpses of some of the sides Olson presented the world. Here is Olson the sexual athlete: "... the Sunday I hauled those two damnes [*sic*] into each of my arms—& what followed, not fr them but fr their 'men'" (letter of May 6th, and a gloss of his poem "The Morning News," *Collected Poems*, 16). And here is Olson the mystic: "... it happened to me that day, Cambridge, when the sun sank into me and henceforth nature was no longer anything that i did not know because it was in me, not out there" (May 20th letter). Even his cameo of the famous reveals more about himself: Olson "drove Buckminster Fuller out of [his house at Black Mountain] three years ago come summer by saying to that filthiest of all the modern design filthers: 'In what sense does any extrapolation of me beyond my fingernails add a fucking thing to me as a man?'" (letter of May 15th).

In all these ways, then, we have open before us a volume jotted down and pounded out by two very different men, distanced by an ocean. They write the news to each other from stopovers well along the methodological way leading them to and beyond the founding of a new poetry. They are Olson's "distinct Travellers," in advance of the new methodology of seeing for oneself and being in openness. Their paths wind into the future, our present.

Richard Blevins

*This volume is dedicated to the memory
of Sherman Paul (1920–1994), who
wrote for love of the world.*

Charles Olson & Robert Creeley:
The Complete Correspondence
Volume 10

Notes to the letters begin on p. 225.

[Fontrousse, Aix-en-Provence]
April 27, 1952

Dear Charles,

At last something set on this house biz; have located
and will shortly move into a campagna about 20 kilometers above Aix.
Will be ok for us, has plenty of room around it, pleasant garden, etc.,
etc. In short, will do. Rent is fair enough, people decent & distant—so
it should be ok.

Well, to get that done with—I feel we bothered you
a hell of a lot at a time when it must have damn well been a nuisance.
Don't feel very happy about not getting there, though any numbers of
people, just now, I don't think we could make. But you & Con &
Kate—that's the damn loss. But soon, damnit, even if it does mean
another year.[1]

Well, ok. It's over anyhow, can face the next months with some
pleasure, at least a place to sit down & unequivocally ours.

I did get to Rapallo, got back yesterday morning after about a day and
a half there with the Paiges. Rather of a confusion—driving all the
night, back, and while there, mostly a rush around looking for some
place. My heart was hardly in it, it is one of the most ugly places I have
ever damn well been; or is now. Villas everywhere, the nobbly hills
they have smeared with them—look up and see nothing but. Town, or
rather city, is simply resort town, rather fancy, snooty, etc. Not very
pleasant. Saw where Ez lived—how the hell he stood it I don't know;
directly on the board-walk of the place, people must have been
crowding past there all day long. But Paige said it used to be quieter,
even the 4 years they've been there have seen a lot of it changed.

Paige himself certainly decent; man about 35, wife the same, look like
any clean-living american couple. Crew-cut, broad shoulders, r in his
talk pulled out, etc. Hard to say. So nice to me, all that trouble; but
don't make much of what he thinks. Though he is by no means of that

17

class of the Simp/ et al.[2] As bugged by such as any of us; got onto that subject with no pushing from me. He writes stories—that was something! The last day, sitting up in their pad, we were talking about what to do on this one place that looked possible, and somehow shifted to the subject of "literature."

He was saying, to be blunt, I believe in a strong construction, plot a la Edgar Wallace, exact & detailed characterization, and plenty of action.[3] Certainly a straight statement. And had that to deal with as I then could. Mainly— suggested this premise, in expansion of his own complaint against the lyrismos, you had hit in the INTRO/ to the stories, i.e., he don't get the distinction: simple egoistic romanticism vs. the SI.[4] Well, anyhow. We were figuring what the line was, & did agree: Conrad, parts of Ford, NOT Kafka, etc., etc. The usual. I sd, Lawrence? And he says, yes—tho object to much of what he says. And then—thought that yr stories showed that influence (smiling, etc.)

Me: yes they do, one man I very damn much admire, etc., etc. Then: what else did you see in there?

Him: I thought there was a little Henry Miller, too.

Me: no, no Henry Miller—what made you figure that?

Him: thought yr rhythms were similar in some places.

Me: well, both of us wd figure the speech rhythms as the thing, etc., etc.

Then some talking, this & that, and then he says—don't think yr things cd be actually spoken. Whereupon I offered to read them, in proof— but didn't take me up on that. No, says he, smiling—don't just now know where the magazine is.

Well, fuck it. Nice man, dull man. Too often that combination. Would do anything I guess for a man or anyone he liked. But dull—unable to either register or show proof of any emotion stronger than the usual run. That's loss; and particular, in man trying to write.

Walter, man who made the trip with me (pianist, and another story in himself, etc., etc.),[5] says, as we were leaving, I'll damn well bet they'll be standing there waving—this, when we were about four blocks down the street. And looking, they were.

That set. A damn hard thing honestly to think of—man so nice, so honest in his attempts—and yet that edge of the pompous, because he has to be, I guess, to hold on. Has to depend on that authority, which, say, he can't be really very sure of. Told me how the Am/ publisher had messed the LETTERS, etc. Added Van Doren's preface—deleted a lot of stuff without telling him. Didn't show proofs, etc.[6] Thought then, stronger man would have done something perhaps—but perhaps he did. Don't however really think so.

To hell with that, for now. See what he now does. I guess he won't do much though—too far from anything we'd much care about.

Got a letter from Lash, that he will print the review of Jack's novel, this June; same issue has Cid & Lohner's translations, etc.[7] He sd, he wrote you on the Kenner bk/.[8] You wd be the one certainly; but is a job which is both dull & a bug.

       Incidentally—how about a review of the Fenollosa? To make a clear hit, back, to F/, *him & the present criteria*. In fact, you have the damn ground work there in that letter I'd copied.[9] I mean, to hit back straight to his premise; not to slight Ez but to get rid of that sense of F/ as only one of Ez' emphases—to get F/ straight on his own ground, and that which is just now ours too. [*Creeley writes in the margin*: That isn't silly, is it? You could do a crazy job on it.]

The thing, that Lash cd have that use; I hate to waste it, in that sense. He is very excited about the idea of you possibly doing a review of the Kenner; perhaps I was an idiot, at that, to suggest it, knowing yr own reluctance to have anything whatsoever to do with any of that. Simply that P/ does get shoved way the hell of off IN this kind of use of him; reader further from any comprehension of what Ez now cd mean, after the Kenner bk/, than before. It IS the occasion to whack directly at these disciples. (Paige cd/ do it, but doubt if he wd/ want to get into that dilemma; I know he thought the book stunk, etc.)

Well, time enough. Just to use this Lash, & the mag, as long as it's there to be used. Which I suppose may not be for very long; these characters a bit shifty, finally. Don't really mean to be—simply too enthusiastic, etc.

Wish we were coming—France not it, in that sense. Not at all. But a place for a year—baby now to be figured on, etc. Guess that makes the place a good one, that we'll have it for a year, is private enough, and we can afford it, like they say.

Letter from Cid on those poems sent; sent everything up to these last 2, and they add nothing, if even make what standard the others have. Anyhow, says Cid: will take 3 (Innocence, Cantos, Rhyme)—I had told him, Innocence was the best, Cantos perhaps too because of parts of the writing. Rhyme is his own choice—not of sd three, but what I didn't tell him about, etc. But to hell with that. What dulls me—he says #10 will be where he'll use them.[10] That means a year & 1/4 wait. Not cool. Maybe will change that—but little dribbling way he prints them, not good either; wish he would let me have more than one to an issue. But to hell with it; can cut those other deadheads with one line! The fact.

Prose he ain't damn well going to get anymore of. It's his own fucking biz, but am not going to tie that up for any goddamn 1 1/4 years while he prints this other shit. Poems, he can have; no prose.

Odd the way he does shift in these letters; the one before this, he offers me the editorship after he quits, around #10, etc. This one he puts me way down—he had sent a poem, and I criticized it like they say. Perhaps that bugged him; also think the deal with Lash did too, tho he gets in, and so why bother abt it. Vince likes his poems he says; ok.

No energy at all to go at this kind of thing now anyhow. No interest at this point. His damn deal; let him do what the hell he wants to. He can't win anymore, he muffed it.

Hope to god staying on means the gig with Rainer can now come off.[11]

But they have to get here first, and not sure they can manage that. Money is the bug. Have to have $250 for that press, and how to get it, I don't know. He hopes to manage it with the radio stuff; two scripts would do it. But they have to eat too. Do you know anyone there who might be interested? He does have a clean prospectus, contracts & all. The $250 doesn't damn well seem an unreasonable figure for such a gig; very low finally. Had hoped to be able to get some of it for him, but had to pay rent for 1 yr/ in advance—that broke us, etc. Also baby now among the other items to figure. Not cool. But can get a little to him perhaps. Have to damn well do something.

Still tired from the damn trip. Half awake.

Could you get me some 15¢ stamps? Thought to try Laughlin with the 3 stories, Grace, Party, & Jardou, for Annual, etc.[12] Will stick in check for $1.50. When you can, & don't bother about it; not important.

Can't see how Ez made it there in Rapallo; Rexroth's comment more or less my own at this point—"Atlantic City," etc., etc.[13] Frightful place, in that way. Only thing possible would be to have a place on the outskirts, along with the rest of the millionaires. But the women— phew. I felt like my coat was about 15 inches too short in the sleeves— and it is, a little! O well ...

Same feeling coming thru Villefranche; just between Nice & Monte Carlo. Big lush estates, etc. Entrances pushed right thru the rock, etc. Mile after damn mile. Horrible.
                                        The town, little strip of docks. Steep hill, on which it sits on the side, etc. What's so damn romantic abt that.

And Spotorno, and poor old Lawrence![14] WOW. Big factory now at the edge of it—piles of sand, gravel, etc. Bleak hard look to it. But they were all there a long time ago, and other people likewise.

But I couldn't make that, even so. Must have the other condition—to be private; can't stand people sometimes even in houses a half-mile down the road. Really damn will get to Oregon or Washington someday—find a place 15 miles outside of town—nothing within 5 miles. That would be it.

Italian Riviera anyhow now is ugly, horrible looking. Damn houses what kill it. And even at that, line or block of land as it comes to the sea is nothing against what you can make in Maine, etc. But it [is] a damn different sense of it I have anyhow—I thought of it in Maine, living there—wild damn sea, in winter. Crazy roar of it, banging in from straight North. Mediterranean IS a lake, etc.

But China, Burma, India. That would be it anyhow, these days. Paige talked about Bunting & his wife; they almost stayed there, in this place which we might have taken.[15] But was that lush—no good for the humble man, etc. And I don't have a suit, or any damn thing; and Ann the same. If you can't damn well wear rags, it's no damn good.

Well, for now; will write you Tuesday, or shortly thereafter; moving into the new place then, and will have the address. Do damn well write; figure you must be feeling not at all good, and wish to christ I could be nearer. DO count on Blackburn, as possible substitute if you want to take off. DO think he would make it, and be dependable.[16]

Things will be straight here directly; can then stop all this drivel & get back on—this just to keep on, ok.

> All our dearest love to you all,
> Bob

Very damn dull letter, forgive me—how are you feeling now, I get worried that it's too damn much. Is there any alternative—certainly Blackburn could fill in, and wd even, I think, be happy to get the break, etc. Not good, so long there—too much they ask of you—you are too damn honest.

Do tell us, but don't make that any more bother for you too. Meantime, I'll keep at Lash—see what can come of it. He is pretty agreeable at this point. You know, he damn well writes like an amiable Cid; same damn sentences! Phew.

[Lambesc, Bouches-du-Rhône]
May 2, 1952

Dear Charles,

Yours here, just as we were talking off for this place:
new address, Pavillon les Magnolias, Route de Caire, Lambesc,
Bouches du Rhône. Not as lush as that sounds; really, very decent
place & damn lucky to find it. Anyhow, are set now for another year,
and hope to god it turns out better than this past one. Well, fuck that.
We have a damn roof, etc., which is the point.

Again, all our thanks to you for the help; it was the only alternative
and did damn well tempt me.[17] But, perhaps not too cool to take on
any numbers of people—very erratic, faced with them—have little or
no confidence about such things. So better not now to try it—or at all
or at least not so hurriedly.

By like token—terrific news that you will
be pulling out, I do hope it all goes ok, and that you all make it to
Wash/. Incidentally, continue to think that Paul B/ is a very fine
substitute for you there. Pretty sure that he would take on that
summer session in any case; and could work out details for longer gig
if it seemed wise. (I do like him very, very much; only that one time
seeing him, but letters are very fine, etc. Anyhow, I would think he is
the one.)

Also, will write Mascolo directly, and give him the new address.
What's this about. Hope to god it means they're moving on yr
ISHMAEL; find that it's a policy of theirs, to buy up such texts—then
not to issue them, hence saving the market for french authors, etc.
(They do this mostly with novels, etc. Five years ago, they bought up
everything, and guess they continue to buy what they're afraid of.

Grim business, but very clear at least. Rene L/ told me some rather
hair-raising stories about their editorial policies, etc. But all french
publishing, for that matter, is a hell of a mess; costs now so high that
they don't bother much with the new things. I think he said it would
cost 1 million francs to issue an edition (1000 copies) of his selection
from the CANTOS—text of maybe 75 to 100 pp/s. Inflation here gets
frightening; costs on everything, or about everything, have doubled in
the last year, really in the last six months.)

Anyhow—will write Mascolo! Little sour about them; had sent them
the stories, and got a nice little note saying M/ would write me
directly he got back from his vacation, etc., etc. And then never heard
a damn thing; sent them postage, etc. Well, fuck them—Gallimard
much like Random House: wouldn't look for a nickel from either one.

Raining here—this room pretty damp; but a nice one, and quiet. Up
under the eaves—probably stifling in a month, but great now. Kids
can't find me, which is half of it. Low ceiling, about four feet, and a
fine little window, at one end, looks out on the trees, etc. Birds & the
works; most idyllic!

                    Whole place is ok, plenty of space, walled in so
the kids don't get out in the road. Outskirts of the town, which is also
pretty cool. Stores & such. Aix not too far away whenever we want to
see anyone. So.

Rain sours me a little, and expect the logical subject, or what I could
rise to, would be that princess,[18] Bottegha Oscura (or how to spell it).
She never sent back that copy of APOLLONIUS. Well....

Too dull at that. Do you think you'll try that review for Lash, or
something else. Very anxious, in some ways, to consolidate that place,
i.e., to have, somehow, tolerance for at least the two of us. What does
bug me is that ORIGIN, at least for me, is drying up altogether; this is
the usual refrain, and forgive me. But his planning to hold those
poems he takes till #10 is something of an eye-opener. It means a year
& a quarter wait, and can't call that very fast service. In fact, worse
than I ever got from any publication—even Kenyon.[19]

What is the
damn answer. God knows I have no eyes to get into any gigs with the
benighted, etc. But how stay clear. The prose is what I'm thinking
about. Feel, now, about to move again with that, or ideas at least; and
now the space & quiet it will take. But idiotic to worry about it, before
I even have anything.

(Still amused by how damn much Lash sounds like Cid; in recent letter
to the latter, was wopping[20] him on one count & another—mainly his
pompous taking of L/—even when sd man is printing those
translations (I shudder at *that* prospect!) of his & Lohner's. And gave
him a little of L/ to show him how damn like was the sentence! Shit
that I am. Ok. But only amusement I get now—damned if I care much
about what he thinks.)

He said the Duncan poem was out, & a beautiful printing.[21] Very
happy to hear that; hope it all goes ok. How is Duncan coming? Do
you make much with him? Wish that I could get something for this
German biz—but I guess there's time. (Incidentally, did you think
anything about that anthology biz[22]—i.e., for Rainer to translate, etc.
But everyone at loose ends right now; it will keep. He has enough to
hold him for the moment.)

Grousing seems only thing possible—
which is strange, but so it is. Let me damn well shut up; will write you
tomorrow, once this weather clears. Impossible to forget it—raining &
all, and fact I have to go out in it damn soon. Ok. Do keep us on, tell us
how it all comes.

All dearest love to you all,
Bob

Writing Bud in the next day or so; will ask him again about the bull
biz. Know he has excellent connections, for same; man who pic'd for
all the greatest (& still doing it) is their best friend there in Seville. Was
taking them to see Belmonte,[23] I think; got them house & all. Anyhow,

will ask again; suspect that settling (getting house & all) slowed them down. But he is neither capricious nor forgetful, so trust that there'll be more news soon.

[*Added at top of letter:*] Did I sign that check sent you?[24] Don't damn well think so; anyhow, here's another, in case I didn't.

—————————

[Black Mountain, N.C.]

may 3 [1952]   lad: beautiful stuff in fr
                you, especially THE SURF, tho, the kicks on the B Globe
sent us both—and on D. Paige (sd C, the pix is beautiful, sd O, ya, I'll
not miss him)[25]
                        It's so goddamned nice to have you boomin, even if i
am—because i am/in bad times: no work, or will to; & grim, fucked
up, mixed by desires
                        anyhow, good news you have a settin place—&
i must tell you how welcome it was here: even a house had been set
aside for you & yrs (& not my asking, done by Huss, spang:[26]
"Roadside, for the Creeleys."[27] Ok joe.
                                And the attached tear
fr the summer bulletin, just in case you did come![28]

Look, I'm so off, I better not push to say anything, I so do nothing but gnaw my own paw. Stupid occupation, but ground down by the terrors of a choice I wish to god had not been made mine. (Not, of course, this place: no problem. Am clear of it.

Point is, those last lines of SURF, coming on top of the preceding, wow, what beauty—and yr troubling over *is* is already solved in the thing itself; from outside, it sets perfect.

And will be back on the earlier things the moment i get up off my arse. This, then, the merest "how are you all," to keep yours coming in here, while i hold my hand, eh? Please keep pouring it to me (I'm back two years ago, actually, and the brilliance of the event that, it was then you came in, makes this whole thing lighted by anything you say.

OK. Love to you all, and love back
from us (Con and Kate are radiant
these days.
((fact is, all i need is a
fucking roaring poem—but you will know that fucking biz of putting off your own deliverance, no?

the way one balks one's own
freedom?
(It is true, COLD HELL is the straightest, but that you shld just now also have something to say for CAUSE is of the matter.[29] For it is such bloody dirty places as that one that I am also born of, and I put off the necessities of that area, and so hang myself.
Not "also":
there I am born, in the other place I grow up. But that muck is crucial to further movement, why I ask myself, and blush—not because i don't know that what is is but because i have always had to defeat my regularity (which I used to confuse—or people did confuse me to think was—with realism!

Have not written anyone, so, if Lash or anyone gets cranky, that's why—am sitting on my hands—& even, when, this morning, a guy (to whom i wrote from Washington, I was so excited to stake out that house for myself for ever) does damn well offer me the 4000 bucks necessary to get the bank to put up the 8500 to buy the she-bang! How about that! What christly luck i do have. And then turn it, and watch it—glum: because I'm damn well *not* squared away.
Just throw this
away—allow me to spit like this once. I'll be back on. Am frightfully troubled. Know all the outs—ins, & outs—but don't take em up, even when they are placed in front of me on a platter! Which is what has happened the past three weeks: everything, offered, just that simply.

Crazy. And I—don't eat! I'll tell you about it, sometime, how a man can have it all, and just sit & look at it! (It wld be interesting if it were not—i ultimately decide—mere stupid.)

OK. Write me constantly— and I'll be out of these woods shortly. Pay it no mind. Keep bowling, high-tailing: it is beautiful.

Yrs,

olson - swede[30]

[Lambesc, Bouches-du-Rhône]
May 4, 1952

Dear Charles,

Getting more settled, but always a bug with the kids; the first two days Tom did nothing but bump into doors, etc., and cried, etc. Dave likewise beating on us in his own fashion, for moving him. But it gets cooler now; nice place, and they have much more room—now to find some other kids, & all will be well.

Wanted to note an englishman I found in a magazine; in fact, that one put out by the man who Cid was thinking of for yr book, The Window.[31] In itself, furchtbar,[32] but this man was ok. This poem, of two, he had there which seemed very interesting, like they say:

ALL DEVILS FADING

All her devils here tonight,
    Duly expected: a sour mouth,

And ache in the head, and her voice
Ceaseless in anger. In blurred sight
Angels on her wall rejoice
      At a sudden end of drouth;
But here, still this blight.

There were no easy years:
      Always, in glut, a vague hunger
At spring. "You were never divine,"
She says, "and over your affairs
The shadows will always incline,
      Closing in. It is your anger
At nature," she says, and stares.

Why then, with her slight smile,
      All devils fading, does she give
Me her hand? and close her eyes,
Thus in her sorrow to beguile
My death. It must be she too dies,
      But with no love to forgive
Me for her own betrayal.

I thought it a very damn lovely thing, very graceful—in not at all the
soupy sense. I wrote him and got an answer yesterday; he turns out to
be living in Mallorca, tutoring Robt Graves' eldest son no less. A
decent man, from what he writes; young, can't be much over 23 or 4,
and this kind of grace seems especially good—very exact in its
character, for someone who can't be very damn far along in the
practice. What did hit me, was his sense of balance—too, the content
is, god knows, something particular to my own emphases, I would try
to get contact with him if only because of that. (I don't think one can
damn well pass by those who are, in any sense, related.)

But he has a somewhat "natural" head for rhythms—damn rare in the
english—or damn rare without a sort of slopping, looseness, etc. This
man very firm in his open things—line pretty hard, though he could
use your own insistence, as lever. (That part is what I want to get to,

with him; because he has this fineness, possible—not to be pompous about it.)

An air to the verse, too, which is damn well intriguing. Not always so clean, but strong in any case. One verse from one he sent yesterday:[33]

I saw her wheeling by a dusk-lit lake
  A child not hers, in ordinary afternoon:
  She was an elegy for some departure, soon
To tear anatomies of love, and make
Each loathed child her own. The sunlight
  Hovered for an instant on the haunted water:
  To leave that child her dark familiar daughter
Who cries out mischief and all ruin in the night.

But I really wanted to show some of what he does with open verse—the sureness he manages with his sense of *equivalent* weights—how he can balance, by that, his divers lines.

As man, or outside sleep, impossible
To descend that path by which, slowly,
The understanding many years have built
Is destroyed, and at the shore
All consciousness of life or time
Lost, private and well-loved despair
Reduced, halfway, to a stunted tree,
Soon passed, and not again in memory.[34]

Something of a damn tightrope he's walking there; I damn well respect that firmness. What do you think? Damn well would appreciate your word; I had thought there was nothing in England, but this man is interesting. Would you go with me on that?

Because it is a content, put here now obliquely, that is something to think about; the perceptions are clear, though their mode is often subterfuge.

He is without pretension—extreme wistfulness, perhaps because I am too, part of youngness, a mark, etc. I like him, I feel him straight, clean to his mark, no matter I can't accept it as my own, etc.

Perhaps it's only my own longing, backwards, after some damn simple lyricism. Finally, to make that—it can be as much a trap as any incentive. But poetry—jesus, I am confused about it. There is a character, to speech, to its continuities, which can invite one to something like what this man makes; I'm not sure it's right, however. I wish one could sit hard on the thing, on that hardness—I think that would be more important, and, as well, no loss of this other character—of so liquid sounds, the passage of them, etc.

(Wonder, too, how much Graves gets into him; could sense the obliqueness being partially that way of G/s. Hope he doesn't go that way—don't know much of G/but this man is already cleaner I think—less the "poet" or wish to be one of such.)

How the hell does he manage that *kind* of statement, there in that blank verse thing. What goofs me. Where is this authority coming from. I would like to find out, I think there is a damn well interesting intelligence making this stuff; I don't suppose he even knows it himself, what he might make. That is, isn't there a kind of attack, clearly in any poem worth the time of study, say, that shows perhaps a slowness but still a premise, or base, of writing which can be developed. You know the quick ones, i.e., those who startle, that way of it—such can be the "one poem" kind, etc. Not very interesting. Yet someone like this, though slower, is likewise much surer; I would insist that there is writing, in any of this stuff quoted, which another man could attack, i.e., could attack as ground for an art, for one man's art—and even show him at least the comprehension of that fact. What else. I know an art like your own is never quick, or even fast in its discoveries—or with myself, 20 poems, and one, perhaps, worth holding on to. It seems that slow to me, I don't see any simple or quick ways to it. Really I don't give a damn about this man's literal diction, I think it horrible many times—but those words are carrying, too, a rhythm, a weight of sound, and that I find very interesting; I find the head which has that in it, the same. Because can't you suggest, say, words to a man, can't you finally say—isn't *descend* and such a phrase as *ordinary afternoon*, etc., etc. too "poetic"—isn't there a harder diction possible? In that, he can change—and with no loss to that underlying sense of weight, balance, & sequence. That seems to me part of a man's *original* balance—the underneath ties of his sounds.

Well, you're a teacher, like they say—isn't this man damn well meat? Wouldn't you like to go at him? He is writing so very quietly, finally; it is a kind of grace in itself.

(I forgot to tell you his name—very english!—Martin Seymour-Smith; also, just done with Oxford, etc. So you see what he did get through, & now there with Graves, etc. Phew.)

A letter from Rene L/ says he's off to the Boulez concert,[35] and can he speak to B/ of you. I.e., thought to see B/ there, and perhaps could tell him about your own interest in his work; would you like to get him a copy of IN COLD HELL—but so much greater for you to have direct contact with him—why not have Rene L/ find out where he can be reached, if, say, he knows any english, etc. Though he could, at that, say you were interested, without making it gushing, etc. But do write what you think; ok.

(Hope to have a radio soon, also that the concert will be broadcast—I think it will. Very anxious to hear some of this myself. Ok.)

So it goes—quiet enough. Will take a little while to get cool again, but at least a roof, etc. Feels very damn good.

Keep us on re your own moves—how things come, etc. Do damn well hope you get out soon, it is too damn much one you—think the isolation so damn much greater. Do write soon, miss yr letters very, very much.

All our love to you all,
Bob

No word from the G/s in some time, just 1 letter since Rainer went back; I can't get rid of that feeling, or guess as to what, now, they must be going thru. Horrible, horrible weight; not human, finally, not what one should be forced to take on himself.

Mon May 5 [1952]   ROBT:

I shld imagine writing something about the Poetry of Dis-
Course, I am so irritated sitting here reading Morse on Stevens,[36] on
these pietisms—both of them—which pass themselves off (like so
much) as modern, as "hard" (that canard—if the word is right—by
which all of them but Bill?—seem to have sought to redefine
consciousness, or at least what they took to be its necessities for them
as "poets"

"That assassin, the heart's desire":[37] dear, dear, right
there they go elite—as tho, someho, they take it their function doth
separate them from it—as tho—ho-ho—something in the desire of the
heart is "soft," perhaps, ordinary, quotidian, is flat:

how they so much *do* come from Verlaine (that
filthy fellow—even when they do not épater les bîches[38]—is so much
more their true penelope than his lover[39]

i roil at all this literacy, even
loving & riding from the bold & subtle language, that, they are
WITHOUT PASSION

(again, i drag my foot in yr rear in
yr statements of faith in Lawrence—that new one, that, i believe
everything he ever said:[40]
how he did not need to trouble these
DIALECTICALS of theirs being able of men's wills

Stevens again

seems—as so often even Ez—supported by what they oppose (how easily they got trapped into the opposite of the doctrines of the revolutionists—the engineers & salesmen as well as the manifesto makers; how easily they permitted themselves to assume that imagination was extricable from the lives of other men, that its practice was different in kind from its non-practice: I would take it that this is only possible to men who have no passion but the passion for words (which is essentially none at all, words being inadequate, and passion proving that an object of love is in fact greater than the impulse, more beautiful than its imagining

it is right there that i would throw them down (tho they erect any number of Erectors of words to talk about value—even ((their ultimate terror to me)) to attack words themselves, not in the inadequacy I have just mentioned but in their own inadequacy—that poetry is inadequate
                         This latter is unbearable in that the WILL is undone, that it is (as I am more and more certain), that they back up on change (or on their opposition, that false contrary) as a sort of paradise when it is not change which is any less terrible than chaos but it is *the will to change*[41]—how that is what makes the lives of all men, not just poets, spring up in front of us

The point would seem to be that by words they prevent themselves! And this is surely discourse. And that "poets" should be guilty of all this means only that they fear revolutionists. I have been one, and have no fear of it, no fear of mass men (having loved my father, and found out how to love my mother).[42]

For the lie in Stevens, however much the pleasure in his the play of words, is his language, that, it is without rhythm because it is without passion which is person (not personae, that further device against mass). (Or is it that this Morse over quotes the blank verse?)

I am at this point so troubled about EP (I suppose it is that I still debate yr suggestion thru Lash to do the Kenner) that I want no sight of him, that Bill stands hugely these days (through you as well as through himself) as a go-er, as a man, as a fellow of the same streets, as a guy

who was not sucked to order by a series of modern fallacies, logical
dialectical discursive fallacies, for ordering disorder

> (DHL as the only prospective man, Olson
> Partisan R, Winter, 1945 [sic])[43]

It gets so goddamned neat instead of a matter of insight by
way of the sounds as well as the petit point

> (even this cult of M. Moore,

this Brooklyn sappho they all sit on their hands over: that spinner,
their last penelope, that the brightness is lighting a la La Fountain[44]

> (Axzolotl,

servant of
water &
to be eaten, not
to be ornithologized,[45]
translated

I rise against em, suffering an old nervousness that I
cannot call the heart's desire assassin but, in that *they* do, sure they
are wrong. For the sun is—not bull's fire[46]—even these sureties
they muck with needle water-blood: Cento longings, Hartford,
Brooklyn, Rappalo[47]—and so destroy by literate ignorance what is
crucial

((Nota: this latter is too broad, but they do come up wearing
no pants but breeches, and cover their walls with books & Swedish
rugs, come out Harlequin & Columbine—and give me the shit Bill
won't, that, plums outlast us[48]

> how dull, when
> It is I who can
> this time anyway
> eat em

All right. Just a beef. But how good to feel how Lawrence stood free of
these errors of order—and Bill, damn it, to the degree of some of those
last couplets, eh? the way he can get in that he is standing too like any
citizen, or cat

> I'll see you,
>
> O

[*Verso of air mail envelope:*]

A   CREELEY   FOR   SPR-
ING

19th Cent(s)-

ury may day
if they ever ex . . . .   now sources

[*Added, filling both margins of the centered poem:*]
P.S.   May 5th: after enclosed, *Origin 5* came in.—& I have just written
you a letter abt Stevens, etc. But just because I am in such a rage, and
will not want to bother with it again, I think you'll get it if I send the
letter to you *via* Corman—just to give him my answer (by way of it) on
his wrong in circulating such shit.[49]

———————   ================   ———————

[Black Mountain, N.C.]

Robt: May 6 [1952]   (Tuesday—yr new address in: & to tell you
I sent off a note yesterday to the old address—and asked Corman to
send you instantly another letter to you i sent via him just to get rid of
my rage over his #5, that damned gig of Morse's on Stevens (probably
that too will go to the old address, unless he hears from you in the
next day or so)

          Wanted to spill my mind to you on a lot of conceptuals
in the metapsychic area. Sat down to do such. But instead wrote this: (I
obviously am in some "Chinese" kick! as a result of yr influence in,
those much more modern verses of yours!)

A robin, berries and leaves
awkwardly cover a speech
as flesh is not awkward
covering a sun

Or, as yr present neighbors might say, *pester entre cuir & chair!*[50]

(No, exact opposite meaning. Only, the idiom delights me as of
my own recent backwards—as of dissatisfaction, and a sense
of lack of courage: "to rail between skin and flesh!"

What a gap that is—and (for me) what a world of involvement, right
there: I have had to poise myself in that *entre*. And the devil tries to
force one either way! I have not been able to budge—as long as I am
old, exactly—and I have had a hell of a time, doubting, as one damn
well does in such areas, being not clear, that is, not clear not in my
acting from the place between but made unclear by the responses
resulting from the poise (base), the responses of those
I have desired

((This suddenly throws a light for me on that biz,
in morning news, of the Sunday I hauled those
two damnes [*sic*] into each of my arms—& what
followed, not fr them but fr their "men"[51]

Got a curious follow-thru of that, recently, in a
letter from one of those men, now in Finland, &
close to 40, biting, at his own flesh—a frightful
thing, that letter, & caused me to dream of him
for the first time twice (Con thinks, from some
night-identification of my own recent
discouragement

(((you mustn't think either
her explanation or my allowance of a state of
same is that flat! I state it flatly simply, that it is
—for the moment—past, and I am bored with it

as i was bored then with both the men and the

> two women, that is, the moment the afternoon
> had left my cuir et chair (their cuir not passing
> toward chair—that thing, that god-damned
> modern thing, the refusal to go in, that tender
> ender of all their pudenda, the selling of same as
> tho it were worth something, as tho it were
> valuable in itself instead (again) as (as so much)
> as instrumentation

We both had a sudden excitement, just now [torn] talking, when it
turned out (it was that fucking Stevens who had provoked it by some
line about poetry to undo dirt) O that dirty Crispin of his—dirtier than
Prufrock):[52] those who keep themselves away from life (again,
protecting a—the—pudenda) that

> Con sd
>
> I don't feel any dirt
>
> And

christ i loved her, for, there ain't none, and those who have it, who
have this thing of original sin hung around their cocks like a dead
albatross, are of another tribe, a tribe of sin not at all of the tribe of
men

> And it struck us both just then that what makes communication
with you so open is, that you have none of this shit in you: you are free
of that

> Which was, I guess, what led us into the business of what I
had busted through to last night—some sense of the identity of person
& myth without loss of a recognition that the diapason of the psyche
and the metapsyche comes into existence only when it is understood
that each have their own laws;

> that they are on two planes

(I could put it another way, in a language more familiar, if I spoke of
the voice of the conscious and the voice of the unconscious, and that
both voices are hearable and improvable—that control like
Lawrence's (that remarkable thing, that he never wrote a sentence
which was not clear, even in the rational way, even tho he never said
a thing which was not speaking the metapsychic, voicing it,
bouncing against it) is achievable;

> again, that he & Rimbaud lived

improves the prospect of the species!)

((Or yrs: the world owes me
a corporeal existence!))[53]

The sense anyway (without developing these conceptions further, because I have to go to a meeting of the Board—and only go out of respect of Con, that, she wants the job of Registrar,[54] and it will come up today, I figure) is, that instead of dirt (even that Genesis biz— which was less offensive than the Xtian thing: at least the Jews then left it as sexual, did not spread it all over the body & the world of things) what Con feels (and I less so or not at all, yet wholly familiar with the areas): monsters

the thing is, that, there are necessary acts of aversion, one does have to maintain a space with anyone or thing

but that this sense (members of this tribe) have not fouled, in the first place, (1) life, & (2) sex: that both of these things are taken as givens and as such are immediately instruments, not pious things, properties—like pudendas or like "poetry" (of Stevens!)

I'll quit & either come back or shoot this off to greet you in yr new house of the camellias![55] with all our love, and also the joy of being back on myself!

yrs,
charles [*In ink:*] C

[Black Mountain, N.C.]

robt: wed may 7 [1952]   Want to try to pick up on what was in my head yesterday (when i had to break off: Con is now Registrar of this hyar place, and it

must sound sinister to you, yet, at the moment, it is

something she wanted to do, and so, let it be: I myself now figure to leave here June 7, and spend six weeks to myself in Washington, returning here for the last 4 weeks of the summer session—I doubt I shall find it good enough there to stay away from Con and Kate that long

> (Kate is such a damn pleasure, a real love-berry, with such snap, such a crow, when she lets one go—I think she takes only her pharynx from her phar[56]—such a damn lovely body— and eyes lit with every curiosity—I even think she is close to speech, the way she has gabbed her way to this point: strong, that's what delights us both ((((you will know how one wonders what one would produce—this seems something I'd not figured on, from the fish-pond!))))

And Con and I are enjoying her, and things. OK. Crazy business, all such, for a man of my mien! (If that sounds fat-headed, it is due to excisions, for the moment)

You will know how such stuff as Mayan & Sumerian engages me. And you will recall that letter to you about sleep & dreams.[57] Also Hermes Tregismetus, & such last signs of "the old science" as Gnosticism.[58] Plus H. Melville, that, I centered the whole of ISH on that Hotel de Cluny passage—and expunged, as—then—too easy, putting beside it that empty sarcophagus passage of Pierre[59] (how, there, I took it he had taken the rug out from under his self

[*Olson highlights the next four paragraphs by drawing bars in the margins:*]
It is that sort of "self" that I was talking about yesterday as "metapsyche & psyche,"—and around which all the above listed curiosities seem to me to cluster.

What fascinates me, at present, is a sense of break-through as of these functions in any of us. Pick up on that old idea [*strikes over* metempsychosis?] metamorphosis. I literally believe in change of form, striking alterations of appearance, character and circumstances. I take it, this is MOTION, in the exact sense of the motions of our selves.

At this point, of course, myths enter the picture, especially such direct ties of them & change as Ovid's.

> But what engages me more, at this
point, than any such "history" (even in our own proper business) is
something else in that business, that moment from which you and I
moved together, when I protested to you, 1st letter, that I took it each
poem was in search of its own language: it is this sense of change of
form which is all that I am interested in bringing metamorpho*ses* to
bear on   (((my guess is, that this

> > is the greatest gain, that I have broken off some proud
> > flesh left of the compelling notion that I had to act out
> > each "change"—

> > this was a quandary, so long as I was
> > pulled to skin or to flesh instead of dwelling where my
> > will keeps me, still keeps me, in between))

And it is this bearing on change, motion, and will—and all in a poem
as the target, as the issue, however much one's person and his
commitments have also to be managed in the face of change—of one's
own will to change—it is this point of it all which makes the
seriousness of it, that we should understand what goes on in the
psyche and the metapsyche

> ((Just here, I wld say, is the real push asked of verse now—that it
put back into itself all that *force* which has been so long scattered in a
series of proper nouns and proper narratives

> > (christ, i am so excited,
saying such things to you, that i am emboldened to make this tie over
time: that the facelessness of the Venus of Mentone or of Willendorf[60]
connects, for me, to a diffidence on the surface of verse which I believe
in. And that such diffidence or coolness or a disarming is a demanded
& superior thing to all those masks, personae, ironies, & dramatic
dodges which our immediate pa's made so much of—that their
positions (poses, even the Dandy and the City Jew opposes)[61] are
ultimately errors, in this sense that, their discomfort in the face of
modern life was some inadequate grasping of their own natures

> > > ((again, environment seems to have engaged their
> > > attention altogether that much—and so, history:

Dioce, in even the Old Man,
stuck in my craw—and only Jim X, took it out—takes it out[62]

(let me make this potential error: that exactly contemporary to them,
the advancing science of mythology was of more value in the area of
such grasping than they were:
which is another way of seeing how
ultimately & always right Lawrence was, how
PROSPECTIVE)

((Again, for me, the
singular importance, of THE ESCAPED COCK, and exactly Part I, how
the Man is delivered from the proper noun—and how miserably II is
not, how "woman" there is still left as Isis or some myth as history
instead of as sign of the force of change in the present;
and, to its
degree, LADY CHAT'S LOVER, that there at least the woman is
dropped down to a psychic depth so that metapsychic echoes
happen[63]
((this is better than my word diapason yesterday))
in this sense, that, I take it that there is a sounding of the sort of
accuracy we speak of in verse, syllable by syllable, and through
all, when the psyche as the most personal plane is in such
relation to the metapsyche (that plane on which force as [larger
than *struck over*] something we are also in the hands of—as well
as in our own hands—as well, in fact, as we are the living
instruments & examples of that force, and as such have to
obey—& obey, like they say, blindly, only in this exact sense that
what we are obeying is something in ourselves that we are not so
sure of as we can be somewhat sure of the outlines of ourselves
on the "psychic" plane alone
and that when these two
planes are in such identity vectors [so?] come into existence that
an individual is a force astronomically different than the
personal alone, the resonances then resulting from the beat and
sound of those two "boards" and strings being comparable only
to the finest speech
to the best, poem

((If it sounds like some shit of the harmony of the spheres, or some
golden number theory, tell me: but it isn't, and if it seems, it is that I
have not yet managed its expression—or can one, except in the issue,
that thing, the ultimate motion, a poem?

((why, if you will excuse
it, and i think you will the more so that it was you who
gave me the statements of its effect, why Cold Hell does
seem the major thrust is tied up with these planes (analogy:
cuir et chair!)

You will know that I know very little about how all same does bear
on a poem, but I am sure that so many of the things we have talked
about about what is a poem these days are subsumed by this factor of
how we are (that is, line, motion, change, field, juxtaposition, conjecture

the last gets a new light for me in this other context of going
blind (say that going by the nose is what we do personally
(psychicly) and that we do it in order to discover the blind
going (meta

I am even moved by the word metapsyche, that it does mean *over* the
psyche, or *along with, after* the psyche. For it is obvious that I have
cared for the care of the psyche, think that it is like a tissue which has
to be paid attention to—that this attention is what used to be dubbed
the moral—that it is as strong as tissue but can be torn, and that the
moderns have neglected the care of same, and so are often pieces of
men, have lost so much from tearing

But now to be able to add this other thing—as if it were *another*—this
echoes in my experience as very true, that there is a differentiation,
and that from that differentiation rises all the areas we cover by the
word myth, and so somehow have separated them too far from the
person.

It overwhelms me to have found some conception to reinforce
my own sense that myth is not or ever was outside any one of us; and
at the same time to distinguish it from that which we have been more
confident of, that the person is the psyche—for i have all along felt that
the behavior of these other forces in one is distinguishable from the

psychic, however much I also believe they are inextricable
from it.

Suddenly, what i think has impeded me in the formulation of
those LAWS we have so much talked of the past year, is evident:

the
care of the psyche is the conscious (such accuracies as you are so
marked in, so much so i am constantly sharpened in my own
movement on this plane). And I would take it that exactly here is
character (in the lovely ancient sense of an instrument for marking,
from the verb, *to make sharp*, to engrave)[64]

and that this other thing is where *image*, true image, comes
out from—and that such image is ultimate only when it is as worked
(as cared for) as is character

That it is these two together that
constitute LAW, the real moral thing, both conscious in the sense that
the metapsychic is as enterable and dealable as is the more readily
admitted psychic

((and—negatively—that neither "psychology"—
which Ez once called a substitute for character![65]—and "mythology"—
which is, like religion, a substitute for personal action—a substitute for
[*strikes over* image] art—do anything but turn attention attention away
from you/me, the going on

Well, I'm getting too explicit, which means the drive is spent, for now.
Let me have said this, adding it to yesterday, and leaving it for you,
sending it with love & admiration (I promise to get to the new poems
as soon as possible

yrs,

C

[Black Mountain, N.C.]

Sat May 9 [*i.e.*, 10th], 52   ROBT:
Curious biz, springing up from finding out more
(accidentally) about SCHLIEMANN—that he dug Troy *before* there
was any methodology of digging, but that it was his push from a faith
that Homer's text was accurate that immediately created
archaeology—in other words, that Schliemann himself was on the kick
which Frobenius and Berard made stick: that written texts of the order
of Homer & Herodotus are as verifiable as the oral
                                                which seems to
me a crucial shift of the base of attitude toward art upon which such
objectism & seriousness as I take it, say, Lawrence stands for, arises
(our own practice, to the degree etc)

                    What has interested me is to find that it
was ERNST CURTIUS's excavations at Olympia four years *after* S 1st
dug Troy that first employed the architect Dörpfeld. And that it was
Dörpfeld who first worked out means of maintaining strata at a site.[66]
So the line, even to that Curtius' son? grandson?...![67]

(Curtius, in a letter to Schliemann, 1872—S had dug Troy 1st 1868, and
was to dig it with Dörpfeld himself in 1882—says: "I am now
gradually constructing our Olympia gable more and more completely,
and I too am experiencing on a small scale the joy of reviving what
was lost which you taught us.")[68]

All of which fastens down a conviction that one can see a change of
knowledge dating from 1870 of such magnitude that it was right to
speak of NEW HISTORY and that its importance is, essentially, that (1)
it created a body of disciplines which can be called THE SCIENCES
OF MAN; and (2) that such science so devoted (by contrast to the
universe, or nature, as its object) restores art to active and primary
position.

Let me graph it for you, for whatever use:[69]

        I ARCHAEOLOGY (digging as image of all act since)

the

primary II CULTURE MORPHOLOGY (this, not sociology—&
sciences   essentially moving from
                                        the cave paintings, 200th
                                        Century BC: it was exactly
                                        the men who uncovered the
                                        caves who formulated this
                                        new, and still relatively
                                        unadmitted, science. The
                                        name [*i.e., the term "culture
                                        morphology"*] is Frobenius's!)

       the secondary (what light the agent and the ambience throw)

        III THE GEOGRAPHICAL SCIENCES (earth, climate, soils,
                                        crops: climatology,
                                        meteorology, etc.)

        IV THE BIO-SCIENCES (of ontogeny & phylogeny, on
                                        animal structure, glands,
                                        composition: bio-physics, bio-
                                        chemistry, ecology etc

        V PSYCHOLOGY

        VI MYTHOLOGY (and I mean literally Frazer, Jung &
                                  whoever, plus ourselves, to the degree…)

(The curious thing about it is that it inverts the old system exactly. Or
at least I have found that the old exact sciences—three of which I wld
here add, as still (?) *physics, mathematics, & geometry*—furnish not facts
but images & vocabulary!)
               end

That's it, there ain't no more: *anthropology* I have found a concept to spread for use, not being able to clear itself of evolution, and "the species" concept, so looking at everything from as deadly an end of a telescope as sociology (from this end): the anthropoid eyeview and the mass man eye view equally ape.

and *art* as it was—and is still generally taken—is too aesthetic—has too much water in its aestheticism—to be dealt with as such, as a discipline.

So, with those two done in (and i take it these new sciences have helped to expose them) there is nothing else: the above disciplines are a university, the whole biz, enough learning, all that a man can find fruitful.

Simply because they all defy the horizontal (kill "history"), are each sciences of perpendicular penetration (thus archaeology as the essential sign), they are instruments of any one of us in our own penetration of our own self & experience. (OK, that flat!)

Let me add to the graph a summary of the men—just to reach the next to the last, to look-up, the point:

SCHLIEMANN   (the archaeology of Troy, Mycenae (1876), & Tiryns (1884)

RIVIERE—BASTIAN—RATZEL—BRUEIL—FROBENIUS (prehistoric art) (1895)[70]

VICTOR BERARD AND JANE HARRISON (the "archaeology"of
                              THE ODYSSEY and of
                              GREEK MYTH &
                              RELIGION, starting the
                              decade 1890–1900)

EGYPTOLOGY, leading to SUMEROLOGY (Breasted, Petrie, to
                              present: began c. 1900)[71]

MAYA, and AM INDIAN generally (marked date, the establishment,
                              by J. W. Powell (who had been

head of the US GEODETIC
SURVEY, and was one of the 4
Hearts (Henry Adams, Clarence
King, Nicolay) of THE BUREAU
OF AMERICAN ETHNOLOGY,
1st publication 1879–80)[72]

FREUD etc JUNG etc.

SAUER, STEFANSSON, LATTIMORE (all more or less
geographers)[73]

AND   DH LAWRENCE   DH LAWRENCE   DH LAWRENCE
DH LAWRENCE   DH LAWRENCE
(for what damn well booms me about this whole demonstration is,
how he is the PRACTICER, the FACT of the matter! how he is ALL
OF IT—geography
    his *travels* (and the books of same, both archaeology & culture-morph)
        his *novels* (what he gets in is what you had there that letter—
            "his immediate world": THE LIVING FACT)[74]
        his *poems* (physiology, all of the bio-s, plus myth
        & his *fantasia of* (psychology & mythology made LIVING FACT)

Nota: I know one book of science so far done which *applies*, granting
        the limits of science, a like density principle:
            C. F. HAWKES
                            THE PREHISTORIC FOUNDATIONS OF
                            EUROPE
end   end   end   end   end   end   end   end   end   end   end

[*Adds along margin:*] rushing this—back on—love, C (stamps
enclosed—plus pix!)

[*Olson adds, in pencil, the following note at the top and down the left margin of the first page of a carbon copy of his poem "The Thing Was Moving"* (Collected Poems, *pp. 263–265*), *which he dates "may 11 52" at the end of the manuscript*:]

Bob—Because I sat down to write a letter to you, let me send this as it came out on the paper, without touching it, simply to let you have it as it felt addressed throughout—(and excuse me if I keep the 1st copy, merely, that I probably shall want to rework it, & 1st copy keeps it more alive, as you'd know)

Be back on.

love to you & Ann   C

[Lambesc, Bouches-du-Rhône]
May 13, 1952

Dear Charles,

So very great to have all your letters, really a christly room that is damn, damn welcome. I do damn well think you are on, and very closely.

Take this, i.e., some unprinted poem Lawrence had dug up for Wake, of that OTHER lawrence—not at all the same!!![75]

(It's called, Resurrection of the Flesh.)

Oh then be nameless and never seen!
And speak no syllable, and never be
Even thought of!—but between
Your nothing and my nothingness, touch me!

They should never have given you names, and never, never
Have lent you voice, nor spoken of the face
That shone and darkened. They were all too clever.
Now let it all be finished! leave no trace!

Reveal us nothing! roll the scripts away!
Destroy at last the heavy books of stone!
Kill off the Word, that's had so much to say!
And show us nothing! leave us quite alone!

Go, go away, and leave us not a trace
Of any Godhead, leave us in the dark!
And let the dark be soundless, without face
Or voice or any single spark

Of what was God! Be gone, be utterly gone!
Relieve us now of all remembrance even
Of what was godly! Leave us quite alone
Within the silence, void of echoes even.

Oh, it is finished! I would like to take
My garments off, but all, even memory,
And what I've understood, and the utter ache
Of everything I've known, even dreamily.

To take it off, this clothing of a man,
This content of my consciousness, this very me
Which I am still and have been all I can
And am and was, shed it all thoroughly.

To come at last to nothingness, and know
Nothing and nothing any more, and so
Not even dream, not even pass away
Nor cease to be: dark on the darkness stay.

And then within the night where nothing is,
And I am only next to nothingness,
Touch me, oh touch me, give me destinies
By touch, and a new nakedness.

I want to know no more. I want to see
Not anything, nor ever again ask: "Why?"
I let the whole thing go! Still there is me!
Touch me then, touch me, touch me, I did not die!

Upon the wincingness of next to nothingness
That I am now, Ah, lay one little touch
To start my heart afresh! Give me the soft, small stress
Of just one touch! Even so, do I ask too much?

It is an incredible poem, it is, damnit, isn't it, all the answer possible,
either to such things, or distractions, as Stevens, or any of them, these
you damn well nail so finely—damn them.

It is impossible to love otherwise, or to even know what is possible,
either of flesh, or what we take to live in it, the what one is, or how to
call it too simply.

I believe it can almost be this simple, granting any wish to, say, pull
apart the last hundred years, or any time, into what is there, is like a
thing is—or what was the pull-off, veer-away, from precisely that
content in that poem.

One can say it: Lawrence, Williams, Melville, Rimbaud, & keep at it,
that way. There is no equivocation possible. What Cid missed, then, or
perhaps what he has to miss, trying to be editor, etc., is that it is an *evil*,
literal, he's called upon to act on—to keep clear of what is not *evil*, or is
of this other thing. NOT believing oneself at least aimed, as one can
aim, at this *thing*, above like they say—it is impossible to either write,
or even hope to.

Evil isn't to be defined by saying it's not good, etc. But it *is*. It is
present, not like black or white—but by distraction, by dishonest or
tampered statement, or by simply this not at root.

I don't know what is beautiful, or can be called so, before it *is* there.
The criteria is so much a muddle, of intents, & purposes—so much
before the issue that the issue never has space to even declare itself as
one, too, present. Speaking so simply about flesh—people, saying it is,
isn't it, on you, and why worry. To touch what? What is it you are
after—girls, or whatever.

But if one looks, I mean, is looked at, looks in that sense. Even to say it, yesterday, in Aix, had met this girl, 22, and young in that sense of—wanting to do this, or that, really wanting it, and only flesh, honestly, for any rudder. What the hell can she put as the straight thing, I mean, that line, which, believing in it, can be used? Even saying—there is no line—yet there is this thing, of oneself, which *is* actual, *is* firm, *is* untampered unless one, oneself, make it ugly.

That—not at all mystic, or hopeful, or anything else. And all, everything, all hell, as real as it gets—you said it, you goddamn well said it—is here.

It's very damn hard to put much, now, as even equal to that poem; I wish to god people could be clear on 1) what IS the thing, what, no matter *any* fumbling, or hurt involved, IS the very thing & 2) what, no matter how expertly said, or done, or broached, or whatever, IS NOT.

Literally, Stevens IS evil; no one damn well knows that, or can know it, better than I do. For about three years, every poem I wrote was said to be, too much Stevens. I learned it that way, I read every damn thing of his I could find.

Likewise, Gide. Both men. And to see it—by god here is one exercise: tell them to read Dostoyevsky's Brothers, and, at the same time, Gide's Counterfeiters. THAT, is a very damn neat little exercise.

Either you hang on, no matter, damn well hold—or nothing. It is not even interesting, not finally. One makes his own way, finally; and that has nothing too much to do with any other.

Literally, Dostoyevsky, no matter distractions in that way, I mean, in the way of his *other* impulses, is clean in a sense, or character, that either Gide or Stevens have, apparently no sense of.

Stevens is perverter, even as they used to say Gide was. Stevens really *is* perverter. Gide was damn well off balance to start with—was, god help him, out to correct that tilt. That, is never any good.

Put it—why read? Why?

I damn well don't ask any man to *improve* his reality, I only want it as
is.

Surrounded, here, with box hedges, etc., etc., that way of saying it IS a
good one—it is the christly tampering—o to adjust, etc. Ode, to adjust,
etc.

By god, that—we who have, perhaps, NOTHING TO LOSE? (Share
with us/ share with us/ it will be money in yr pockets! (Go now, I
think you are ready!)[76] I mean, that, is damn nice; Williams always at
least that clean, in trying—his "failures" are failures NOT, or never
really, of any "over-writing."

(Wonderful poem, and I just get to see, that it is: begins, on my 65th
birthday, I kissed her, while she pissed.)[77]

To get rid of this sense—even—that the surface form of a man's work,
should kill him too quickly. Well, not just like that—I was only
thinking, that that Seymour-Smith, for all his 19th century flavor, IS a
more honest man than Wallace Stevens.

You can say it like that; and he could learn, couldn't he. It is not that
he is willful, or intends any damn kingdom (what all those want) but
what is immediately his own.

"… but may be too floating …," Cid writes me—not jesus, not to be too
glib about what he *is* trying to say, etc.—about The Innocence. He calls
it slight.

No, christ, one cannot worry about that. Slater once wrote me how this
same Sappho of Brooklyn used to nag at Hart Crane, on all the things
he sent to the Dial, etc., etc.[78] Isn't this word too strong, isn't that
adjective too strange, isn't this line weak, isn't that not what you
mean, isn't—fuck it. Fuck it UTTERLY.

                                        Really, the man who does

presume to tell me, me damnit, who wrote it, what I *mean*—not to be taken, not goddamn well to be taken at all.

Well, he doesn't call "it" slight, he says, the whole bunch is "modest ones...." I am not modest? Phew!

Let me damn well mark up these last two letters, and enclose them with this. Ok. I can't certainly IMPROVE on you—it is damn, damn crazy stuff. Reading it—really wish to god I was there, I feel much, or pretty much, an idiot not honestly to have grabbed that chance— seeing that thing from the bulletin[79]—I felt somewhat sick, it wasn't till then I really got it, what it could damn well have been like.

But space, right now; even this somewhat trim one, and all the hell of language and all. Frankly, I just can't learn french, I don't seem at all to want to.

Anyhow, do keep us on—hope it all goes ok. DO compliment Con on her new job; wish to god it had been possible for us all to be there too.

(It isn't any simple thing here now, there is some damn fear, one has it, about doctors and all—simply prejudice perhaps, but it's dull bucking it even, or even that, when it's a time you want only some damn ease & simpleness, and no damn worry about anything.
                                        Well, christ
knows, like they say. (And where the hell is he?)

I damn well think we *would* have got there, if it had not been for that hellish prospect of getting there. With the two kids, the baby coming— it might have ended up somewhere between nyc & washington, say— it was too damn much.
                    Also, I hate to give it up here, having nothing to show for it, at least let me batter away for one more year; then it will be something harder, etc.
                    Agh, anyhow. The simple propositions. But here I am, and there you are, like they say. It doesn't ever seem too damn clear.)

Write soon, all our dearest love to you all,

                          Bob

———————————————————

[*Below is the only surviving page, typed on both sides, from Creeley's response—probably enclosed in his 13 May 1952 letter—to Olson's letter of 7 May 1952.*]

[*After typing out that portion of Olson's letter that begins "(let me make this potential error ..." and ends "... to the best, poem," Creeley comments:*]
(To quit there—really, statement, "and when these two planes are in such identity vectors, etc ..." is wild. It is something I never damn well thought of—this "time." Perhaps the ONLY time.

                          It is very damn interesting stuff; I mean, just like that—it is very damn wild. —And yet, too, beyond, I think in some damn definite sense, a too simple "law" of coincidence, or of the propitious, etc. There is confluence; some tune, really, some actual flow—not simply, damnit, Heraclitean!

            Anyhow, that is the edge? Right there, that sentence. Both of the character, of the sentence to there—and look how *geography* does jump in there—again ... It is damn wild. That is, also, a crazy "adjective": "astronomically." Again, very damn interested.

Well, ok—DO keep on—it is getting back, or again that thing of, sleep, isn't it. Isn't that a possible ground for this—or what, ultimately, it must insist its way somehow into.

                          (It is *not* too relevant, but this mistranslation I had. I just found it again, from Holderlin:[80]

...to say something new, about form, the
character is the nature—to tell them the
[torn] of this e[torn rest of page]

[Verso:]

Re that Holderlin, backside: I really fuck it: here it is—
... neues zu sagen nach der gestalt, die
abdruck ist der natur, zu reden
des menschen nämlich ist der nabel
dieser erde, diese zeit auch
ist zeit ...   That, is something?

—from the letter/ last one.

[Creeley copies out an earlier part of Olson's letter, beginning with "What
fascinates me, at present, is a sense of break-through ..." and concluding "...
and only Jim X, took it out—takes it out." Here the fragment breaks off.]

[Lambesc, Bouches-du-Rhône]
May 15, 1952

Dear Charles,
          Feeling very damn great, and hope to god I can stay
up here long enough to do you justice on these last things sent; I do
take them of *immediate* use, I don't see the slightest possible shifting on
this *list* to hand. Well, it *is* excellent & it *is* damn hard. Many, many
thanks.
          (I have to get these books, I feel an ignorant idiot, lacking
them; shall try these english bookstores, etc. Anyhow, somehow. I do

not know anything but what you have taught me, and it puts much too much trouble on you—i.e., for much of this reference, I feel I'm pulling down too much, etc. Well, that can be solved, and will set about same directly; have asked Heffer's to look for Waddell, & Strzygowski, & also F/s Erthyra[81] (or how to spell it)—anyhow, will see what they can dig up—would be cheap, buying from them on the $/lb relation, etc. Ok.)

Pictures, too: wow! You have a very damn bright kid, or so she does look to us. Do love the way she looks up, there, in that one where you are, apparently, squeezing out her life-blood! Why not, eh? Anyhow, goofy! And damn fine to have a picture, at last!, of Con—ok.
                                                                It is
that it is something to hang on to, lacking you all closer. I am very damn teary about pictures—almost a fetish, at that.

Here's something: magazine called INTRO,[82] which damn well moved me to write Cid, and tell him why, in 6 pages, he *must* do better, etc. The fact was—general level of interest, I mean, what could excite & produce *usable* reactions in reader, was about, call it, a good third over almost any issue of Origin. A shameful fact, like they say, but one I damn well do think *true*.

                    In other words—how the hell manage a magazine that constantly insists on its commitment to its one major contributor—and then go on to knife him in almost every *other* item then printed! There is a *non-sequitur* between the issue of Sam's gig on Stevens & yr own HU, that comes to interest me more than the content of at least Sam's gig; obviously, that is not at all true, when it comes to HU.

        But there, again, is the problem: is it ultimately necessary to issue the magazine simply for one man's commitment, and prove an utter incapacity to show anything like to it, for the remainder of the pages?

God knows it is not a *happy* state, etc. Well, I did get eloquent. I do not believe that you should be compelled to pull all the weight—it is not, god knows, simple to get anyone else to—either, or even, capable. But it forces you into being all there is—and that is simply not true; and why Cid feels it necessary to either censor, or simply not notice, relevant additions—has got me, at least.

I mean, finally—you are the only critical voice in the magazine. It is, by that, a limit. I don't, to make it clear, suggest any, put it, "contrary" opinion, etc. For christ's sake, like they say—almost every other item he prints *is* that *already*! The idiot who said "the man from whom our creative impetus must spring ..." and then continues by printing his own *most* lamentable, Insurance For Wallace Stevens, is a goddamn liar *somewhere*.[83]

       Hence: 1) to get very clear on what *is* the critical position of Origin; 2) to give multiple & precise instance of this critical position *not only* in these damn simply not-critical poems, etc., etc., he *insists* on printing. I mean, finally: *reviews*, anything, any instance of overt & clearly related comment.

       (A review is, or could be, any comment whatsoever on any publication whatsoever, pointing to, or giving illustration of, or dealing in any way with, some aspect of sd publication. It is *no* limit, either to possible area pertaining, or any "form.")

IF on page 29, say, of an issue, there *were* a man saying, a poem *is*, isn't *it*, some occasion for an evidently determined statement—then on page 7 we *might* be spared any such idiocy as Cid's own po-ems.

Well, it is a headache, I don't see any very quick solution. Why INTRO now excites me—that it does, in spite of a lean on Korzybski, the 4th dimension,[84] and divers other & equal problems, say *things* which interest me very much:

"Today, without speaking of totality and relation, we do not speak of culture, but cult."

"Selfconsciousness will achieve instinct, instinct will achieve intellect."

"U dont bring depth to a story by tailoring in symbols. 'Reality' itself is a symbol if it is not used as a constant."

"Yr story wavers between probing this which u know to be the inside gut, and the general story which is there because it was there to begin with."

"In our time it was E. Pound who discovered the initial gaps—he no longer wrote literature—i.e., something continuing from naturalistic or pre-naturalistic tradition. He wrote in the *Cantos* through a structure of comment and conversation—which alone in our times can hold the ability of a powerful, wellread, assimilating mind—something that functionally harks back to primal times, the tribal saga, the epic of a society.   —And this is the theoretic difference between the *Cantos* and the *Commedia*. The *Cantos* makes the *Commedia*, in an *absolute* relation, into a personal affair—the difference being that there is a space-time world in the *Cantos* which could not have been possible in Dante's time...."

Well, it is interesting, I'll damn well get you a copy, and see what you think. Origin too long damn well rests, on a most hopeful "creativity"; and what the hell *is* that. I don't, at all, pretend to know, etc. I grant him, any issue of Origin has better work, of poems, etc., than does this issue, to hand, of Intro; *but* I do *not* think that relevant to *any* excusing of what are, literally, Origin's lacks.

It is *still*, persistently *still*, amateur in its total front; it will not, as yet, attempt a literal, & incisive, attack on what is its immediate circumjacence. It is too pure? In any case, it is—something!

(Originally—a magazine that would handle the going-on, as well as that which cohered, I mean, the poems, the stories, etc. And the going-on: those relevances, hits, strikes, hopes, etc., that can come of any instance of stimulation—from another man, a letter, a book read, or whatever it may, or can, be.

It is to put that, squarely, etc., against what is now to hand, this present set, of Origin. I don't know that reviews are the actual relief wanted—I think, by that same disposition of his contents he has managed, now & again, they could become part of the move, with no loss at all.

(Too easily—he equates the plan for his own "form" with

what those other magazines he dislikes are *not*.)

There must come to damn well be some place for what I, or any of us, want to say about a book, or a thing, which has excited me—or got me to some active form of condemnation. Really, it can't be left at, too simply I damn well believe, the poems & stories themselves, *however* clear, or incisive, in character, they may be.
                                                        It is as necessary to make, as Rainer had put it, a climate possible to the work in question, as it is to give that work itself. What he said *was* pertinent: "The climate of poetry, or the general intellectual climate of a country, is not produced by the poetry of one man, nor of a few only ...

Certainly the individual work also lends nuance, but what one forgets is that it does *not* create, more than that, *value for* the work. Or it is ineffectual in a desert of bathos—goes under unrecognized."[85]

If we had *clear* place, for any such hitting—and this was a review, then how goddamn simpler our *literal* defence, of ourselves, would be. What else is it—isn't there a literal, an utterly actual opposition, to what is attempted.)

Ok, I do get pretty carried away. Writing to him, I was, perhaps, too blunt, but I am tired, altogether, of having to find myself some tone which will not offend, when each of his letters is, in effect, tantamount to an intentional insult. It is too one-sided, to put it like that.

My own guns are big enough, are all that I have, anyhow, to shoot with. Will shoot, accordingly.

Writing, too, to Kasper & Horton—they sent notice of this Mullins bk/ etc.[86] Really, which Mitch pointed out to me, last summer: "internal financing by industry has grown to such an extent that already several large corporations behave as banks with respect to other sections of industry."

I.e., a quote from an article, America's Garrison Economy, Contemporary Issues, #11.[87] I've always felt Cid exceptionally *narrow* in his reading; but I may be unfair.

Kasper & Horton have a like problem; the Encylo/Brit/ does, actually, make clear the *main* lie in the Federal Reserve System, by inversion of point.[88] Not that everyone, etc., could find it there, or whatever. It is, in any case, a problem removed, quite literally, by this *further* phase in the *credit*-system. If General Motors can finance all of its own operations, from the ground where the metals come from, to the distributing of their cars to a public—and this *without* recourse to any bank—then I do *not* see that banks are longer as relevant as these very industries themselves.

These same two, according to Paige, who reported to Ez, after his request that they look into INTRO to see what it was all about, etc.— that the Louis Brigante who edits it, is a Freudian—hence, *not to be touched*.

The idiocy, the utter driveling idiocy, of such insistently narrow concepts of USE—I don't know, I go dull, blank, staring, horribly ANGRY, even thinking about it. It kills me utterly.

If there are to be *so many* untouchables—then who in christ name does one finally hope to address himself *to*???

Well, I did Paige a pretty damn vicious & certainly needless disservice; I had little enough right, put it, to write to you what I did, I mean, that finally too simple lampooning of him. He is easy enough to do, he is dull; that is fact, and even now, can't see its simple removal. But he is decent god knows, and attempts an honesty, of mind, I don't think at all in these others.

It is, at that, a bad damn time to suggest this switch on my own part, he just now writes, he's been asked to do a series of Am/ books, of approx/ a 100 pages, etc., for an Italian printer who is to come there to Rapallo: "I expressed before opinion that your prose (as visible in Origin) was not MY cup of tea. And I think I said I wished you well on yr. road. So that it is not flattery when I ask you if you can prepare a volume of prose pieces (yr. best stuff), say about 100 pp. for eventual publication. You are careful and serious, and that's what matters."

I feel it impossible to now make straight my own damn dishonesty; it isn't only that he says that there, though god knows it is as decent a thing, the last of it, as any man ever has said to me. Before that, writing about Russell, Kenner, et al, he says: "Re discipleship: Russell, Kenner et al. (poss including YVT)[89] just kill themselves. Should we weep?"

Guts, to put that in: YVT. I damn well respected it.

So christly lonely, finally, any one of us, if that is to mean, all there is. Someone writing, in INTRO—impossibility, and he asks why, of not staying away from all others. I'd felt that so actual, I put it in the notes on prose, as something literal to my own experience.[90]

Kenner has friends I guess; I don't think Paige has very many— he is too honest, on the one hand, and not very exciting, on the other. It is hell to be that way.

Ok, this for now; I enclose check (Gallimard: was 12 mille, at 350 to the dollar—this am't, and check me). And also pix: for the kids, & to show you, literally, how the hell I do look with people! (But I am eating—my mouth full, but nice at that to [*continues in margin:*] know people do not like me, for the way I look!)

[*Continues along margin, in ink:*] All our love to you all, Bob

[*Adds along margin, now typing toward top of last page:*] Have just written P/ abt yr poems, in case Cid does not make it—tho it looks like real fancy editions—he gives sale price of $50 each! But that wd be great too? Wow!)

[*Typed at top:*] (11 kids now here—a misunderstanding Ann tells me— but that's another story, and figure I should be done [*down?*] there, too—holding the fort!)

[Black Mountain, N.C.]
May 15 [1952]

Robt: The point is, the feeling of the motion & the space around him, that is—in this sense—dance is an action and a thing[91] (in more sense of the same, a poem is)

    that this is what emerges when man takes himself no longer as either the measure or the end but as instrument of, force

    that he is not nature & not super-or-meta-nature but is *the* thing by which each of these (so far as they matter) are most interestingly expressed to other men

      but that he never does get a breath around him, his space, until he has the modesty, the acknowledgement, the wonder, that he is himself beholden to both nature and whatever that meta is (what I very much think it is, the power he can show & feel when he is in command

      that he knows what he is when he recognizes that he is also in himself nature (the way his blood enters his heart and departs from it, say, that beat—or that the sun's arising each morning is a part of his necessities) and is the thing force can do to him when he is its proper instrument, that imperfection

    but that his irregularity is his individuality, is his manhood, like they say, and that it is what matters—if it is not overprized, as i think all lyricists do overprize it, and as i take it Ex remained finally uncertain of it and had to shore his doctrine up by, say, Confucius, that indoctrination (which, having just seen the "Stone Text" of his two translations, just published, rankles in me as his misuse of "stone," of Fenollosa, of ideogram does rankle—[92] that i take it he prevented himself from the proper push his insight led him on to,

and so, by not using these things, that properly, by using them
however improperly, he has harmed them. And harms them more in
such late peddling of that proper noun

that any of us is the only noun,
and the degree to which we accumulate to ourselves—and so mark
it—what is to be known, we give it vitality (the inverse is what is not
noticed, that, the degree to which we leave it—out of some false sense
of honoring others—is indoctrine

((((i am distinguishing a careful
exactitude about what another has done, and any use that we might
make of another, the latter being the act which involves us in totally
folding it away into our own self as the only proper noun)))

which is where, i felt so strongly this morning, your
concept of conjecture comes in: that just that is action behind any proper
act, and that the arc of conjecture reaches out and comes back in from,
anything which draws our attention. This that duality of self &
experience, or of external-internal, is shown up to be the shit it always
was

Or this distinction which has lighted up for me the last few days:
that expression & communication have to be understood to be of totally
distinct orders, that a failure to distinguish them leads to all
aestheticisms, as well as to all the rot of design of the present, to all
technology, either of machines or of men

that what makes a fragment
of a Massacio somehow a containment as complete as the lost full
mural,[93] is that that man, and some others, did their job not to express
themselves but to communicate[94]—and that the difference of these acts
is crucial both to the resulting thing done and to the take-back into
yourself

that the dimension of any act is the amount of desire in it to
communicate

and that expression is not the same drive, is
somehow inevitably short of the demand

that translation stays somewhat expression, and that
men who lack this other will—to communicate—fail to transpose
anything all the way over into themselves, thus are left hanging with

some desire to have their self the signature, instead of the thing being
the rifler of all that ever was, including oneself

that somewhere in
here is the simplicity i keep chasing—in the thing made to
communicate

that transposition (the destroying of any other proper
noun) is the proper act toward anything or anyone

And that this is
made possible when a man is seen to be the thing strung from those
two poles of which he is also a part, nature & metanature

For force is
what anything is—what is "behind"—and so makes us, or any thing,
historical or otherwise present & immediate (that compass wiggling
north with every slam of my keys)
: instrument.

That those "new sciences" are analogues, that's all, of
what i find out—and what i think you find out, you are so disposed,
your attentions are cool:

it excites me, and tho it all comes out like
metaphysics, it holds in itself—i hope, to you—its items, where i
got it
(that place, cuir et chair, or, between my nature & my
desire: that we do use that phrase, human nature, and by
it state, in the adjective, the essential differentiation:

I am so
moved, that man stands up (again?) right there: that he is that huge

Boris Aronson is here, and we do nothing but talk theatre[95] (you may
know him as a stage designer, from being also a painter, but what I
have discovered is, that he is all Russian, and it is like a hedgehog, the
way his rhythm is, he rolls as well sidewise as forward, and it is
beautiful, for the end of each of his hairs is sharp, even as he rolls)

and
i have been restoring speech to his comprehension of the theatre, of,

drama, reminding him as best i can that speech is—language is—what gives all men on stage dimension

and it gives me back an increased sense of what language is, to put it that way (what blank verse was, the excitement saying to him—he wants to do THE CHANGELING (Middleton-Rowley)[96]—that I would coach his actors:

that blank verse as Shakespeare pushed it (until he came out the other side of it, and wrote that verse of THE TEMPEST that no one has ever dealt with, perhaps that it can only be recognized when, from another practice, one gets, as he did, to the other side of what is the dominant speech form of his time)

(((nota: let me have a say in a moment about what i think is happening right now—your own new work has cued me, as well as the curious closeness of, say, GLOSS, and this latest one sent you two days ago,[97] to blank verse line)))

as S pushed it, it got to be *a vertical force* by which any person was not only held up but given that dimension Aronson argues is lacking in theatre (he sd he did not think Moses could be put upon a stage!)

(what i did was to try to show how a given speech, say, in Lear or Antony, whatever the provocation for its beginning—dramatic necessity, even—though it does go by five-feet horizontally, finally uncoils itself in strength from the top of the speech to the bottom, or wherever the image, idea, or narrative comes to end

that the directional of the line is one thing—one axis—but that the accomplishment of the force (due to the whipping, say, of the line, the flex of it, the pushing around of its elements) is another axis, is a vertical movement

and that because it is, all people who speak are properly in size, because only the vertical is the measure of human force

I place this (because i am like i am) against phylogeny,[98] thus: it is demonstrable that when man came down out of the forests on to the plains (my Plateaus!)[99] he ended evolution: he had got his hand as far as he proposed to take it, thumb opposed to digits, and thus a hand could use stones, and also make tools; and he had stereoscopic vision, what no other mammal but the anthropoids did have, does have, the ability to see things instantly in three dimensions.

(He also, I learn, was unusual in another respect, that he already had lost litter-birth, had settled on bearing one child at a time; and had done a further thing—had slowed his child's growth, had ceased to mature at 4–5, and so somehow had given his brain a chance to increase itself by thus lying so long fallow as children do: the sutures of the skull do not close, finally, until one is 25 years old!)

On the plateau, out of the trees, language got invented: he invented it. And it happened in two parts: he had speech first, words, and so could pass on what he had found out about how to do things as well as what he took it it was all about, by precept in addition to example. Thus continuity was born, from father to son, say.

At that moment, evolution was buried, and the other part of his accomplishment (one beside which agriculture takes secondary place)—written language, or sign, as it was first—brought into being the methodology which erased evolution: culture.

(I am tremendously moved by this opposition of culture to evolution,[100] as you would guess, knowing how very deeply I abhor its resurrection not only as a historical concept but as an attention, a disposing of attention, now—that the last 100 years are a dirty reversal of man, and until this is seen to be true, we stand in huge danger of exactly the projections of science fiction: the substitution of [*crosses out* culture] evolution again now 50,000 years after man outreached it: for culture, for the very thing which made him the delight he is, and has been, in—the interim since ape

And I think the opposition is of such greatness and clarity that I want you to know from whom I suddenly found it, Monday: CFHawkes.)[101]

What it does, of course, is to intensify my own overwhelming sense
that the struggle for language today is THE PRIMARY, that it is
speech which is the warrior against all evolution, that it is
the Poet (Dichtung)
DICHTER[102]
who is the one final responsible agent of culture, simply, that it was
language—words, goddamn it, WORDS—which freed man from his
hands and any further extension of same.

(Seen this way suddenly all machines are what I might have
   known they were: picking up, 50,000 BC, anti-culture.   —I drove
   Buckminster Fuller out of my house here three years ago come
   summer[103] by saying to that filthiest of all the modern design
   filthiers: "In what sense does any extrapolation of me beyond my
   fingernails add a fucking thing to me as a man?"

And what equally delights me is the sense Hawkes gives me of the
relevance of the brain to speech, that tie I so believe in and have had to
struggle to keep my faith in, the mind is so ignobled in our time (or
was) exactly as sex has been, the way both of these joys have been
turned into mechanics, too, when surely, by our own testings, our own
deepest knowledges, loves, these two, the brain and the cock, are what
we stand on, more than our legs—are what man is glorious in having,
that, he can go so far with each of them and yet, when he gets that far,
he knows he is instrument, he knows that the beauty is something he
is only tapping, that, however far, it is still far—and he must travel it,
that it goes on and on, and that if he lived to 130, he'd still be
moving,

         moving
                  (that these two are rhythm, those
                  two

What you suddenly see is that the brain—that thing by which man can
organize his senses and his responses—had to have speech—that the
tongue is the life of the head; and that what happened when the brain
was able to swing from the hand and its tools to speech as the ultimate
tool—the first & ultimate tool of culture—there was no longer "tools,"
that technology (& so all design) are cheap by comparison to speech as

methodology. For, like the body itself as instrument—dance, say, or handball, baseball, those two, the sports I made my body by—suddenly man contained all inside his own wonderful goddamn "universe," his skin. When that happens—and such mastery is what, finally, is the analogue of our own progress—to be the self, (a real skin-full!)—man stands up,

> stands, he
>> this little mammal,
>>> can look around, and, because he's got
>>> it, he can crow![104]

He has space and then damnwell goes on and acts—as surely he has, terrifically, for 50,000 years (those paintings, there, Altamira,[105] and his feet in the dirt before those paintings still showing, until right this goddamned minute, those fuckers, in spite of them we are still in business, how long I don't give a damn so long as we still throw words, and our cocks, around

Anyhow, language, that beauty: look at how she shines, against that background—and in the face of all—any—damn fool of a "human" son of a bitch (Shahn of a Bosch)[106] who would use anything but a word exactly to lay out what's on his mind!

((At this point, quote Creeley, working out different drops for his verb *is*: BOY O BOY, THIS is IT))[107]

okay. only go back to back of this page 4 [*i.e., Olson resumes his typing on the back of the page*], and i'll try to whip this hungry stomach into saying that biz, of what speech as base of verse now is moving on love to you all, c.

language, now:

three things lead me this way: yr own new things, yr quoting me those shots of Bill's, and—like i say—what GLOSS, say ...

that what Ez and Bill did by going down to live speech as
base (De Vulgare Eloquio)[108] ... going below stanza or whatever was
for so long from the necessities of memorization (the oral, before print
as record).... that blank verse was almost on it, in that, there, rhyme
was removed, and so one of the two terms of the old necessity.... (that
Whitman was not (so far as line went was weaker than b.v. [*blank
verse*]), but was he who cut the first trees down, simply, that he took
some enlarged stand, even if the cause was onanism, yet, he did a
thing which meant something at least to Ez, and that's enough to
credit him, even tho the onanism, and that dirty line, the "naturism" of
it, is for me to this day a preventative).... that it was "American"—
and I'd swear still is—just that here men did gather anew, and were
also placed anew, so far as the terms of experience went (this Plateau,
and so, again, Language

> Plateau my extension of, de-
> terminant of, Space: "The
> Plains" (excuse, mere notation)
>   (for myself)

[that the combination was this double newness, vulgar speech |||
and vulgar man

             so the double drive in both of them and in us (why
Whitman in his pose of New Man does move—or did move then,
1912)[109]

             why we are what Lawrence also was, half prophet, or better,
have to be Prospective as well as Poets (prospectors, that,
consequence, not facts alone, or truth, is our people's thrust—the same
as it was the species thrust, once (something, here said, throws against
that letter, WCW, to Corman, abt your our work, & my own)[110]

                                                              why
Bill is after, has always been after, New Found Land Man

                                                    (and why I
always feel a detraction when i say Ez is Cento Man, is Gemisto to the
New Found Land, 1429 five hundred years late[111]—why I am sure he
drags up Confucius, and does let those idiot Kasper & Horton throw
that sticker you sent me, that, the Commies have outlawed C there:
that he's "dead," and that force, what men are, is more in that
outlawing, in the negative sense, than all this cultural literary

positivism of the Master

I am only embarassed, flatly, don't get a
laugh out of—anything but a feeling that Ez has a hair across his arse,
when i stumble on this stuff or see this "Stone Text"

((that what
keeps me boiling—redballing along these days—is the complications
of just such senses of wrongs, even on "our side"—let alone last night
having to put up with a new terrific slick, a magazine called
transformations, a fine package of Bauhaus turned Backhouse shit—and
Cunningham, Cage, Boulez, De Kooning, Heisenberg in that same
paper—christ. . . . .))[112]

all right! that, what they damn well did do big, those two, was to say,
down the perpendicular, in, below, lies form in verse, not out, not in
any line going sidewise, and being arbitrarily stopped, or, vertically on
the page, going so many lines and then stopping, but go down

and
that corrolary this enforces, there ain't nothing to say except as you
penetrate your own damn self

(that combo insuring speech,
significant human speech, "serious character")[113]

ok. i take it now the hidden premise neither of them did
completely acknowledge was,

(1) that there ain't no end to the necessity to keep moving personal-wise,
character-wise—that you can't stop for
cultural formulations (there's no totalizer
on this race-track, "civilization" ain't
worth the bother

(note, this was most Ez's
mistake, that, backing up
only to wall, Rimini, 14–
29—so Confucius, 500 BC)

(that Bill's error was only not going
to the Pelasgi ... ok)[114]

and (2)—tho i am sure this was explicit, to each of them his degree—

that in live speech there is metrical shape to be discerned
which will probably become as decisive a series of con-
ventions as the old oral & memorizing forms were

(I emphasize this aspect of it merely to suggest a conservative
principle which, once recognized as a limit implicit in vulgar speech
itself, in human language essentially, frees one into the radical
principle of the human thing, that, far is never anything but the
creation of more far
                              thus what Ez conspicuously failed to do with (1)
is avoided
                    (and thus Bill is seen to be—as these poems you have
                    recently been quoting me open my eyes to—more right,
                    in that (DREAM OF LOVE punctuates this) he is more
                    open, has not let his mind & his itching desire for
                    attention to his self alone close him

anyhow (I begin to lose edge, the edge of my hunger is so great):

                                        that a dimension of simplicity is
reachable in the common speech (as it was in blank verse) by driving
down into it
                    and that that dimension is arrived at by way of the very
complexities of rhythm which Shakespeare broke through, finding,
that (THE TEMPEST) he'd settle for a conservatism of speech in order
to keep a radicalism of life

                    (unsatisfactorily sd, but i did want to add this: that EZ's
concept of a poem—a constant with variations[115]—is somehow rigid
as against what i am trying to see ahead is what that base of speech
leads us to
                    OK. Enough for today, and i dare say, too much   O

[Lambesc, Bouches-du-Rhône]
May 19, 1952

Dear Charles,

Poem & letter in, and wild, wild things. In fact, it is
on what I was trying to write you—mainly questions, because it gets
to come up, as, say, those poems sent, and now this one enclosed.

Have felt, precisely as you say it here—alternative necessary to present
taking of either rhythms or their structure in aggregate, etc., has got to
be from the ground up. A hay-maker, if nothing else. And in what
damn little I get to manage—constant bearing of this, if no solution
yet, etc., in poems sent.

(Item: I get harder than *ever* this constant
emphasis of yours—the vertical, and/or, the
perpendicular

As instance, and no matter whether "poem" is poem,
etc., or makes it all the way—what lifts, for me, item like THE
INNOCENCE is that it makes *no sense whatsoever* unless it be *this sense*.

"Life," finally, of no other bearing—or literally *how* otherwise. I
couldn't understand it in any case.)

I think, I don't know if I could prove it, etc., that ultimately Ez' use of
the "ideogrammic" extends nothing that isn't literally evident in
Stendhal.

(German reviews, for example, neither make any such thing
as plot summaries, or character descriptions, but only state whatever
each man seems to have thought of—and have that sense of
"relevance." (But really, Rainer's reviews I'm thinking of; though
much of that in Curtius' review of the magazine's lst issue.[116]
Anyhow, may not be at all true of usual German reviewing.))

But the thing: sequence get to me to *in what sense* shall we say a *thing* has reference to *another*—this, to note it, in the more "general" positions of any continuity.

In other words, *if* the "ideogrammic" stays, still, horizontal—the milk bottles still on the doorstep, etc., no matter the jumbled "order"—then what the hell is the gain.

Too often—ideogrammic merely, or only, another means to an old ordering—much too familiar.

At least to think of some other use, implicit in the old idea of Ez'. What I was after—since Stendhal, in even something like this:

"Voilà un genre de mérite *littéraire* dont nous ne voulons point. L'auteur n'est pas entré, depuis 1814, au premier étage du palais des Tuileries...."[117]

is doing, at root, what Ez does in any of the essays, and, more importantly, in the verse itself.

I am myself interested in Williams, because I have felt, often in reading either his prose or poetry, the ground *itself* shifting. IF the method be of such kind that in itself it is capable of such shift—then we get warm.

Goddamn well "historically"—attempts to fracture old lines of logic implicit, explicit mostly, in any damnfool attempt such as Dadaism, or, as Rainer tells me more seriously, in German Expressionism.

Likewise obviously—Gertrude Stein is of little use in her *results*, but what she had her eye on, often, seems to me of great interest.

Well, it is damn interesting, and the further your own premise of the perpendicular—with its damn well HUGE implications of an entire ordering, actual, of one's quite literal existence—sinks into my skull, the closer I damn well feel to working it out at least for my own uses.

Perhaps not at all relevant: " 'You should have seen him come from

the tennis court, striding along'—here the waiter demonstrated by
several long energetic strides—'with the arms of his sweater knotted
around his waist, swearing and smiling. *Un brav' uomo.'* "[118]

Any idiot capable of picking up that detail : both writer & waiter offer
little enough to choose from, etc. But I like to think of ole Ez in that
way. It releases me, you might put it, from any *personal* obligations!

The chance to teach there, BMC, etc., was not put down easily, I get to
think, given these attentions and now seeming what, only, I will have,
etc., I am perhaps pretty hopeful not to jump in all the way. Perhaps
teaching isn't that—but one can make it into that, or back to what,
ultimately, the whole gig was supposed to be in the first place.
Reading past letters, from you—instances of when you must have
been giving them incredible chances—and wish to christ I might try it,
even if I have no surety, or even much hope of being literally able to
speak (audibly) so one can understand me.[119]

Yesterday we cut the field out by the house here; family I'd written
about back last winter—that Christmas party of sorts[120]—here too in
Lambesc, and will use the greater part of it for a garden—have no
space for such where they are, etc. Man of course worked like crazy,
he did the scything, and I followed after, with a pitchfork, etc., picking
up & carrying it off to pile it against the wall, etc. I hadn't done
anything that like since NH, and was pretty dizzy by the end of the
afternoon; but he was too, so we made out ok.

I'd written bulk of poem to hand, that morning, i.e., yesterday
morning, and he came by about noon, to check on cutting that
afternoon, etc., and then back again about 2 to start. At least, after it
was done, and could look again at the poem—I felt, feel now, no
embarrassment, I wonder, and do say it snidely, how many of our nice
poets enjoy a like complacence.

Well, I came up from the bottom, rock of sorts, and feel, now, I am *not*
going to toss out the one thing I got from it : speech. No man is going
to get me to let that go. I heard everything, as a kid, and felt, then, shy

& unfamiliar—often started by any words too hard, or couldn't find those flip answers my friends could, etc. In fact, my friends: one was in prison the last time I heard, another working in some garage in Acton, the rest I don't know. But speech, I heard the craziest, shouted, or whatever—the deepest, most permanent contempt for any "written" word any man ever wrote.

(Paige had, and how the hell should he know, written me: "But surely you've heard good story-tellers in bars go on and tell their stories, even illiterate tellers, with no style at all (thank god!)...."

Wipe that drivel off yr chin, etc. He never listened, not like I did, not to every idiot who wanted, even didn't want to, open his mouth. He tells me, then—this is what we're supposed to imitate. Forgetting that the one point is: man telling what he means to tell, & for his *own* good reasons.)

The "vulgar" speech, in their sense: careful mimicry of the least bothersome of the slang, etc., etc. Williams *never* bought that one, and is to be ultimately respected if only for that fact. He nailed that damn lie right where it started, he wrote his own damn "vulgate," and how else.

Ez with those hideously studied dialects—a little sickening, and a rot I can't think too escaped in other conclusions.

I don't say anything I don't say, I don't imagine "characters" to relieve me from my own reality.

When Henry Miller got self-conscious, and he always was frankly—he dragged a hell of a lot of trusting imbeciles after him. You said, and it is obvious truth: the point is not that a speech should be common. Point is—we could learn in so-called "common" the rhythms we might *then* make use of.

Nor is the "point" otherwise—simple or homely truths, etc., likewise of *what* use. Fuck them all.

I mean to make it stick, I mean to make every damn man who writes in this most careful manner wish I never was born.

Lawrence's use of "dialect" is, and not at all easily, record of his own horrors. I wouldn't jump on that one, anyone, if I were you.

What dialect I have I use, and can use; we were, if only a little, out of it. Mother being district nurse gave the whole family that impersonal look; anyone could call her up at any time, etc.

From the ages of about 7 to 14, when I went away to school like they say, and was shocked, scared to death finally, by that loss[121]—I can't have said more than a half-dozen words to anyone more than three years older than myself. My uncle used to be bothered by it, he was so much of a blowhard at that point.

In this sense, and it doesn't have to do with the poem, at least I don't think it does really—problem of recall, and how to use it. Do you think one can make it as you have; I was convinced, for myself, because present relevances are the head, and all shots are to that purpose.

THE RITES

                       (Hogpen, deciduous growth, etc.
making neither much dent
nor any feeling   :   the trees completely
(or incompletely)
attached to ground

During which time all the time sounds of an anterior conversation
and what are they talking
about

Cares mount. My own
certainly

as much as anyone else's.
                                Between
each & every row of seats
put a table
and put on that
an ashtray
                        (Who don't know what I know
in what proportion, is either off, too much
or on.
            Look it up, check
or if that's too much, say, too time-consuming or whatever other
neat adjective to attach to any
distraction
                        (for doing nothing at all.

The rites are care, the natures
less simple, the mark of hell knows what but
something, the trace of

line, trace of
line made by someone

Ultimate: no man shall go unattended.
No man shall be an idiot for purely exterior reasons.

End poem, etc., and me too for the moment, but back on directly, ok.
Do damn well keep them coming—it is wild, wild stuff; and very
damn grateful.
                        All dearest love to you all,
                                Bob

(Both Dave & Tom down with some kind of fever—a little tired, etc.
But cool in a day or so, voila.)

Chas/   To go on a bit—I say any of this with much too goddamn
much bravado, or that tone. But so much of yr letter, here, makes a

case I just don't see made by anyone else—or no one, that I know of, but Williams. "Therefore each speech having its own character the poetry it engenders will be peculiar to that speech also in its own intrinsic forms."[122]

The fact has been that, putting himself as he did & fixing, I think, even quite definite limits as to what area he would, then, allow himself—the "literary" usually divorced or if got to, then offered on any instance or simply without, perhaps intentional, an apparent selectiveness—that this might have him appear, and did god knows to many, as incapable of any "large" range, and hence not much to be listened to.

He had & has, other than yourself, no one literally writing precisely on his own attentions, on what they brought him to. If there is, and god knows there is, a jealousy of Pound—perhaps it is because Pound could have done it, could have finally directed the attention to, quite precisely, the *peculiar* problems of the damn metrics—of their peculiar relation to literal American speech, its fix, then, and now, and the quality of it making it so fit for use, in the *new* context.

I don't think he did; not in the line, say, or really too much in other senses. In my own imitation of Pound—certainly often enough—I get to think what solution is made, in his work, is personal, or no ground for any continuation. Well, obviously unfair: the trochee, that basis for lining, etc., what it did literally do, etc. Ok. I don't so much mean that—I mean, say, that in point of *non*-classical innovation, Williams outweighs Pound on the basis of about 10 to 1. He has experimented more completely, in his attack at least, than Pound in this area.

And it is the area that counts, at least for me. Reading you on the whole works, and now this poem to hand: actually this relevance is pretty unmistakeable. The mistake, or what there was of it, was to look at it, Williams' work, in terms of either complete or "overwhelming" successes. Against what he's attacking, etc., I don't think it too happy a hope, or simply not much of the matter put against what *is* there. (I *don't* have the collected poems, lent them to a man here, etc., but reading them the past weeks—certain that I could prove that.)

Look at some of these, i.e., lines from divers items:[123]

If I do not sin, she said, you shall not
walk in long gowns down stone corridors.
There is no reprieve where there is no falling off, etc., etc.

The perfume of the iris, sweet citron,
is enhanced by money, the
odor of buckwheat, the woman's odor
is enhanced by money, etc., etc.

I should come to you
fasting, my sweet—you
to whom I would send
a rosy wreath not so much
honoring thee as lending it
a hope that there
I might remembered be.

Whereas any art—or perhaps not any—but say painting, cannot come
to rest on too much more, finally, than *any* man's apprehension of the
divers weights & relations of color, line, and mass—this poetry is *how
much*, in parallel particulars, a discipline many men don't even damn
well remember the terms of. Myself the same. I couldn't have said
what meter, put it, I was using, but that I was using it was evident
enough.

Against this Williams' apparent sense of density, and the means to it,
are relevant, are very damn relevant. IF, and certainly right in many
instances—line does not seem good, or enough—what *else* is there—
and isn't it that, too, we might try looking at.

The line is often a mess because it's trying so much. It's trying, among
other things, to be NOT classical: "a reply to Greek and Latin with the
bare hands ..."[124] The man who thinks Williams can still be called a
"primitive" can hardly expect an answer—this, or this question, after
IN THE AMERICAN GRAIN? And that date: 1925.

Williams had *a much more interesting* sense, ultimately, of the "ideogrammic" method, at that date, than Pound has *ever* had.

At least I say that for prose—and talking to Paige, could say that was a basic book for a "prose method."

Lawrence had not yet got to it, and never really did, in fairness, advance method in this sense of its particulars; or didn't, put it, do with exactness in the literal writing, what Williams did in this book. It was not only to save time, etc.

Perhaps Williams wanted to be POE;[125] perhaps it is because Pound is more "Poe" than any other writer since that man, that Williams is a bitter man, etc.

"I've accepted the job of whatever the hell it is: The Chair of Poetry at the Library of Congress for 1952–53. I take Conrad Aiken's place beginning about the middle of September. They pay $7500 now. This will enable Floss and me to live in Washington next year. I shall do what I can—at my age. I am very conscious of my age which will be 69 then: my birthday is Sept 17."

The loss of the past, say, 15 years, with respect to Williams & poetry in bulk, has been that they took off on his content, remarked that—at the expense of his method. Against the *Cantos*, and that seems to be what his work *is* read against—content is perhaps "smaller" though what *is* size that we should so excite ourselves with it, etc.

A poem has to say something, and it is hard to read any poem which does not; it is damn hard, too, to see a rather idiotic delight in a man's mentioning what anyone could damn well have heard, and did, elsewhere, push out a more *serious*, shall we say, concern with HOW that man was trying to say it.
          There is a *basic* difference between the organization of the material in Paterson & that used in the Cantos; I am *not* now just sure what it is—but I will be someday. It is, or seems to me, very damn important. SOMETHING allows a range of TONE much GREATER than THAT in the Cantos : WHAT IS IT???

Not simply the man, etc. Men all get lumped together IF means are faulty. Distinctness of both Pound & Williams relates to a care with means, etc. In fact, I can damn well quote you a poem[126] which shows the same, say, sense of organization & means to density which this one you just sent me does—and by that, I don't mean any easy similarities:

Winter, the churned snow, the lion
flings the woman, taking her
by the throat upon his gullied
shoulders—shaking the weight fast
and unmolested plunges with her
among the trees—where the whiteness
sparkles—to devour her there:
transit to uses: where the traffic
mounts, a chastity packed with
lewdness,
a rule, dormant, against the loosely
fallen snow—the thick muscles
working under the skin, the head
like a tree-stump, gnawing: chastity
to employment, lying down bloodied
to bed together for the last time.

To get it, so it can be read: literally. What you can bring so much IN ON, etc. The breath is what's out, though that one, not so bad.

But principle of how to make it, just so, v e r t i c a l : very damn interesting—what would you say?

The other half of that one, first half, I always have damn well loved:

Traffic, the lion, the sophisticate,
facing the primitive, alabaster,
the new fallen snow
stains its chastity the new shade.

Use defames! the attack disturbs our
sleep.

This is the color of the road, the color
of the lion, sand color

—to follow the lion, of use or usage,
even to church! the bells achime
above the fallen snow!

—all follow the same road, apace.

It makes me very damn naively wish to cry, it is so christly close to all
the sadness I've damn well known.

Not so naive at that: You Aigeltinger/ you were profound[127]

I passed over this one too quick at the time, i.e., intro/ to WEDGE,
reprinted now in LATER POEMS, etc. (I wish I could now do over
review of same WAKE will print, but they wouldn't print it;[128] two
men I want someday to write, if I can, at length on, some kind of
respect if nothing else, i.e., Lawrence & Williams. First paper I ever
wrote, of any length, was on Williams, for Matthiessen at Harvard,
etc.)[129]

"When a man makes a poem, makes it, mind you, he takes words as
he finds them interrelated about him and composes them—without
distortion which would mar their exact significances—into an intense
expression of his perceptions and ardors that they may constitute a
revelation in the speech that he uses. It isn't what he *says* that counts as
a work of art, it's what he makes, with such intensity of perception
that it lives with an intrinsic movement of its own to verify its
authenticity. Your attention is called now and then to some beautiful
line or sonnet-sequence because of what is said there. So be it. To me
all sonnets say the same thing of no importance. What does it matter
what the line 'says'?

"There is no poetry of distinction without formal invention, for it is in the intimate form that works of art achieve their exact meaning....."[130]

But I am, finally, more interested, now, in what you note of communication, and this distinction, between it & expression. Few nights back, had felt that such concludes; in some sense, certain maturings, and one comes from "expression" (simply to talk to oneself) into a conscious act of communication (where nothing short, of that, will satisfy).

It is what Rainer nails with Orphic, and likewise all that genre of poetry which has, ultimately, only an extasie for purpose. It is not, on the other hand, at all Rimbaud.
                    And, by Rimbaud, I get how peculiar is the ground now damn well open to anyone of us—against what he had. At least how exactly there.

Any man going back, it has to be going back, to a relying on achieved forms, no matter their perfections, misses 1) that change is more fixedly our condition than it can ever have been before, though it hardly matters what it was "before," etc., and 2) that no gain can be possible until what is to hand has been secured. Practice in one or two men's hands can't be final; Shakespeare doesn't seem to have saved any of his fellowmen, etc.

Elath's sense of *classicism* seems ok: "The old man looked at it as maturation of all the knowledge u are capable of, in an adequate style—not as backsided romanticism conceived and dedicated to justifying the past."[131]

That's the *one* side; against that—to project, certainly prospectors, the peculiarly relevant, the particulars of which any one man, you said it, damn well is.
                    Ok: end tirade, etc. To get on with it anyhow.

[*Typed along margin:*] Hardly necessary to bang off Ez—to extricate Williams from him, wd be about it.

[The letter's last page consists of Creeley's unpublished poem "Voici," its title clipped from a printed page and pasted in, plus two cartoons (referred to in the poem). See the photograph following p. 160 of this book.]

VOICI

what it don't take is
style, inverted or uninverted

commas (which I never damn well
understood anyhow:

get a load of Tough Shit
before the Book Store Window!

Concerns honest or otherwise,
what is the import

(not to bother no one, but
likewise, perhaps of the issue, what

is it all about

You tell me

concerns no one but
who wrote it, and if, say, they DON'T?

That wasn't the point—which comes to,

alors:

the Greek fishmonger.

[Added, in pencil, in the space between stanzas 7 and 8 of the poem:]
thinking that David will be 5 in Oct. and of school age? Am wondering
if both French and English will be taught in French schools—

[Black Mountain, N.C.]
May 20 52

ROBT:

That one of yrs in (including the LAWRENCE), and the
movement of you (of him!)—by god, much, to have back (especially
how, this poem of his throws what light on Rimbaud, there, that
ordered derangement … and, the other side of, despair: that they join
(for me) at this moment this way is huge (myself getting off, finally—
getting clear—about that thing, the sun)—that Rimbaud changed that
one, CREDO IN UNAM, to LE SOLLEIL ET LE CHAIR[132] (that,
interchangeably, if this one of DHL's speaks for the decision of
Rimbaud to stop writing poems, that one of Rimbaud's is what DHL
did not manage in ESCAPED COCK II

But let me see if i can get down for you what was swirling
yesterday, talking with Con (we had such a day, with the baby near,
and asleep, and the two of us going on about things). I had waked,
from a nightmare, before dawn (a fitful night, light [sic] they say!), and
she was awake with the baby, and came in with me (I wanted her to,
to put that presence between that dream and new sleep) and i told her
what i remembered of it.

The point is not the content of the dream
(manifest or latent, like they say) but what, later, I had to say about it,
Con, in the afternoon, bringing it up, what a business, that apple,
which I reached out for, on the table in the Sullivan's house (where my
mother died),[133] and it turned out to be artificial, actually made of
metal!

You will see I am back to what you carefully put, sleep. And
what I swept on to was—for the first time—an incisive sense of the
limits of allowance we can give any mystery in the presence of that

mystery which is no such thing at all: force, that reality which is as present awake as asleep and into which we learn to subside or we do not stay alive: (subside or sink, in any case, right up to the rose hips!— above which we wave our arms or tongues or whatever, to speak.

I have this sense: that to all manifestations of force (above ground and underground) we are susceptible

(same susceptibility to be distinguished from openness, that the former is the weaker half of the latter.

yet, that just this weakness or invaluableness is what requires responsibility, both of any one of us toward ourself— as keeper of force in terms of ourself—as well as any one of us toward any other, that we do not invade or mislead another by preying on the susceptibility instead of playing it straight down the middle to the openness)

that such susceptibility does not disappear (I would imagine it does decrease), and that just such a decrease is what makes possible what i propose to try to say here again about dreams) but that the more a man manages to keep in open, the more he is both an agent of responsibility and the more his acts are direct, simple and compelling

now, for me—for my tribe—there is a third proposition: that for him to move, it is necessary that an image of the arcs (which vision is the name we give to their describings) be located in himself (it happened to me that day, Cambridge, when the sun sank into me and henceforth nature was no longer anything that i did not know because it was in me, not out there[134]

(i am sure this is why objectivism is right, that, such life is what any live thing has, that, privilege

Going back, counting in susceptibility, especially
where it is such a tendency—dreams (especially those using our own
intimate [terms *typed over*]

which come from underground, these dreams, or magic—even
the magic of poets, what they do to us when we read them—lets
the revelation acquire (because of its potency) any least sanction
in the face of that other sanction which is the greater, his own
blind & stumbling pursuit of responsible act

I don't know that this is getting the proper light on it to
make clear that i am talking about intimations which lie at the
root of all experience—that i am not talking about such easy
aspects of it as those conceptual ones—god, devil, incubus,
succubus, whatever
that i am trying to come from the other
end, from our own terms, our very bowels, as the Hebrews had
it, and i do not like it, thinking that such, too, are ultimately
sentimentalities, even though they grab on to themselves the
putative force of physiology, our own mortal organs (that
dirtiness, which, finally, is where i have had to meet the Jew,
that, I don't take them so, in fact that it is because they lost the
sun—put in its place that monster, the mono-theistic figure—
that they mug their blood)

But let me cut back to freedom, to this new sense i have of how life is
free in exactly the degree to which, in the face of all forces which tend
to show a face distinguishable from your own face, even when they
come as dreams wearing all the features of your own life (yet you do
feel separate from them, and i am saying that *this* is the true

revelation—is not any schizophrenia—is not ourselves as observers in the self—as tho the self were a theatre, and they performances of us)

that we are *separate* from all things (all those three classes) *except* in our acts

and that this is freedom, that, only by our own imposings (however carefully we read the directions given us, by our own dreams, or as i was by a tarot fato,[135] or by the sun, or whatever)—that fate itself (as i say, allowing, that force might have a pattern—a beginning and an end to which that Creator was pushing all, including each of us) even allowing in that superstition, in the face of it one finds that fixed fate itself is no single pattern but is the pattern any man imposes

and that if this is a freedom in fixed fate, it is only any one of us who chooses to work it out according to his lights not according to any acknowledgement of commands—that his lights are the commands, if he does them responsibly

and that the limits of his freedom are only the limits of his willingness to acknowledge force— that force is limited in the tremendous sense that any man's irregularities are no more than he can make them into acts!

Or say this; that i will not be intimidated by any assumptive pattern, even the most pressing dream, let alone any agent or expression of force outside myself

that i take it now there is only one form, what i make— and if this is to any degree less than the "plan" (thus granting plan, god or devil), it is not all interesting, is not the equal of my own wroughting

that this is freedom, this insolence

[*Remainder lost.*]

[Black Mountain, N.C.]
Thursday, May 22 [1952]

Goddamn it, Robt Creeley, those sounding 12 mille francs were
not meant for any damned x'change, for any damned international
bankers to make pennie from, but for you four and ½ to make a party
with—and i so intend it again: i hereby tear up yousen
check
    You can't deny me this crow, that, once in my life i am ze franch
riter charl olsonk (see Les Temps Modernes, October. 1951, #72)—and
that at the same time, by one of those intersections we owe it to the gods
to observe, and have some fun of, you, the American writer, Robert
Creeley, are in Provence, with family, where, somewhere there south
of Lyons they must cook blue trout, or something, and I and Con and
Kate want you to eat it for us. Or something.
                                        They sounded, anyway,
those 12 mille francs like i was a banker! with an account at my
publishers! WOW: i must have worded my letter to you badly, didn't i
say Gallimard would be sending you something from me, not for me?
(What impresses me is that Mascolo, this once, jumped like a
headwaiter!—which pleases me, for that is just what i want you to do
with that stuff, USE IT[136]
                                        OK. And it is a damned fine feeling for us to
be here watering our mouth at what you can do, there. Eat. (Which
brings me to yr pix, yr look—was trying to state that look to
disappointed characters here who would have come next year, they
swear, had you been here—did i get to tell you the proposition i had
already moved thru the Board of Fellows? that (to make the paper
balance) i had suggested i move over from writing, leaving that to you,
and i become teacher of american civilization! or proto, pre history! or
anything, so that what characters might have you fresh, and me
become salt fish, in some barrel!

(i must say the prospects here—and
Con & my jump (the joint's jumping)—have put my Washington drive
a bit askew: simply, that the place is more no-college now, and fast
becoming a Chinese monastery or hill-fort (like in ALL MEN ARE
BROTHERS,[137] that beautiful book I don't know that we ever chewed
over, but which you must put behind you, one day, for, the dimension
of its heroes, and *the motion*, the damned terrific geographical motion
of same huge critters

> (what a piece of theatre such would make: must
> pass that on to Aronson—as well as try to get
> done for him my old play (four years ago,
> Washington, attending the Budapest, playing
> Coolidge Auditorium: a beautiful natural Noh
> theatre, bored by all music except Sam
> Barbour's,[138] I started
>   THE FOUR
> GENTLEMEN[139]
>   the idea being to put four
> men on stage as set as four men playing. and
> then, by having same do nothing but talk
> (intersect, not converse) make a time interesting
> enough for people to sit thru it)

what's happening here is something no one without nerve can stand:
the likelihood of students for summer & fall is so small (the factors are
two: (a) education as a whole is feeling the pinch of the fall of the
births at the depression; and (b) black mt is not albers or rice's
institute: if it is anything it is mine, that is, i have poured in here
(Shahn was the only real help, formulative help: Huss, the runner of
the place, is a fine financial beagle, and has lowered its sights, at the
same time he has fattened its farm—so that we at least can live off
that! in lieu of sd fat heads—and as a result, whatever formulation it
has, sd formulation is so new it has only begun to show draw—as
against that design biz, "art" crap, which may have fit the 30s but
don't do for now (Rice, finally, smells better over the years than J
Albers, much as I cannot sting him, that, he was flexible enuf to have
me here once a month that first year: that showed pedagogical

instinct

Anyhow, the (c)—third factor—is the one i have kept my eye
on: that Am education stinks, and more men & women who want it,
get displaced, and some come here, more & more after other places.

It is that i have thrown in with, hammering at a necessary mobility of
teachers, students, and program, renaming the place The Institute For
General Studies

and Huss rode up on that one, pulling out a program
for next year which has interest: to divide the year into 4 institutes;

    I   (October-Nov): Architecture, Pottery, Weaving, Graphics:
       CRAFTS, or whatever

                (the spine of this is that biz, which
           came out of my continuing correspondence with Leach[140]
           —after that go last year for you, there, Cornwall:

                               he, and
           Hamada (Jap potter) and Yanagi (head Jap craft & folk
           stuff) come here from England October 15th for a two
           weeks seminar—and Wildenhain (Marguerite) Pond
           Farm—the best living potter of them all (for my lack of
           change to buy her stuff) as our host-potter)

    Eames—the chair guy—may be here to govern the whole 8 weeks

OH shit: it all sounds dull, by comparison to other things closer to our
hearts & heads. But you will understand what a temptation it is, in this
precise case, simply, that I damn well could, just about now, push this
whole damned place forward by my own steam, in this sense, make it
Olson's University—and with one plane of my interest, you can
imagine what a appetizing thing that is. But that i lose for an instant
the LOSS such a turning of my energy is—it is merely this idea, that, if
i could get policy fastened on, such mobile arrangements as, say, that
you, Blackburn and I alternate here as "the writers," we could, each
one of us each three years, say, have a place to sound off, have a place
to make moxie with hyewth....[141]

                    (Let me finish: Inst II, the Theatre
                    (December & January, with Boris

> Aronson as "boss guest" and Huss as boss
>
> III, those Sciences I shot to you *before* I turned it
> over to those people! (February March) maybe
> Hawkes, from London, as guest, and me
> shoving
>
> IV: ECOLOGY, with Taschdjian (algae as food,
> etc!) as g. [*guest*], and Sprague[142]—the biologist
> now here—as half-ass organizer (this stuff is
> close to myself, so i push here to: I have to lay a
> little low on theatre, simply, that Huss is scared
> of me!)

What I wanted to talk about is pictographs—ideographs—phonetics.
For I figured out last night that these are the proper progression, and
that use of words like hieroglyph and cuneiform are of another order
(one is the class who had language in their care, or more, perhaps, the
intent of the writing: "sacred carving"; and the other characterizes the
tool: "wedge-shaped writing."

And in what sense this interest of
writing now (it is also interesting that painters—by calligraphy—are in
here too) discloses a *principle of simplicity as the issue of complexity,**
rather than as it all seems to have been taken, as elementary (the
pictograph lying behind all terms—mother, say, death, beloveds,
genders etc.); magic (tarot pack, or, such witcheries as when some
other strong person says some essential thing about us); or, say, such
penetrations as the moon, or a flower, or northern lights will awake us
to (to switch from you & me, take what E. T.—Miriam—tells of
DHL,[143] that, he so gave his attention to a flower that he seemed, to
her, to disappear with it, or, that night, of a full moon, when they were
making love by an oak and she felt him go, go off, as thought he were
no longer human, was metahuman, was something like (if more) what
they once covered by lycanthropy or by Endymion, such
metamorphosis)[144] [*Olson underlines the phrase* "principle of simplicity
as the issue of complexity" *in pencil, and adds in the margins around the
circumference of the page*: P.S.:

What comes out of these vocabulary
accuracies is one fact: that Egyptian, Chinese & Maya all kept the
vertical axis, & so never went phonetic (properly speaking); while
Sumerian & Semite each shifted their axis, in their 1st 1000 years (one
90° left, the other 90° right),[145] & so seem to have more readily went
"abstract." *(the pictograph lying behind all ideograms. When I
remind myself that man painted & sculpt 50,000 years before he
WROTE!, then I am prompted to ask in what sense was his first
writing SIMPLE? Myself, I wish to write with the simple as the
consequence of what I go through. And tho I am using pictograph to
ideograph as only an analogy, I am wondering what is true of it too, in
this respect!]

Now these three classes are, aren't they, underground (dreams), above
ground (the last), and magic floats in some purgatory between. I make
this point merely to declare what i think is a neglected likeness (in the
face of too long a tendency to see their differences). For overall, they
tend, when not so seen as one, to reinforce what i take to be the most
sick of all the dangers of susceptibility, the superstition of a Creator—
that these "mysteries" of "straight line" and of letter have to be
explained (because causation is the way they are dealt with) by a
Cause, instead of being dealt with as *what is,* and sufficient unto the
day and night thereof (the thereof being you, me, whoever—anyone
who takes it up—as he is alive to have it

          ((((this sense, of what a damned fine thing it is,
     led me to this, last night—which i would very much like
     your analysis of, hard:

FOR US

I am grateful that I was given life, that they gave it to me, those two,
that they met, and that they selected each other to marry

Now I ask that my daughter shall be able one day to feel likewise, that the day will come when she shall be able to know why

))))))

I ought now to be where i wanted to get us (in the face of our susceptibility to dream, say) :

it comes to the old conundrum of fixed fate & free will, i should imagine—however much it is something else than those conceptuals

this way: granting teleology (not that i do, any more than i can tolerate mechanism), but granting it merely to engage the tendancy i feel in everybody to put fate or pattern in at some point in the disaster of the struggle of form (that tendency constituting, no matter how the divine or the satanic is brought in to ennoble it, superstition—note Michelangelo, the last sonnets[146] doing the same)

if i allow that my dream yesterday morning was a clear statement of one part of the structure of my psyche—a lesion there; and if i allow that that dream (like others i have had) was a warning—a signal—a picture given to me by the meta-psyche of where I err, I have got to this liberating position: that I am not at all sure that obedience has to be at all strictly in the same terms as the revelation

in fact (and i walk here as quietly as a man must) i think that the loveliness is that the determination of the "pattern"—the accomplishment of the figure of oneself—that IMAGE—is ultimately *only* what he imposes—that he is finally not alive if he, in any degree, lets the revelations (even those in the sun, the above ground, as well as these [*breaks off at bottom of page.*]

Nota: if all of this, or any of it, sounds metaphysical, or moral, or conceptual—comes across so, i can assure you that, yesterday, by that dream, and by these observations, i saw an end to a struggle of exactly two years duration which almost put a finish to me!

And that the crazy thing is that it was a dream two years ago which, with this one yesterday, might have garroted me, the ends of the two of them!

But that what excites me is, that—despite the terrible havoc (and i do not speak of myself, to hell with that, but on others)—the damn thing did work itself in the sun-light! by stumbling dumb acts.... and, of course, is no more finished than anything is, in fact even as i say this i am scared pissless that the ground i think i have under me will be stolen from me the next minute (that just this, is the superstition & susceptibility i mean, that, we do get scared, the damn fucking job is so much *only & all our own*

        ((((one literary relation of it all:

                I read THE CHANGELING
                (Middleton-Rowley) Sunday, and
                was so bored by the way the logics of
                the deaths of Beatrice & De Flores—
                even tho they are logical—are finally
                so backed up to the wall of fate as
                governor

                and again, Shakespeare, how clearly
                in LEAR he extricates the King and
                Cordelia from this sense—how
                definitely he even gets Edmund clear
                of it, even going so far as having
                Edmund say, I have come full
                circle[147]

o, Robt, there is so much springs up—right there, for example, the circle as image versus that thing, the straight line, which, i swear, is the hidden premise-image behind all that stuff i was trying to see a way through in this letter

that the sun is of such moment anew as image that it
does say what the flesh is, that we must walk it

that any gain is
only a movement into a new circle—that circle, in its turn,
involving us in new dumb circlings until we come to the end of
it (a circle does have an end, i know that now: it is a lie, that it
doesn't: it is on one plane

even a sphere is changed for another
sphere (and so three dimensions are busted)

that life is so
multiple that we—no matter when we do—do little, but that
recognition and obedience to the multiple is what makes us as
huge as we can make ourselves—and all others likewise

that
this push is eternity, the only one—and that this movement
from sphere to sphere is infinity, the multiple possibility of our
force, there, the astronomic

(I'll quit, and sorry that i have not borne directly on the matters you
have given me. But I wanted, too, to speak of a distinction between
plural & multiple as of all images, especially those of "gods" (which
are how forces have been allowed to be used. let me say this: (1) that,
monotheism ((that man Amen-hotep, who gave it to Moses,[148] is
another to explore!)) tends toward pluralism, in this way that any
anthropomorphism goes domestic, eventually, & (2) that the only
offset which keeps multiples in, is the sun as sufficient image—he
breeds, mythologies! (I shd have let the principle of multiples have
much more play (above) ((the whole letter)) as why the pattern is not
fixed except as we fix it. [*No signature.*]

[Black Mountain, N.C.]

Robt: (Saturday, May 24 [1952])—i sat down to write you, but had a complaint of Blanc to meet, a Washington character who had a painting in a show sent here—and the upshot of answering him was something which extended itself, and wiped out much of the afternoon. (It is on the back of this letter to you, just scrabbled fast, to make notes of it—& I send it with all apologies for its carelessness, merely, that I thot it might be fun for you to see the thinking.)[149]

It burns me, for I wanted to use the afternoon to set before you some new stuff about language which pushed itself up yesterday—which I went after, to get.

Let me at least take a whack at it. I pick up where I left off that one page to you Thursday, (1) that hole, 50,000–3500 BC: how come?; (2) that axis is Egyptian, Chinese, and Maya; and (3), the SIMPLICITY, the pictogram, behind the ideogram—how simple was it?

And these are some of the first tentative results, guesses I want to get out of my head to you, for what use ...

I have been able to locate some things *behind* the first pictograms—or along-side them.

            Certainly the most crucial is this: that the Sumerian sign for sheep was no pictogram at all but an arbitrary sign (like some of the hobo language, that mixture of representation & convention)—a cross inside a circle.[150]

            To throw the big switch, sometime ago I stumbled on an old article (1875) by an American named Rau about cup and ring symbols carved on rocks[151] (apparently from a time exactly contemporary to the paleolithic paintings)—and the same signs found in America, Europe and India!

(Bald Friar Rock, in the middle of the lower Susquehanna, in Maryland, has some of the most beautiful of these things I shall draw and send you, another day)

Now add some other things to these termini of the 40-odd thousand years:

(1)   such knot-languages as the Peruvian quipus—strings suspended with different lengths, and knotted at precise interval differences, which are assumed not to be abaci but some "language" system[152]

(2)   that wampum—those beads, at intervals, sewn together to make a belt—was not so much "money" but was like a musical score, by which singers remembered song[153]

(3)   notched sticks—here, my best example (and it lit this whole thing up) is not of "language" proper, but is those "maps" used by the old Polynesian navigators across the whole Pacific, nothing but rectangles made up of squares (like latitudes and longitudes) only made of sticks tied together in the proper angles to tell how to make passage across each of those "quarters"[154]

my proposition: if man could "tell" how to cross space, how should he have been impeded, for 40,000 years, from telling other things, by similar devices, in lieu of written speech?

(4)   all such arbitrary tokens as hobos use, as the Dakotas used to make a calendar by (1829 is, "The Year Red Jacket was Killed"— and is represented by a drawing—a *photograph*—of a red coat with two arrows in it dripping with blood[155]—and what excites me, to connect to what went on in Sumerian—is that they added a determinative to make sure that coat was understood to refer to a man: they drew a straight short line from the coat down to a pix of a man's head!

(The Sumerians had a series of such determinatives, in addition to their pictogram-ideograms and (as the language developed rapidly) their phones of phoneticals: for example, "ti," which meant arrow (as well as certain other instruments) was accompanied by a sign which by itself read "gish" and meant "wood" but which, used as a determinative, merely indicated at an instrument of wood was referred to. Similarly, place-names were accompanied by the sign "ki," meaning earth, divine names by the star-sign, "an."[156]

as (to continue) mathematics uses arbitrary signs ((this is really using the big stick, to get the point made, hard!))

and—what is certainly the most curious anticipation of Morse code I know is the pure "language" sense (leaving out, as I have here
purposely, such "sign languages"
we are all more familiar with,
such as semaphore, smoke,
mirror- reflecting, hands, both as
mutes used them and as the Am
Plains Indian used them,
apparently both for signalling and
for conversation)—
a language I never heard of until yesterday, called—I think it is—
OGHAM, a Celt invention based upon the Runic alphabet[157]
(((which,
by the way, was itself basically the Greek alphabet, in other
words, our own—got into Europe from the Black Sea
sometime around about 600 BC)))
in which the alphabet is given a wholly notational value, thus:

a line is drawn as the determining horizontal bar (like one stave of the five of music); the letters of the alphabet, in groups of five, are given the values 1 11 111 1111 11111; now if you arrange the first five above the line, the next five below it, the next below tipped at an angle right above, the next five angled left below, you will see that you could notate any passages by this cryptographic system very easily

Which brings up home—even brings us back to the cups & rings, of 50,000 BC. For these are placed in degrees of precise spaces from each other, and as well they are joined, in some cases, by deliberate ligatures. So one could start speculating—against all these other devices—that these ubiquitous cuttings on stone were paleolithic man's "language" system, his written equivalent, the earliest pictograph-ideograph—even possibly phonetic (?)—system.

And when you consider that the Am Plains Indian was (by contrast, say, to the Maya) a stone-age in the nomad state (in other words, stood in the same contrast to the agricultural Maya that paleolithic painter-man stood to the Sumerians—the first people to invent a language in the sense in which we use the word

(((—use it, this whole line
of thought suggests, altogether too "literally"—)))

then the clues the Am Plains Indian offers are valid to bring to bear on the whole question, from the cup and ring symbols down to that sign for sheep there, Erech, 3500 BC.

OK. There is it, as far as I have got it. And what it leads to, I don't know. What I do know is, that it helps me to reinforce my old feeling that the pictogram is so vital in language that Western Man [(as distinct from the Maya, the Chinese, and—maybe—the Egyptian)—and above all, as distinct from the Sumerians so long as they had their language—(((it was lost to them by passing over into merely the recording system of Semitic language about 2500 BC)), in other words, they had the things straight for 1000 years, and only lost when the power began to shift northward and westward ((which led to the defeat of the last Assyrians, the Persians, in 500 BC, by the Greeks and thus Western Man was born))]

that W M bred what he was—what he has been—Abstract Man—when, in two instances, the axis of his language shifted from the vertical of the basic pictogram, and became, in the Sumerian case, syllabic (that happened about 2500) and in the "Phoenician" case—(it is more exactly called the Seirite case—they were those miners, Sinai,

2000, to whom their Egyptian overseers passed them the beginnings of our alphabet, the story I sent you last fall[158]—) the effect was decisive about 1500, the date of the birth of the north and south Semitic tongues, especially the most powerful dialect of all, the Aramaic, which was the parent, by god, of—look!—Indian, Persian, Arabic, Greek; and so, of all languages which ever were (it having finally swamped Sumerian) EXCEPT CHINESE, MAYA AND THE EGYPTIAN FROM WHICH IT STEMMED—the Egyptian stayed hieroglyph and essentially vertical until it died with Egyptian civilization, about 400 AD.

It comes out a sort of gauge of all cultural history interesting to me, the more simply, that it is the history of *language*, and, because it enforces anew two distinctions, the solid and the vertical of, or implicit in, language, and so should make clearer how far back into the dirt we are leaning—Big Trains—to make the pitch now![159]

There is one last kick the idea of a world-wide token speech filling the gap between 50,000 and 3500 has for me—that a certain *mobility* of mind and fingers, a certain *plastic* quality, was the necessity of that other system by comparison to what at least alphabetic-syllabic writing has— a quality more akin to just the beauty of the brush in Chinese (& so, from the tool and the medium, preserved in the living language), the power of those Maya stela, and behind that excitement of mine about those earliest poems and stories of all written poems and stories, the Sumerian myths and epics.

love to you all,

C

[*Olson enclosed the following:*]

THE ATTACK, NOW, IN PAINTING & WRITING

Taking painting as a writer will, as analogue, say (and by so saying not cutting the least ground out from the validity of the observations, I knowing, from experience, that it is painters who tend to throw most light on myself, so far as it shows in the work) ...

I sd to a friend who had a bird in a show,[160] that his, more than any of the group with him, was some pepper in the pot, simply, that the others seemed still to be moving from the work of the immediate predecessors and that that could now be called visual maneuvering, and to show no push toward any vision of man at all, "no attack," as I there put it, "on two-dimension as it is now more than a field for visual maneuvering." (The degeneration of that immediately preceding advance is design, DESIGN that falsifier of the true formalities implicit in any valuable extension now, beyond the work which was done between Cezanne and the present.)

Cezanne was the last huge painter, in the sense in which Giotto then, was the terminus (as Dante was, in my business, Giotto's immediate contemporary). After Giotto and the Sienese, painting & sculpture & architecture became what they were, in respect to what I shall say below, right through to Cezanne. And what seems still required is to say what that is, in order to get clear what difference now is. For I am so often bored, right now, with shows, that they disclose a lack of understanding of what has happened due to the change the vertical axis the Renaissance rested on has gone through, passing as it did, I am dogmatically saying, from such an axis to a vertical emotion El Greco lent it (exactly contemporary to Hamlet, on what a handiwork is man)[161] to what it strikes me it is now, a vertical motion. (What it now is is something neither as mechanical as perspective nor as [*types over* mystical as] aspirant as El Greco's literal vertical human male bodies— like crucifixions, yet without loss of a capacity to secure the vertical law and at the same time keep in such vision of man as, though differently stated and how somewhat inaccurate, Hamlet and Theotocopuli's Christ showed.)[162]

The horizontal, too, has shifted, due to the shift of the use the law of
the vertical has come to. I call the vertical the law, just because i think
it is the law of art for man, the more so in the plastic arts, that, there it
immediately relates to that which man acquired by standing up off his
hind-quarters, his eyes at right angles to his spine.

(This is the true
equivalent to the law of gravity in man, that he stands up—to see, to
move, to act humanly, as distinguished from those things he can also
do animally.)

For if the vertical has thickened itself into a motion, though staying
axis of painting & sculpture & architecture (much present practice
would belie this, the ameboid in painting, the spreading of building,
the mobile & stabile in [painting *typed over*] sculpture—these can be
shown, i think, to be false faces of the present necessary push) then the
horizontal has changed. And the other lack i see is a lack of awareness
that it has become not frame but direction, the direction which
qualifies the vertical motion, qualifies it, not confines it, and so restores
the frieze or dado or vase, say, to interest.

My notions here can be put more explicitly, in terms of what
happened from Piero or Uccello to, say Picasso. By Uccello's day, man
as measure had so informed perspective that only the sky above and
the ground below him limited the vertical axis as it stood in any
canvas as image or principle of man. And the horizontal was only,
essentially, man's environment, the one big one then, the countryside,
landscape, Nature. By now, in contrast, man knows he is only
interesting as motion.

(My hunch is, that the error I call visual
maneuvering comes from a failure to see that motion also affects the
old horizontal, breaks it out of the rectangle, and so forces painters
and sculptors, in order to justify that limit—to use that limit—to
reconceive space as something else than what it looks like, fields, or
whatever.)

One could mark these fundamental changes noticing one
such thing as present painters' interest in calligraphy, or writing as
decorative art, especially their interest in the Chinese language. Now,

though this entails black and white—black on white
(this needs to be emphasized, now that one of the two men most
responsible for putting the Chinese language back in circulation in the
West has made the gross error of publishing some of his translations
page by page with plates which pretend to be rubbings of stone
tablets and are not only some cheap mechanical equivalent of same,
but are also, madly, white on black!)—actually it itself brought about
the restoration of the recognition that black and white are colors, not
merely poles of grey as a color. And so even here one is dealing with
what any painter worth his brush these days is a howler in, color, that
wondrous thing paint, as color, not even any longer just a means to
register light, but itself, color, pigment, that thing, flesh practically, it
is so movable.

But, at the moment, my switch is—to the language
aspect of this thing painters are arrogating to themselves, the
ideogram. Now I am one of those who are pushing this thing in as part
of the writing act, from a common inspiration to the first to do it, from
Fenollosa (Pound, however, is now falsely pushing it, though in his
earlier position he was more right, using one face of the ideogrammic
art correctly, that is, as a further push of imagism, simply, the demand
that a writer see at least as sharply as a painter—that a poet write at
least as well as a prose writer[163] (—that he see as well, remember as
well, and transpose into sounds which keep the same definiteness of
outline, the light)
        I push from a wholly other insistence, that the
medium (stone, or brush on silk, or on fig-paper, or papyrus, or clay
itself) is an analogy to the need of men who write to take up from—
and keep in—the *resistance* implicit in language   *cf End
itself because he came out of mouth, that diverse thing.

Which will get me back to what i had to say to this friend about
that show. This way:
                that it is my impression that what is crux
now is how we take a man anew—which means that each man must
put in hard for himself on exactly that level of vision I don't see many
shows disclosing (technicals are no longer the front quite as precisely
as they were for Pound & Picasso

And that this has overwhelming effects upon
how one takes the paper, canvas, or block in front of one

                                                        my own
obsession is that all this has restored the two-dimension surface as a
field to work in (not the box it was from Uccello's "Battle of San
Romano"[164] on, and not what falsely replaced that box, or theatre of
perspective, the visual game which is played today with the rectangle
like someone playing hopscotch with no feet) but literally a field to be
ornamented, as that Scandinavian chief did, who had his sledge and
his child's cradle carved, those panels there,[165] the simple pleasure of
using up the whole space

         that such an art of ornamentation has behind it a tradition as
rich as the Mediterranean thing out of which Piero and Uccello started
that other business, a tradition of which Chinese language, Japanese
screens, say, are only the Oriental face of: that from Turkestan
(Malraux, in the 20's brought back from there sculpture in brick, mud,
and from cave walls, tombs on the edge of the Gobi),[166] from there it
came through Russian and the Scandinavian countries down to—and
was half of—the Gothic
                           not to speak of those utter masters of the
principle—the vision of—ornamentation, THE MAYA (sophistication
is the quiet thing, which only comes—never comes from outside—
issues only from inside the single human being, his sense of courtesy
arising from his knowing that he has needs—is not dramatic, does not
feel any slightest need to put anything out as theatre or even as such
rollings as, say, even that moving place where Shahn has at least put
man back in as struggling creature, so curiously stunned, as his people
are, so pathetically looking lost, however much this is, the proletariat)

         I say any of this—and am about to stop—only, that i believe
there are men around who, by the nature of a wish for vision and by
the care they devote to paint, are ready to push beyond that old
perspective confinement and the newer false freedom—of the visual
surface

who—placed there at that point, that one-dimensional stand that a painter or sculptor or architect is as he stands before any surface as he is also, a man—stands where his audience also will stand—works from that point not for perspective (not to add that dull stereoscopic simulation to that surface, or avoid it) but to inform it by the only three-dimension which ever properly mattered, that cultural one (not that evolutionary one of two eyes without a snout): that man is round, two eyes, a nose, and a mouth, like any pumpkin or like any man who ever lived and sought—light.

*RC: furthering this analogy of the medium of language (man as a man the "stone," and himself as self the tool, chisel, or whatever, brush, if he be silk), I don't know but what I should want to identify something else as a resistance even under these more detachable upper parts—silence, as the thing from which—and against which—all speech plays, that thing if a man talked steadily his whole life long he'd only chip at, it is so buried, so much as the earth out of which any stone comes, to be carved. And so much the fact of rhythm, that, in speech it is silence which is the interstice, the space, the variants of stress, the thing that we mean when we say (say Dostoevsky) he gets it all in. Or what we call the breath, the breathing, there—the taking of breath, like they say, how, this is allowing in that factor which the word silence is altogether inadequate to characterize, it is so fat and moving a thing, even though it only shows the top of its head in speech.

[Black Mountain, N.C.]
Monday May 25   52

Robert:

The feeling, just now, was of a break-through, and i thot i'd get it down to you, to have it for myself also. But you will know that curious fact: that the moment you do have such a lighted sense, you also kick yr arse, for in the next instant you are able to say to yrself, but of course, just that is what i have been doing, up to now. So i would assume that the process of break-through is merely the coming to the surface of the drive, which, until it can so phrase itself as law, is actually doing its better work below. What is then, becomes the value of the sight & formulation of the sight, the law?

So far as i can see, only two things, and only one of them much good to any one of us for himself: I'd guess the main value to the man concerned is that the coming to the forefront of what has been the practice, unbeknownst, the coming up, merely clears the way for new practice, is, in fact, like the proud flesh, a peeling off for new stuff to have its way.

Which leaves the damn excitement of, the sudden lighting—lightening. And I figure you, too, are a man to tell someone instantly, or as soon as possible, what has been discovered, "look, the bright thing ..." etc., the shining hawk's bell [*hawksbill*?]. So i figure the second use is PRECEPT—pass it on to the next guy, for what use, etc. The secondary function—tell 'em. (Tho i am more & more moved to believe that this teaching or critical function is going to be less & less interesting. I would honestly surmise that such activity is demanded only when men have got mighty ignorant of the simplest things. The truth of this will not be apparent to most, still, simply, that for so long just such spelling out of what goes has been needed, so much so and so long that i am persuaded that we still tend to think of the critical or pedagogic function of twin to the other. Or maybe this is peculiarly personal, to myself, having been so much such a sort of hybrid. In any case, I take it it has been dominant in our parts since that Socrates at least, Christ only such another who made so much of precept and who, like Soc, seems to me by just that fact intrusive on another man— that thing, which i do not like about the religious figure (exception, Buddha, who, said, dying, what can i say except, you got yr own job to do!), that, because they don't make things, they have to put all the package on their own damned selves, that thing, that they lived, only that, that their life is the thing made (as though a life was that potent, however potent, knowing myself that the sense of size—it seems to be felt most in the chest—is only an excuse for getting on with more work, not, the prizing, even in the modestas[167] of a doctrine, of one's own life as anything more than a bearer, and not, as such, those two, a sort of knowing use of their death's

                         ((is it true, what i heard, that Socrates' reason for refusing to fight his sentence or taking exile was, that if Athens kills me, they kill themselves:[168] jesus, isn't this the same deal as—the use of a life, of its mortality, as the big stick—as that other, the crossed stick, and the hanging, a Roman law offender))

You will know (knowing how i have been pressing myself to the statement of LAWS) what is going on here, in the person of ... And it got a damned funny light thrown on it this morning—the beginning of what i wanted to write you was, the light, for today!—when i came to the end of this man Hawkes' book on the prehistoric foundations of Europe, in which i found him setting a principle of Europe against what he would call the principle of Orientalizing—that Europe has been, from its mesolithic beginnings, a culture balanced on instabilities which have kept European adaptiveness to the front, and so, he says, that "instability of balance has been the measure of their success under the law of all life"[169] (that last phrase arcing back to what man had got to by evolution—as distinguished from culture—up through the paleolithic); and that the civilizations of Mesopotamia, Egypt and Crete went static fast because of a tendency to organize themselves in cities under king or priest ruler (the European doublet is warrior—each man his own strong arm—and trade—have magic things, amber, gold, in other words moving strength, not cities, and exchange of goods, not accumulations of same, said accumulations tending to settle and raise empires on city bases, or valley places)

Now the thing is too well argued to take its top off this way, and leave it at that. But what i wanted to indicate by it was a sort of change (which, as you'd know—knew, and saw so incisively in G & C—I would not put as Hawkes does, so late as the Greek attack on Knossos—Theseus, in his picture, becoming the forehead of Europe, the First European Champion[170]—would not make into that too easy biz of West vs East, but would make a story in a circle, and that we are back to that point of stance toward things more like what went down, there, Mesopotamia, 2500, than what has been true since that warrior gang got their metaphysical tongues going in Socrates, etc.

In any case, it comes out, to me, that it is more in the nature of something like precept overcoming made-thing—thus the distributive function out-running the productive—than two chronological or historical
orders, two geographical ones.

>   (Further confirmation, by the way, that ignorance of
>   writing—art—on the part of contemporary men of
>   learning is what licks their new science, as it licked the old
>   natural sciences

>   that *mythology*—where, surely Waddell
is strong, and where i have always had my own correctives of those
birds—from Homer, first, then Herodotus, then Pausanias—last, the
Sumerians—is the circle which bends the iron of their progress axis
back into proper confinement.....

All right. We are starting home. For suddenly, again, getting myself to
see this old history which i got into G & C in a like sight (the language
go i got off to you yesterday must represent the beginning of a new
push, and that push *backward* from Sumer!), I had to ask myself the old
question, why do you spend your time nailing down these bloody
goddamn things?

And it shot me, once more, to my faith in the instant, in what one does
keep going at as, measure, I, know, not so much fool as cupid, blind.
And it threw light, this way:

>   joining you, that surity of yours, that time, in the
>   act of narration, is from the writer at the instant of
>   his writing forward, what Ann sd, the reader's
>   time, what about that, that beauty there, the way
>   you have it—get it in—that, this going on
>   ((((((((I sit exactly N by NW, ¼ NW))))[171]

What humanism was was the self dragging—arrogating to itself—that
other factor, the instant—and thus, by that appropriation, starting to
lose both the cause and the effect of the doublet, self and instant,
which is, is it not, multiplicity (and its other face, diversity)—what i
would again call the metamorphic or the arrived-at change

Take it from my own quandary, why I interest myself so much in time backward. I have never felt this as a pursuit of history, in fact have, as you know, taken it as more some space-pursuit than any time one. Yet one does weary of one's own cliches, and so i have always questioned the whole deal. So if, today, I felt the whole pressure suddenly as a bringing to bear on this instant—as an essential act of my nature to inform any moving present—you will imagine the sort of relief. And connection. For precept, suddenly—lesson or law—dropped away as issue. And I felt again pushed toward that principle of simplicity which I still don't know the content of, no matter how moved toward it i do feel, these days.

                      I felt even something more: that perhaps the reason why that piece to you Saturday on the other language was in such a better prose than the obverse of it on painting & writing is itself sign of a jointure, in myself, at this point, moving in two directions, forward to some other sort of verse and backward (as I said above) so far as that space-time—which had led me so far to Sumer— now takes me *behind* the Mesopotamian Valley.

                    (Let me toss in, here,
        as probably the left-out counter, is, *image*. So far as I know,
        it is the only thing i am after, in any search, act or learning))

What struck me was, that, where we are, in our practice, as against that humanism which has been observed for so long ((which i damn well do trace to sometime *after* Homer and yet not anywhere near so late as it generally is put, the Renaissance, to my taking, being only the sudden surface sight of what had been making even behind Socrates and Christ:

                 (picked up one fix today which excites
        me very much. Did i put it to you that flatly, that three
        figures interest me for drama—no, do *not* interest me, I not
        finding it possible to create by negatives, am not that cool,
        do go, as you know, to some figure like Apollonius,
        instead—but three figures who, antithetically, serve to
        define the sort of figure I would create:

Socrates, Paul, and
Akhenaton or that pharaoh of the New Kingdom who was
Amenhotep IV, and who twisted himself and turned a new
sun worship into the monotheism (which, argues Freud,
Moses picked up direct from this guy—Moses, says F, was
general of the Sinai or East Egypt areas for Akhenaton)—
1370–1352[172]

Anyway, this bird is the true fountainhead, I'd guess. And
what interested me, was to learn from Hawkes that
Egyptian trade and objects in Europe cease just with this
guy's predecessor.[173] In other words, I back up to the same
point, on this line of tracing humanism, to the one I did,
first, in looking for the rear of Homer, and second, the one i
did in G & C. So that that door of the Hebrews I got out
through in that shove I sent you called "Culture,"[174] is the
other proper end to the search to the one—through—the
Greek kitchen.

There may seem to be some confusions here, but they are due to
differences of time planes, not to essential differences. That is, the
break-up of the Near East (which can be seen all over the place to be
dated by the fall of Knossus, c. 1400 BC) is only—as i tried to put it in G
& C—the consequence of some earlier loss of coherence which already
was setting in a thousand years earlier, c. 2400 BC.[175]

Now, out of the
rot, around 1400 BC, came monotheism—Akhenaton & Moses, 1350 on:
HEBRAISM, the earliest sign of the West, simply, that it was the
periphery of the Semitic thing which, 2400 BC, knocked off the old
Sumerian thing.

GREECE, on the other hand, was, 1400, exactly the power which
destroyed Knossus: Mycenae, the capital city of the Atreus family later,
the ones who, 1220, knocked off Troy. Homer, then, as our best sign of
what used to be, is so because (1) the Myceneans—what he calls the
Achaeans—were the direct continuation of old Crete on European soil,
thus direct pipers from old Sumeria; and (2), because, when, later, the
Achaeans were themselves knocked off by the Dorians from the North,

they holed up in Ionia—a backward movement, so far as the base pattern of migration westward is concerned—and by Homer's day (850 BC), Miletus, his home town,[176] was still telling those tales.

That was what these birds call Helladic Greece. But the Greece we have had to put up with is HELLENIC GREECE. [*Writes in the margin*: just here, then, Europe finally clearly shows itself.] And that twin of Hebraism was altogether a local Greek mainland product—was in the making, independently of Miletus, at the time Homer wrote, and showed itself finally with the defeat of the Persians in 490 BC. So Socrates (who fought in the battle)[177] becomes the SECOND MONSTER of humanism some 800 years after Moses (Akhenaton). And the THIRD MONSTER, the Christ, is the sign of the accuracy of this geneology, is he not, being, as he was, the mixture of Hebraism and Greek which Christianity itself is, and has been.[178]

OK. Then, to come back. What seemed pertinent, today, was the idea that the restoration of instant as now (which is what I am charging humanism with disturbing, by (1), a single patriarchal god; (2), a concept of Ideal or World Forms (Socrates-Plato); and (3), Future, that thing Christ most did havoc with, Redemption)

the restoration of instant as now restores the self to both its edge and its multiples, thus giving it back its force, not an ego or lyric bird-mouth, but as density proper to our own sensation of it

and that this condition forces on any of us a wholly other space-time disposition, such an other one that I am delighted at the wealth it shows:

      (1) that the downward is the place where form is to be found (not outward, either in the acts of men—power, etc., as rule, gold as not precious, but finance, etc. etc. —or in the acts of communication—not stanzas, or canvases, no exterior boxes—

WARRIOR!

(((extension of content, then, is intension of same!)))

> (2) that the multiple as several selves demands
> change or metamorphosis as autobiography,
> not biography, that history of men by law of 70
> years

TRADE!

> (3) that the time of man is not history but the space
> of him, and so is as crucial a way of severity as
> is required of each of us about ourselves, we
> being only analogues of all men, actually more
> than analogues, being, containers of all men
> back and ahead

> &   (4) that time as axis is only this now, every new
> instant, that it is changing, not washing, or to be
> stopped—not that Heraclitus image of into it
> you can't step twice,[179] which is outside, like all
> Greek thought, even Ionian, *after* Homer—but
> is to be participated in as wholly as space is, as
> it was all men, and will be

I'll shut up, with this quote I stumbled on, from lovely Lawrence: "I
like the wide world of centuries and vast ages ... mammoth
worlds beyond our day, and mankind so wonderful, in his
distances ..."[180]   Love, C

[Lambesc, Bouches-du-Rhône]
May 27 [1952]—morning

Dear Charles,

     Very damn good to have yours, it moves a lot.[181] Am
not at all sure, put it, in this area—I wish one could be but don't yet see
how, beyond this of the responsibility—which is the base in any case.

To get to the poem quick—it is only that I am again very damn
confused, i.e., I don't see clearly how I can take my own life, or
another can, except that it is there, and that is all there is.

It's the problem of the third line—"Now I ask ..." That is, who? It is
that character of the address that I don't think can be used, and please
don't think I jump too quickly, or without seeing what I am bothered
by.

    I've thought a lot about it, I can't look to anything for anyone but
myself; it's not a selfishness. Not believing in any god, or even a
structure beyond "All flows, etc."—I couldn't ask anything of anyone,
for anyone.

    To me it cannot matter. Neither what Kate will come to
feel or know, nor what Dave or Tom will; not in that way. They are
very distinct from me, anyone is, must be. Their reality, call it, is
lodged in what they are, not in what I am. That they keep somehow
live, is all that seems relevant or that I can, like one does, hope for.

The literal problem of one's aloneness—not as any queasy uneasiness
but as damn substantial fact, is what I think I have here. Or have as
objection to what this poem is after. I can't thank my own parents,
perhaps that's simply myself and my own particulars, etc. I hate that
coincidence which obliges me beyond my ability to feel very deeply; it
is no question of love, or that I do or don't.

    If my parents are at all
what I myself am, and I don't believe it—then they force me out from
them, will that to me as necessary act. It's impossible to feel grateful
for my own life, it cannot be expected either of me or of anyone; it is
the horror too damn often asked of us, that we thank anything for
being animate. We are. That is what it is. We damn well are. There
must be an act beyond gratitude.

At least I can't feel that my own parents gave me life in the sense here
offered. I am—that must be ultimate. Beyond anything else, this
being—with no reference to undo it, say, or say that it is at all too
much another's choice.

I believe this because I think that no one can be open, in these senses you damn clearly indicate, unless there is *singleness* in him. Somehow *a distinctness that does not avoid contact*. It is very close to Lawrence's, his emphasis here, the *non-isolate singleness*, what must be.[182] [*Adds in margin*: Perhaps saying that—I make clear only my own confusion—trying to see how to accept even that I AM alive. Anyhow. To begin it.]

In that sense I have no children, and want none. I don't believe one can have these ties clearly; and I am [*no*] more instrument in their being there than I would be in any other act or thing—their issue through me but not to that which I am.

                    Animals are very clean here. Each thing is, that is what it is, and all that matters.

I don't think I make much of it; very confused here, and impossible to work through it very quickly. The poem worries me because it posits a gratitude which I cannot accept for my own acts, or really for yours; and it involves another being, your daughter, and asks too much of her because it asks *anything*.

Forget it anyhow, I am not at all cool on this subject; but damn well do argue it with me. This thing is almost my hysteria at that; I will *not* see it, that we have any need to thank anyone or thing for our life or that it is not actual loss those times we feel any move to. I so loathe what can use it—just what damn Christ and all the rest of it which I hate because it hates me, what I am, hates literally that I or anyone can *be*— in spite of neglect of the supposed rites.

When you say, "Now I ask ...," it is I know only that form of speech, yet it is too close to that other form of speech—o god almighty, etc. It scares me.

Only for myself. That's all I can deal with; I can't do anything or hope anything in this sense for any other. That is where, in what, he is. Let him act it, that is what he is.

I am, damnit that IS enough—damn well enough to work with. Not anyhow to say, fuck you, etc., I'm too busy—but that how can I have the audacity to hope for you or any other. How the hell should I take on that—to hope you are what I am in any part. It is too goddamn simple, I don't believe it.

It is damn well the fierceness, and the mystery if that word is the right one. My damnit MY persistence in the literal act of life. Anyone's. Who's to thank.

At least it is not fine, and damnit I don't mean to get snotty about it. Life is not fine. I don't see it. It is there, and I don't see anything else. *Kill me, ok; until then, I'm here.* [*Adds in margin*: much too simple.]

No one has any mystery, either in his hands or in any other part of him, until he acknowledge that he is himself, and that ultimately, and that nothing shall ever relieve him or even thank him for being. That anyone dies, or anything, and he is there still—as long as he can say it or feel it with his body. That he must register all that is given to him, that nothing can be expected, that no matter his calmness or sureties, it can be infinite in its gradations, of pain, or of anything. That to be stunned is to die just then & there; to act is fierceness, that force which he distinctly is, and no one else can be. [*Adds in margin*: about it all comes to, now.]

I get hit by Laubies' work (litho/s for this book just now in) because he can acknowledge it—not simply as fright. What he did for 3 Fate Tales is a more deep acknowledgement than what I did in writing it; I mean, I wrote it down, and he acknowledged it to be there. He made it of, or from, his own character; it is a damn deep thing.

Acts between men are mostly acts of sight, [*In margin*: not true—but a "right" of sorts.]—but it's impossible to thank any woman for making love with you. A damn odd phrase to begin with, but accurate at that. How to live with anyone is the problem, at least I was damn honestly trying to be exact in that poem A Song. It is what I continue to believe. I mean it has its positions, the granting is that there is continuance, and that this continuance is multiple, "gross" in its manifestations.

Either I am, at each instant, precise, and all that I am, all to that point, or I give myself over to an actual limbo, or waste of movement. [*Adds in margin*: what you teach me.] It is damn well grotesque to think about—what one can do, by not doing it.

I try not to say it all too simply. Life is so goddamn evasive but in its acts. You see a man alive, etc., and then dead—just that simply. It is impossible not to see what had mattered, or what anyone is. Times, literally, in Burma, etc., seeing so much death it had no value but that it was *not* life. Odd & sudden grotesqueness: two men dead on the ground, blankets over them, and a crazy flower or bird very close to them. How to express it. How a man dies or what is the literal thing he has lost in that act; not only crying out, the shock of that, but whole strain and retch of the body just then— what it is after just then, and doesn't get.

To accept responsibility. Every damn day you get it. Cleaning out the reservoir here, lot of tadpoles, etc. Watching them die in the sun. You take it all on because you must. That idiotic injunction, do unto others as you would have them do unto you, or really its 20th century evolvement: I want to do things so that no one anywhere will be hurt by them. My sister said that one to me, or something like, to act so that it will involve no other unpleasantly. That sense. It may be an honest hope, but I don't see that it is at all possible. Fuck general rules anyhow—do what you can each time. The philanthropists get screwed with particulars; they are too nice, etc. (Lawrence's rules always damn well impeccable, i.e., his revision of Franklin.)[183]

Right now thinking of this poem, what it is, and fact Williams has always put himself directly to it, and doesn't ever go out.

Just damn well remember the copy is still with that man; anyhow, it is that one (and do read it) in Later Poems—Come back, Mother, come back from the dead. Something; this winter moonlight is a bitter thing. Frankly I do not love you. Do read it; it is a damn fine one. Toward the end of that book, title is I think AN ETERNITY.

Also what he had said in Paterson: (that damn book too not here, fuck it) *It is almost the hour* I.e., I think it's beginning of Part Three, Book 4.[184]

Both Williams and Pound so clean here; Williams particularly. Very damn great respect for them on this particular. And a huge one.

For the moment, or let it go just for now; am in knots trying to think about it. Not to let it go—but that I am damn well sprawling, etc. Too defensive, etc.

Cid answers it looks as though ORIGIN is not going too good, no money, etc. Figures not too much more.[185] Wish to god we could think of what then.

Rene L/ has litho/s done for that book; as said, 20 copies, and don't even know if we can get that many printed. Real great job; was very much taken by formality of any such lithographing, against his structures—wild thing. I mean, formal surface, and then what he makes of it. I think he is a very great painter, but god knows I am mostly feel on such things.

Look: yr letter just in, all about what's going there, and I can't take it much longer—damn well do want to come if still agreeable as soon as we have this baby and have loot enough to get back there. Well, not to make it too rigid, etc.

I just don't make much here, I miss any stimulus, and feel too displaced. It would I know be work there, to manage one's own time, etc. But here it is simply off and so no good—just don't see it for too much longer and this place, though pleasant, quiet, etc., solves very very little.

I tell you what;
about the middle of December we will have loot for passage, etc.
Any time thereafter would be cool for us if also for them there too.

What I suggest: I could even bring the G/s with me, damn well an
idea I'd always had, since G/ IS terrific printer, IS real sharp on
European literature, and so is Renate; it wouldn't be at all a favor to
have them there, and it would be so great for them too. I damn well
think I could get them to come, if you see any way to use them.

                                                                                 I
mean it. I'll take on getting them there, if there's room & food for
them once there, etc. Could all come together, if that wouldn't
inundate you.

Also, Laubies is likewise looking for some way to get into US for a
few months, and there again, crazy man.

Both, all three (Laubies, Rainer & Renate) would have full academic
status i.e., have degrees, etc., etc. Rainer some kind of great one I
think; very good man for the list, etc.

Rainer could teach, say, anything relating to European culture,
economics, printing, writing, etc. Renate very cool on French, and
much the same material as Rainer.

Laubies is the same—with painting added. Honestly, sharp men to
get in there. Young, able to look things straight, etc. No set or warp,
etc.

Also, Renate and Laubies speak excellent english; Rainer a little less
but no problem—two weeks he was with us, was perfectly cool in
all conversation, in fact, he used to start about 8 any evening and
wind up circa 12! Not bad considering he hardly knew how to say
hello confidently when I got to Freiburg.

Is it too screwy? G/s probably could stay on for as long as it
seemed ok; Laubies, if he could get in too, for 2 or 3 months. Would
be real wild collection! Too much!

Well just for now, and say
what you think; forgive MY DAY, etc. I get much too damn pompous,
simply scared. And WILL find some BLUE trout, and many many
thanks. All our dearest love to you all;

Bob

[Adds, in pencil, beside signature:]
MAKE IT: I could get there (B.M.C.) beginning middle of January '53
as the latest; Gerhardts (and Laubies too) if it is feasible. Makes sense.

[Adds, in pencil, at top of letter:]
Had not got yr last when this started—see END. (noon)

———————————— ════════════ ————————————

[Black Mountain, N.C.]
May 29   52

Robt: Yr superb letter, and that—is it not #1—poem, THE RITES—god,
it's beautiful, the way it comes to those things finally said—how man
leaves what he leaves, and those cares, the doubling of it

And I am
full of this, yet, will you permit me to let more spill out of these
preoccupations of my own, hoping, that there is an end to them soon,
and i can get back to these things which you have raised in front of me
(as well as Origin matters, which have got into a pretty state, i have
just let the whole thing slide, there being no impetus with you
absent—and simply that unless one can feel that one's days of writing
go home there ((that huge error he made, not to keep his damned
forms open until the last minute for anything you or I came up with,
each new issue, that result of his failure to do what you have analyzed,
make it live instead of literary. And this news that he proposes to
"present" his own work in #7 [186] leaves me in such discomfort that i
do not honestly know what to do. Goddamn the thing, without you it

is the old fucking thing, publication, which i never did push for or value that much. In fact, it gets worse: I have this wish, to "publish" to [*i.e.*, the] Creeley, and let the rest go to chance. It is that flat, that lonesome. And yet it is more than anything. It is the way, for me. (I wish it was you that was still in there, Origin, instead of me, and could mediate for me with this priest—for i can't do it anymore, can't mediate for myself. And yet am in despair—a sense of doom—to lose this second volume of verse. Shit on it, shit on him for spoiling what was such a thing: origin, boston. (Still the ring of it rings for me.)

Ok. Not feeling well today, but want to see if some of the things in my head will drop out for you. They cluster around three propositions:

(1)   that jazz was, from rag to yr Bird, say, composition as
man as instrument as backing up to "gone," goofed off, bongo—
and so free of what all those Composers (excepting my boy
Boulez: either, they get that good or, they go back behind those
boys, Krupa[187] or whoever there, a twitch twitching how to
make the nerves obey, not the ears the feet, fast feet, beat

& that dance, likewise, that formal dance is either kinetic in the
absolute sense (i have not seen it, but, say, Nijinsky:[188] I believe,
from what he *says* …). Or it better go behind (like Litz, & I
surmise Cunningham—tho i shall know better in August) what
Millicent Rogers once told me about a three-night go at Tao[s]
Pueblo,[189] the strength even she took as the thing went on—or
any African gig, like say the Dafora group i saw once 23rd street
do KYKUNKOR just as they came off the boat—a left benefit, for
Spain.[190] (Or, merely to get what i took fr jazz dance
acknowledged, the night, Cafe Downtown, I was gone, with [*rest
of paragraph typed in margin:*] Meade Lux Lewis &—what was his
name, wrote Blueberry Boogie[191]—taking turns playing for me,
with no one else but us, and the redhead I was swingin—out
(just about the one time i was in there, that way, back to the
backbone, dancing with those bones, the rest all appendages
doing what they will do when they go free, and get exact
in other words, some first sighting here on the state of those two

"arts," as put up against verse, or certain painting, say: what do they rest on?

(2)   Aristotle, the Poetics, that the tragic flaw in a
        hero of an action is not properly either from a
        lesion in the character or a conscious sin or
        perversion, but from his "ignorance" or
        finiteness[192]

(3)   & Benedict, there, on rites & dances of the
        Pueblo Indians as distinguished from their
        Plains neighbors, the small difference, in
        discussing which she lets out with the concept
        that what any knowledge of different
        "cultures" impresses on one is not the
        extensions but *the limits of human imagination*[193]

What this beats back to—around—is what the play is (I take it we know *where* it is, that is, in any one of us—that this is what finally makes uninteresting, all these "scientists"—even maybe Frobenius, tho I have not yet, because of German, read enough to have any sense of if he shows limits of this order—Jung does, flatly, that he had no other choice,[194] knowing what he did, but to use it as in himself, not make it that public knowledge which they all do and so defeat the end of any such knowledge, that, it is only known & disclosed by acts and things made, it is that responsible—we are, who know it, have to be— metamorphis is

What it is: Lawrence only is the present gauge, co [*Olson*]. (I would limit Ez's push from this side more, perhaps, than i would from that side you do in this hot job of yrs on Bill & he: that Ez lost his gain on that side where he stops with Sigismunda or Ulysses as the active principles and then starts adding those conceptualists like Confucius, John Adams and several Chinese emperors)[195]
                                        as you are the more
impressed by Bill's verse, these days, I am, currently, the more by Lawrence's: that he wanted, or did, in his verse & his prose, get communication not by a form which simulated the process of

penetration out of which his sights came but by something one can call
forms in the public domain

(there is grave danger here now. I am of
your opinion—i think it is true we coincide, in this respect—that any
largeness has to come from the "where" of it, and that any *what* is no
more than that *where,* he or you or me

and that the what of DHL was
exactly the degree to which he had wrought himself—and, by god, by
purity of act, severity of same, and no literary matter—that came *after*,
was *his* consequence, and has the extraordinary magic of not asking art
of anyone but life of them[196] (this, surely, is the thing which makes
him of the greatest, what Homer was (tho Homer is something I shall
want to come to, out of these propositions—including Ez—that Homer
was able to carry that accomplishment—DHL's—with some
*un*necessity of stress which I would take to be the thing which even
Rimbaud, in some way, did not arrive at, nor Melville, even though he
does in certain powers of Moby-Dick, simply, that his language, there,
was, at those times, the conduit to force as life is the best expression of
it we know—that maybe Dostoevsky had it, even though, for me still,
his vocabulary of the soul is something which, by contrast to image (as
in HM) or personage & event (as in Homer), I am not able to follow to
the full ((tribal difference, I'd set it down to, knowing a Christian, and
having had to go through all the troubles that such tribal difference
creates, yet, having gone through those passages, knowing that a
Christian, in the Dostoevsky sense—or a Catholic, in the Rimbaud
sense (the distinction is pertinent, in him, that the sensuality there is
not so much a gate *as* in DHL (a Nottingham or American Christian),
or in Dostoevsky (Melville, again, is a hybrid, was a sensual man, and
the Mass would have relieved his unbelief, and so removed it from
him, and let go more often that force from language which MODI
[*Moby-Dick*] permitted him: cf. Rimbaud's Le Soleil et le Chair, earlier
called CREDO IN UNAM,[197] to mark how woman was the controlling
term: it throws much light, to me, on why he did make so much of his
mother & sister in those after years—why, in fact, I'd say he gave up
verse, that, he hated its sensuality, its perception, that, it did not stay—
production as man act—did not stay as it did in Lawrence, enough:
Rimbaud wanted—would give up anything for—that thing, touch me,
that—& without that final question which kept DHL producing?—"or
do I ask too much?"

(Rimbaud's mother's love:[198] when one thinks of it,
it must have been, from beginning to end, the thing against which
nothing else was as good

      —I am pressed on to say that Catholicism is
that form of Xtianity which keeps African and Hebraic knowledges
more alive in itself, and that Protestantism or Orthodox bears more
Greek & Socratic individualism in it than that what i loosely call, for the
moment, sensualities

      and that at least in the Jewish and the Catholic (I
know too little of the African) the mother thing is apt to get a stress
which, say, Bill more than Ez discloses

      (again, Melville, that curiosity,
how his mother & his Hebraism are intimately joined

Think of each of these men as they draw woman: DHL, who fought it
all the way through, and made it, as much as any man might—made
that, "Frieda" of Kangaroo![199] but how, finally, it is his men (his self)
who have the richest echo, the individual mark on them: The Man
Who Died, etc.—how that other thing gets distributed, sort of, is more
from Tortoises as from any of those women, even his mother or his
Friedas[200]—((that he took such a fierce attitude toward his having
children—god, how beautiful, that he seems to have thought his own
paternity of his self enough for one lifetime! how fierce he was, how
damn stiff pure he was, about the male rebirth, that feminine look he
gives Mellors' backsides, there, when Constance sees him![201]

      (((how the absence of this in Pound—any sense of
      these pushes—as tho he was Apollo, or something,
      the lack of Eros in him, the lack of that
      engagement—how Amor becomes the metaphysic
      instead of the fact, the involvement, the
      problem—
one feels Ez skipping in these areas, not at all getting down,
actually enjoying himself like some All American kid, just all
any of it, on any hand, and it all very damned dull

Dostoevsky, that damned queer light all his women have for me—
exception, those Magdalens of his, Sonya and Grushenka (though the
latter joined to Dimitri, makes something else than Sonya, but i think it
is only the addition of that pinchedness which the other women—the

Katerinas[202]—have—what spinsters they come out, not in the American sense, but the English sort of sense of those many unmarried sisters, sort of aunts of women

but there is that other thing in D, that, despite the lack of women portrayed, one takes it that D had a very beautiful sense of woman—that he was damned modest about them, had in him an act of recognition of them—of what they go through—which is most most rare, that he never for an instance set himself above them, on the contrary, because he was a very great man—not mere male—he felt life—I was going to say, through them, and i don't know but what that is it, that, he had had the reality of them, that it was in him and that, almost a mark of that modesty, he did not know that it was his business to disclose them, that he assumed that the day would come when they would, if it seemed worth it, disclose themselves. So their presence or their absence is not of the moment it does seem to be to other men: they are there, through him, through those men Alyosha, Dimitri, Ivan—and the father (and Smerdyakov[203] not there through woman—that quality of S is most a distinction from his brothers—but through the father) through the way men are—that damned big sense D gives of men's doings, and women in there behind them, however

(((this is something Bill seems to me to show like effects of, that he has known the woman thing and yet figures his business is to say his stuff

tho i feel, again, some American sort of inaccuracy there, even in Dream of Love, "Flossie,"[204] some lack of knowledge on Bill's part of the incisiveness of woman: he has the sense of what they put up with—a little of their ultimate outrage at the hands and feet and cocks of men, of their minds—but more a man's sense of how they maintain their thing in the face of men than a woman's knowledge of how that is done (what Dostoevsky, of them all, of all these men of the order of our reality—post-1850—had)

Lawrence had it, but with some color of mother on it than that thing a woman has when she has an individuation achieved in addition to what that love demanded of her as mother can give—and i do not mean, by such a phrase, to localize such love to only her children: it is something

the word love diminishes, for it is a disposition toward all realities
different from any man is capable of, rather than mother-love, in fact
just because it is backed up to generation, locked up in that act, it is
different, and is a source men (this is where I think Dostoevsky is so
very scrupulous) had better leave alone—or they start sliding, as so
much and all the dirty moderns do, and lose both their own damned
thing and woman's for her too

                              (jesus, when i think what a deal women
get now)

Ok. Melville is a queer one, simply, that the American thing then was
such a pisser, and he did the damned best he could, so good a job in
fact that he never slid, and in the reaches of MD had a lot to offer, in
fact so much that he arouses huge source which it is difficult to talk of
genders about (read one day his thing AFTER THE PLEASURE
PARTY, with its moving sub-title, AMOR THREATENING,[205] to
gauge how damned severely the sex thing had him in its iron hand,
how seriously he did take it

                      but he was not the man to meet it that
way or even to be as quiet and alive to it as a Dostoevsky—he couldn't
have managed the victory DHL put himself through:[206] all he could do
was to ring those changes on force which make MD the rich obscure
world it is

It is not accident, that, here, I put it [*in*?] Homer. For I would take it his
coolness in such handlings as Circe, Calypso, Nausicaa, N's mother
and maidens (I am of Bérard's opinion, that the Descent into Hell, and
confrontation of his mother, is *not* Homer, is a later, another man's
addition:[207] it is too Euripidean, too "modern" in its consciousness of
the individual and his exact relationships to be a part of a man who
could shed such ease of reality on all amorous and erotic event and
person: Circe is, for example, set beside Medea, the *real* presentation of
jealousy, that thing which woman is involved in as surely as man is, in
his vanity, that thing which is always driving her to wreck life, to
bring it down as no good, as ultimate affront, like man has to his own
powers—that Medea is woman giving in, where Circe is just the thing
itself (and that both are witches is so sound, for jealousy is so much the
way woman does know, not her intuition, but this pool of blood in

which she looks and reads all things—reads over all distances, and
sees things & events that I, at least, as a man have learned from this
sight of woman what communication is—how it is so much more
than memory or light, that it is something a man can only go to
form in the face of, to image, as his equivalent of that incisive,
conscious absolute knowing which woman has from her jealousy, that
exactitude she damned well feels which a man, if he feels it, has to
watch, as she does her jealousy, that he not think himself a god as she
has to think herself a demon, she knows so much

And then she loves,
she plunges into man, I'm sure that that focus that woman has in love
is from, or is the like thing to, that sight jealousy gives her, that
narrowness (I speak here as a man, for man can never endure that
jealousy, it will beat him, he has to take it, and go on with his motion,
he has to put up with it, and, goddamn it, see this thing it is—stop his
assumption that, because he doesn't ultimately have jealousy—in fact
is, when he is a man, generous, the very opposite thing (but never as
generous as woman is in his love, never), he is generous and warm or
he's a shit of a male, and woman is cool & hot, that beautiful thing,
cool and hot—and neither of them ever cold or they are dead, just
goddamned dead things cluttering up the earth, impeding those men
and women who can live, never cold or small

For jealousy is not
small, however it chains man—it isn't, simply, that it is hot, and has
such sight in it, such goddamned wild reaching as far as anything is,
the track of it is so much not only from the focus but out to anywhere,
even to abysmal depths of reality as any individual takes it as abysmal
at those times when they are not productive or to the lineaments of the
moon or of any god face (Demon always, for woman, why, I'm sure,
they do go for these Dionysus' or Christ's only to deliver themselves
from the sense that God is the Devil—a sense I do not think man has,
due to his other thing, his pride, that he can do what he does, that
raising a man has to do, and because he does, because it is only on his
own one leg that he stands—he stands on nothing so solid as woman
does, somehow, that she generates—because man damned well has to
do the whole thing himself (even free himself from his mother and so
from woman) he thinks only finally in terms of life & god as triumph:
this is what makes him the rider he is, and why woman can look into

his face to see something the pool of blood will not show her, what she
herself cannot see, the damned glory of what she herself makes

a boy
is a woman's slide. And I swear that she never settles for it until she
has worked her way thru men and found not one of them as big as she
knows they are!

and i distrust all men who don't go beyond woman
as girl, who stop there where we all begin (Lawrence, I surmise, went
over a certain distance more than necessary in his push—went over to
woman as mother plus wisdom—curious to me, but one does not
sense, in him, knowledge of woman as courtesan, what one does feel
some of in Dostoevsky, but only most in Rimbaud—and in Homer,
that Calypso, wow, what a gal, what a one—and that he has those
three, has the power to have Odysseus rise to that girl Nausicaa
looking as full of chest and shoulder as he does look, being cleansed of
the brine and coming out covered with an olive tree—and yet the
clarity of him that this girl is nothing for him to go to bed with as Circe
was, or as Calypso was (his refusal, even there, to stay, to eat her god-
food and drink her god-water and wear her god-clothes, but no, says
he, I must stay man[208]—jesus, who amongst any of these, or ourselves,
has this firmness in verse or narrative, this size (I am aware the clarity
∴, but the size of it)

and where it comes from—came from, I don't
know, but I sure figure to find out, for, if I would see what I am always
talking about (how dimension is in there without loss of particularity)
there it is

there is the what of it, the fullness which makes the limits of
human imagination something I'll stay inside of, and not let any such
concept lead me to any social action or any individual despair, I'll stay
with Odysseus, saying no even to nature (if it is fair to call woman
ultimately that, or Calypso), saying, the where of it is the what, and it's
all I got, no matter what you got, I got this thing I am and I have to
make it bear my way, no way other than that, no other man, or
woman's way, but this that I am stuck with

(take out woman as
nature: 'tain't so: we are both something else than it, however much we
are involved with same: we are more involved, each of us, with
ourselves, thank the maker, that, that is what we are, and it is something

different than any species, and as each of us is it, something different than any one else, each one of us, each man and each woman, this is it, and all such sights or insights nothing by comparison to that limit, that, we are it, for whatever use, that use to be our own choosing

                                        OK. Christ,
what a speech. Hope there is sense in it. It is what speech I got, these days, Olson's speech!
                Love,
                        O

———————————————————————————

                                [Black Mountain, N.C.]
                                Sunday June 1 52

Robt: I guess i am as bummed as i was last summer when i wrote with a pen.[209] Certainly not so, or, I wld not be jumping in this way, having read yr letter fast, last night, on receipt, and not back to it, jumping in ahead of it—yr biz, there, of how you took these four lines, that speech (of yrs, of mine). But what kills me is, that it is Williams you have used again as counter, and I riz up, hackles, ready, for the same ole fight.
                OK.
                        For there it is. It stays, for me, a matter of song, how you sing it. What I asked you for—hard—was that, was how the singing goes, not, ... but there we are: I do not separate, and so the speech i got back is what you give. (Where i rub is, that, you hear "ask" as not said word said sound but also this, for christ's sake, do you think i ask anything, any creature, any—ask Kate? Jesus, Creeley, without dropping back, it would seem exactly that Olson does not ask period. And so—no?—thanks are also to whom addressed? To those two? Imagine. Or to thank or to ask anyone.
                        The fact that it says all these

things this flatly—should it … look, to hell with it: if it don't work for you, ok. Then it missed. I damn well was on the shakiest ground, had obviously put myself on that ground, not shakily, but damned nervously knowing that, just such terms are just so obviously what you have read em as.

What bigs [*bugs?*] me is, that, you don't tell me a thing. Creeley don't tell me a thing!

And when you load it with Bill, I'm for bear. For—shit—do I crowd you—or him—off your spot, that I must have doctrine back? Was it doctrine I was writing there—or was it (the very four lines of it) an American Chinese chrysanthemum?[210]

I don't know. I'm fucking troubled. For with such extensivity as I am damned with, when you give me the doctrine of personal intensives— that via (not you, anyone, always, the same thing—I say that knowing what I am saying—i hear the plain-song, not the division, I go bloody, I know this is you but you don't come through, you get to be the crowd, the enemy. (It does seem to be—any answer—all that I said to you then, last summer, that handwritten go: fucking well don't even remember the provocation—ya, i do—but what i said back i don't remember, except, that I'm sure it fits. This new situation feels like. And so, to hell with bothering to say it again.   It is too damned close to my own worst fucking moments.

The thing is, as you damned well know, one's stuck with what one is. I got what I got to say. If it don't fit, another can't wear it. I can only make what use I can of it. The rest is over there. It just breaks my stride, for a minute—my gall— whenever it's you that can't use something. Fuck it.

I'm sure the trouble is I shy whenever anyone rears up a philosophy at me: I damn well take the particular that thoroughly, that I see any of us exactly the thing—Creeley, Williams, Olson. I don't know that I am any more than Olson—have never been able to take that further step of conclusion, or a wisdom out of it, even the phrasing of some truth supposed to cover experience as such

(and in saying that I'm sure

you'll hear all the questioning that this fact confronts me with:

it is

why i have never managed to speak in any other voice, why i do not
write stories, why all i can do is to stay particular, am in this trap, and
so—if i speak to others—i cannot say that i think it has to do with
anything any more than that there are some others who appear to take
experience by some like handle, so, I speak of tribes.

More than that: I
do not believe that i am wrong (i mean the 1½ negative: i do not at all
know that i am right). I only know that I can do nothing else than what
I do. Beyond that, I have no certitude—not even in what I do.

Have just reread those three pages of your letter, and see the
irony of the duplication of statements—even to the "too defensive." Yet
I still burn: fuck Pound & Williams, even on this. I cannot use their
lesson.

Nor that animals are very clean in this: exactly they are
animals, and we are able to see a thing around it: what the hell else is
consciousness, even, seeing around the fact that we are alive—and
that, surely, is the flatness of that thing there, those lines, that, we do—
and so are post-animal (the shit that comes from any failure to
recognize same, i see in much amount around

Or take it, that when
i talk so much of ornament, I mean it. I mean to speak of such things
too, such objects—put stucco rings flat on the facade/

Why i should
argue an instant with you is no good. Just, that i must speak back. I
can forever hear you, but I cannot, for an instant, any longer, have
you or anyone quote me anyone as text—or quote me text. Conjecture
is too deep a part of me, and particular. I am that ground—honed—
that I am so prepared to feel i am not right, I cannot stand to endure
the notion of how far I am not right. And so, like any fucking idiot, i
spit.

With one last thing: even, your quoting Lawrence, at that point, as reinforcement, or—that's not square—as usable extension of yrself:

the only literary matter between us—allowable, in such hot points—is the mss before you or me, no fucking fact of the "life"of that or any other man, merely me and you, what life you bring or what life I did not bring.

The practice, yes: anytime, spell me how to say "I ask" and make it stick. Or "I thank."

But the package, that's me or Creeley, and Lawrence, Pound, Williams—are terms, in other situations. I don't live them or they don't live me. Nor do you.

Shit, god damn it. It is a damned nuisance that I should stick you back. Forget it. But I cannot omit it, or we won't have the thing we have got. I give it to you, and won't add anything, just, to make it be the dirty end of a stick it goddamn well is.

be back.

Olson

—————   ══════════════════   —————

[Black Mountain, N.C.]
Wednesday   June 4   52

Robt:

with all my boasts, can't see around *that* thing, any further than that i wrote those four lines to begin with, and would defend (not them, but the direction out of which they come

yet i so hear

any of your judgements, that

it was narrow of me to put it back to you that way, god damn narrow—and a sure sign i feel cornered at the moment, that i should have flashed off at ur suggestion i pay attention to Bill's practice in an area which the lines put you in mind of (despite apparent activity & possible advance in some areas of perception, i am not making poems of any importance, and it always leaves me weak and irascible)

in fact, i am damned boxed (craziest thing of all, too, is that the WennerGren came through with a check for $2500! just like that, in an air mail letter, with no strings, just "for site examination of Mayan glyphs"![211] jesus, you shld see such a thing fall out into yr lap!

And tho I rode, for the moment, I have so hidden the fact even from myself, that you are the sole person, beside Con, to whom I have mentioned it—haven't even acknowledged it!

The reason is clear: I do not want, now, to go back to Yucatan. I want to do one thing: be isolated (as I used to be in Washington) to do no thing more than write each day. Yet here I am, and these new moneys cannot be used for Washington. So I am in the position of banking the whole damn thing, and let it sit, until such time as I can take them up, and go back to the sites.

(Therefore, by the way, because they don't represent live money unless I go to Guatemala & Mexico & Yucatan, do consider it private to you, Ann, Con and myself, until such time— ((when, now, i can't, for the life of me, figure))

Which goes straight to (1) what i do this saturday, when this place is over, and (2) what abt yr project of you, Rainer, and Laubies sailing here (right up the North Fork of the Swannanoa,[212] as one smart one had it, last night, when I announced your plan to all & it was welcomed by the students ... it came popping out of my mouth, in an open meeting, before i had said a word to the Board or Faculty. And I think I was right to open it that way, for, as you will notice, your arrivals would coincide with just about the opening of the 3rd Institute i layed out to you. And as that Inst is now considered "Olson's," another wise guy sd, "just in time." Which it damn well is. And is mighty right.

But the trouble with all these things (including the fact that Con is now Registrar) is, that this place more and more pulls me to make it my center—that is, sucks me towards itself, not, that I have yet, or I take it, ever would center on such a thing.

My own working plan is (1) to go to Washington shortly, and stay four to six weeks, to be by myself, and see if I work well; (2) return here for the last four weeks of the summer session; (3) then wrangle out of these people the same visiting plan of four years ago, visiting here from Washington once a month; and (4) return for that eight weeks Institute in February and March.

So my suggestion about you, R, and L, would be to keep you three in there (so far as the College goes) as guests of that 3rd Institute, at the same time that I keep all three of you in the minds of the Board and Faculty as replacements (permanent replacements) of (Laubies to replace the painter, you to replace me), and Gerhardt to be pushed for the vacant printer's position (one which has never been held for itself, but always a combination of design & printing.

So that it works out, on that schedule, that I would figure to go back to Mexico just about a year from now (in other words, that I will have to lay that gold on the shelf that long!)

Such a plan pivots on this wild deal, of buying the Washington house, simply, that I could not afford to pay a rent in Washington, and come here (the place having so much less money now than it ever did ...

and the bottom of the birth curve of the early '30's about to hit the place—as it is hitting all such (Marlboro College, in Vermont, just folded, and Goddard is reported to be close to it)— next fall (Huss and I differ in our guess of full-paying students in September: I say 10, he 12!)

((((((Not that this actually would hobble yr plan for the three of you, for the place is—how do they have that phrase—dirt rich, and cash poor, or something—that is, housing and food is not their problem, but cash. There'd be place here for all of you, and food. So the only problem is salary and position (the latter is what takes the maneuvering, simply, that the paper position seems to be something a "Faculty" can't get its minds free from, anywhere). So take this as my doping, and let me give you usable word to go forward on when I can get it moved along into the formal place. OK?

The other mechanical news is Corman: a letter in from him yesterday on his intention to turn the mag into a every two months "journal." I'm not quite sure what "J" [*i.e., journal*] means—he says his model in format is the German NEUE LITERARISCHE WELT!

In any case, I swung him off a letter immediately (the first time i have felt able to write him in months, the dying off of the feeling of the thing being that grave).[213] In fact, I welcomed the idea, taking it as an opportunity to renew some principles of editing, and also to make damned clear to him that, if he does argue, (1) it will give him a fresh alertness to possibilities, and (2) a more rapid instrument to move "new writing" forward, then he has to bank on you and me, or there is no chance for him to save himself from (1) the "foreign trap"; (2), the "review" trap; and (3) the "creative writing" trap.

I put it that flat, yet, I do not find it possible to hit him where I imagine you do and which is obviously the only way

i find his utter carelessnesses so thoro that the details of them is such a welter i cannot engage myself with them. I can only make *principles* of editing as clear and bald to him as I possibly can, and hope that a little of it gets through, (holding back my despair that he can do anything else but operate—get out a mag as he did get out 5 nos of ORIGIN THE FIRST [*SERIES*]

But I feel, as you do, that we are already off in some other directions, and that Corman is behind us—even tho i am still ready (and I damned well hope you will be) to push as hard as possible to make his new thing (16 pages, but I gather more of a newspaper format, and so equal to 64—with this added gain of only two months between issues) to make this thing what he won't make it IF YOU ARE NOT IN IT (I am not that decisive)

For INTRO does make the difference. The crazy thing is, that I had it, and this Elath,[214] just about the time you did (Jack Rice,[215] in Mexico, had sent me the thing, with his brother, on that spring vacation and I had gone right with Elath. And I propose to send Brigante those two copies you made from letters of mine in the last two months[216]—what do you think? and have you any other suggestions? for I take it, this sheet is the best one we have in these parts. (It is such a pleasure, to have this guy Elath laying down those sentences of his—damndest bite. Strikes me he is a German, or something (tho he obviously ain't), but the only like *temper*, and true exasperation (it is characteristic of the man capable of the principle of TOTALITY, as he has it) is this guy Zander, whom I wrote to you about and whom I stumbled onto in CONTEMP-ORARY ISSUES

> (it is wild, how, suddenly, there are those two,
> at least, who are all the way clear—no. hold on, I do
> not include Zander. He is merely political. What
> gives Elath his seniority is his totality—and he
> means it. One can test him, and take his
> thoroughness, both of interest and investigation

Let's pick up, between us, on this prose of Elath's (what I was getting at by "German" is the severity of his mind, but his prose is something unheard of—true illiteracies of syntax allowing those pushes of hard thought to sit there to be worked for—it is so damned nice, how climax and all such rubbish is set aside, how he doesn't raise from this real welter.

> And his wildness for methodology! By god—that (if anything ever did) damn well demonstrates ZEITGEIST! How abt that—a guy using that word!

> And his hammering on dimension 4, his acknowledgement of science.[217]

> This is a lad, for company

Note, to explain remark above: "am off." I feel down, but not down the right shaft, and so not free to move off in the proper galleries— the galleries proper to me—and this, finally, is always wrong. Am

crazy to be down the right one. Know it, godamn it. A fucking fact of
how to get living in place to leave me at the door of my own shaft,
not something the company's property also makes available to me
for descent.[217a]

        Will damn well let you know when that happens.

                                                     By god,
having sd that, I now do see around what you laid home to me, there,
Saturday: it is, finally, not my business to make those attempts at
flatness. You did hit me, once, hit me bull's eye, when you put it, too
fucking honest. And it makes only one business mine: the invocation by
image. I have no way of delivering my conscious stuff except straight—
and this is only of use in critique, in a sort of incisiveness, no more—
because of that hideous straight-on Swedish flatness (what damn well
did kill my father, "happiness"). (Memory, & Pa!)

                                        The other thing, it's
something else.

Feel damn much better, and hope this will erase that dirty letter for
you, too.

Innocence, & simplicity. Still those two. Am sure they are what have
made it impossible for me to get a word to dub what i keep calling
ornament. They are what I am interested in, not, such "statements"
as this recent stuff you have had to look over.

                                    And they do not lie,
for me, on those levels of statement. That shit of honesty prevents me,
there. (Justice, I once called it.)

        I shall have to find their foliation in that other place. The art of
aversion. It is animism, not spiritism on which i rest and which has
been the clarity for me to come to.

                        (One crazy moment in which this
sight was needed, Sunday, and wasn't then known: Paul Goodman
was here, to examine a student.[218] Came Friday, left Monday. First
time I ever met the guy (no, saw him once, at Breit's, twelve yrs ago,[219]
but no matter—remembered his 1st wife more, the sort of straw or
prune she was, that wrinkled redheaded thing—like these Southern
straw blonds, pitiful creatures—(and i never able to believe a redhead

can be that way, having lived a floor above the most luscious piece of
woman I ever saw, when i was 7, a Mrs Shorey, who was put together
like the brick house, and a flesh better than any i have seen since
((actually believe this, thinking, a 7 yr old damn well knows

                                                              (or i
dream of Negroes slouching in a convertible, and the marked one with
a hard on, from Con standing beside me, either on the running board
or in where the steering wheel is—(((the harassment of these
Negroes, and a driving through a country unknown, even though very
American, with a direction of intent to go some long way toward such
keys as the Florida ones, yet off in some landscape like I have known
precisely in other dreams, a place like some Holland, tho not that
exact, merely, that sort of unreality

                            ((This Holland thing is crazy, in
this sense, that Shahn and I, last summer, acknowledged that, of all
geographies, that place is, as simulacrum, the same place for both of
us!))

         (crazy thing was, that Con and I were sort of camping out—
driving long distances, and having to find place for the night. And it
was in these involvements that these Negroes appeared. At first pissing
behind one of those temporary pissoirs circuses or carneys set up, a
mere grey canvas sight-break. But the end was coming down hill to the
center square of some unknown city—tho I would place same city in,
say, Georgia)

                     to hellwith it

Back to Goodman. Sunday night, after two days of sparring on his part
(he has an inordinate desire to close with a person, and drives any one
but some open fool, some lowly lonesome man or mineral woman,
immediately to their rear), I brought him in to a discussion of the
draft (several of these guys are now having their classifications
changed, and are damned bothered, were asking me questions about
what to do). It was fun, I figuring this was G's strongest ground, and
my weakest, such a subject. He came into the ring of us with a bad
opening (calling me wrong, having been hearing the latter part of my
remarks, about why there was no international underground
movement of fugitives from the armies of the world, with fake
passports, etc., and resting on an international secession principle ...

not at all anything I would organize, simply that I take the other
position toward the State, beat it, and the only law, survive, with all
agilities

which position turned out to be Goodman's (somewhat to
my surprise, I having the sense that he had played papa to NY
anarchists, a sort of Rexroth of New York: he acknowledged, at one
point, that he had very much wanted to go right into the Army, to do
it as much harm as he well could, but, that he hadn't (had, in fact,
played it smart, at Grand Central Palace,[220] and got himself off)
because he couldn't do wrong by his "public," the anarchists

But
what wowed me, was, that, when I pushed him on was his position any
more than the substitution of a psychological revolution for any other
kind, any old-fashioned kind (he argued the job of any individual was
to set aside any rigidity of response to the State simply because it is non-
human, and admit that one is afraid, and, from that clarity, one could be
agile and survive, invent devices even inside the Army

(i remained unable to let go my own experience, that, it is not
at the [draft stage *is struck over*] service stage that the thing
involves us, but at the registration stage, the sudden sense
that some force exists which has such a right over us, that
outrage, that sense of a loss of identity, that "style" question

—and that, therefore, anger—that old thing behind revolution, that
non-psychological, that straight social opposition, the feeling, that all
the rest of the creatures are being pushed around as you are—that that
drive is not included in his proposition

And to my surprise, he backed
up on Taoism, or Zen! and started that thing i just can't go with, ANEC-
DOTE (that thing Jews do still get such force into and do rest their
humanism on—whether it was in that still unsent Sunday letter of last
July,[221] in another, but I worked my way thru this thing with Shahn last
summer ((((tho i ought to say Goodman is not that dimensional, lacking that patriarchal thing, that power, S has. ... Goodman is a cricket, another grillo like Cagli,[222] tho, again, not of that moment)))

At which
point G did the thing he had twice done before: say I was different, in
some need of himself to get us set apart as poles! (You will know that

fact of men, and how second-rate it is, to have themselves some position by opposition to yrself! It is the chief device of the weak, all down
the line)

But by this time, his 3rd attempt, I don't remember that he
was at all sure he knew how I was different! (O, yes, I know how he
put it: he sd Sophocles was so alive to him that he could even change
an adjective, as tho the play was a mss. in his hands—and likewise, he
wrote tomorrow in imitation of the successes of a scene of Sophocles.
And—sd he—I imagine you take it differently, Olson!)

That one I
went by fast, and pushed back to where I did sit on such a thing as Zen
as base. And could do no more, then, but say I was unable to satisfy
myself with any such vocabulary of where I stood.

(It was a damned
curious sensation. Suddenly, my particularism felt very strong inside
me, yet, in my mouth, I was weak—felt, as I always do, at a certain
point, even, say, with Elath, how non-verbal and non-literary (or non-
sophisticated) I damn well am, the Irish Giant! Just dumb, and a
bullock in the mouth, even if there is an adrenal complement
below!

And I damn well do feel that loss of words, at just that point!
And it seems to me right that, at such extreme points—where
humanism is tested—I should have no easy word. For if one does not
use either the old spirit as the sanction of identity or this new
psychological thing as capable of producing clarity of being, then one is
without vocabulary. It hasn't yet been invented.

(Elath's "totality" is as
loose as our own words—except, I still feel, for that one I attribute to
you, the single intelligence.

Ok. Better sign off. Am exhausted (the heat of summer has come, and
it takes me a few days to come up on it. Besides, this place does get me
into too much waste of strength—even tho I say this uncomplainingly,
merely, that there is an alternative.

Con and the baby are fine. The
baby sleeps out at night now, in a carriage on the porch, and sleeps
right through from 7 to five. And Con has had to give up my night life.

It makes a strange business, that I never have either of them in a time when I am not going at some tilt. But it is over, soon, however it is over,

      love to you all,

           charles

           [Lambesc, Bouches-du-Rhône]
                June 10, 1952

Dear Charles,

          Not very cool at present but I've been off for too long. I felt miserable about that letter, I know what you meant and can't excuse myself. No right to say it like that, it is too simple. Reading your:

      "It is animism, not spiritism on which i rest and which it has been difficult for me to come to."

                Clearly enough there. It is my own answer to what is beyond either of these sets, intensive or extensive, and I believe them at best qualifiers, of what is at root here.

Anyhow very shaky these days, Emerson finally came through on that booklet (due out now in October)[223] and it led to several things I'm not at all confident about. I had to add more poems, in fact everything of any use up to RITES. Present contents are these:

Still Life Or
Hart Crane
Le Fou   (title)
Littleton, N.H.
Hart Crane (2)
Canzoni

The Epic Expands
Guido
A Song
Love
The Crisis
For Rainer
The Riddle
The Surf
The Drums
The Rites
The Sea
The Cantos
The Ball Game
The Rhyme
The Innocence
Something For Easter

It was a very damn lonely business, spent one night at it, spread them out on the couch downstairs, and tried to pick them up again in some order or other. Not at all happy. Anyhow that's it, I think this will be the end of any further changes. [*Adds, in pencil*: Or something—I damn well don't know.]

Very damn fine news about the WennerGren, and damn well makes sense. Even to them. I know what you mean about not now wanting to go into it, but it will hold, certainly. It is very, very wonderful—and damn well about time too.

Many thanks too, about the thing there at BMC, it is very damn kind of you and hope to god it works out. I just heard from Rainer, I haven't yet said anything to him—I think he & Renate may get back here sometime pretty soon. Past months have been a hell of a mess for them, they lost their room in Freiburg, kids now with the father-in-law, and he's not much. [*Adds at bottom of page*: not the phrase—but in any case his "vocabulary."] It would be so great to be clear of it all; hope this is the chance.

Anyhow I will talk it over with them when they get there. I know

Rainer very much wants to get the small press going, but no money to do it with to date. That might conceivably keep him here, I don't know. In some ways it would make a great deal of sense. But not to keep on with life like it's been for them—that not at all good.

Anyhow I'll write you on this soon, Laubies also to be here sometime in July— he'd written me earlier about wanting to get over to the States—at least he would have nothing to keep him as Rainer might—though I know R/ [*penciled, in margin*: I honestly think he'll come. I would not have said anything otherwise.] has it as his own hope to get there sometime, and why the hell not now when it could be like this.

I had a letter from Elath, and he sounds ok—letter is confused, but I like him very much. He's trying among other things to translate Trakl, I take it he is not german but has that tie with them. Incidentally I had just been reading CONTEMPORARY ISSUES, they sent me a free one, and I finally got everything they've put out. Zander is, I think, translated from german, that problem. Otherwise, E. V. Swart is very interesting man, in fact they all are.[224] Swart wrote a very decent letter, put him on to Rainer for material re abuse of charity groups, etc.— Rainer wrote he had heard from him and was going to try to do something.

Seymour-Smith, that englishman, wrote again; some idea for small pamphlets but don't yet know much more about it. Will tell you what happens.

Problem of Smith is, again, what you find reading anything like NEW STATESMAN, etc. So-called "journalism" cuts so-called "creative" writing five ways to Sunday. That CI group very cool sometimes in just this point; I like their punctuation, if that doesn't sound too silly, very damn much! As for example, that way of theirs—"not to fight it in the name of—the lesser evil."[225] In fact only yourself, otherwise, I'd ever seen do that and I figure it works. Much the same feeling for most of their use of exclamation points, prose rises and drops very damn effectively. Also use of dots, in sentence, much like Elath's—or saw some here & there. Such makes a very great deal of sense to me, as implement. Anyhow, some—day!

Just now broke off to go look at the garden, half asleep, could only smile in lieu of something better. French is horrible, and man about the same being Spanish. He doesn't like it any better than I do. Allons.[226]

I like Paul Goodman's prose, or some of it, I only met him once. Both Buddy and Leed knew him; Leed very well, he used to go listen to P/ talk, then go to bed with the wife. Fair enough.

Can't see that it matters too much in any case.

Just about on my face here, have to cut this for now—really only to get you some damn sign back. Do send that material from the letters to Brigante, it makes a hell of a lot of sense to me. Will tell you what happens with Elath as soon as I hear again, and WILL write to you again tomorrow. Ok.

You are a very damn fine man. All our dearest love to you all, [*signs, a caricature of shaky signature*: Bob.]

The Sleeping Beauty.

[*Adds, in pencil, along margin of last page:*] Have you heard from LASH on FENOLLOSA? / perhaps not—I thought he might be editor of Dinge der Zeit.[227]

[*Adds, in pencil, in margin to right of list of titles for* Le Fou:] "TOTALITY" *ONLY* TERM WHICH CAN BE SAID TO *ALLOW* THE "S.I." WE MAKE *THIS* VOCABULARY. ELATH'S REMARKS ON *REGIONALISM* ARE VERY *INTERESTING*. WILL GET THEM TO YOU.

[Lambesc Bouches-du-Rhône]
June 13, 1952

Dear Charles,

Still hauling myself up. Utter damn dreariness of the
life hereabouts—impossible to tell whether it us or them, but it makes
no difference—christly flatness is there in any case. I am anyhow
without much damn energy, or have it but can't use it. It is hellish to
start out for Aix, say, feel good driving in, even in this old hulk, etc.,
people along the roads, cutting the hay now, etc., a kind of pleasure to
have them at all close lacking any better contact, and then once there—
end of every damn pleasure, flat dull & insipid bullshit of the
conversation, even with a friend like AB [Ashley Bryan], etc. Tho best
to leave him out of it, he holds himself very damn close these days.

Well, to hell with it—never again to ever get into a fix like this one—I
swear by the living GOD, etc. Ok.

I finally got some books from england, mostly penguins, etc.[228] Some
of this current trans/ which is very readable, at best. Rieu's reads
better to me than Rouse; Graves makes a very pleasant book of THE
GOLDEN ASS, in fact that part, of Psyche & Cupid is as lovely and
close as anything I have ever read; it is very wonderful to find it. Also
have finally at least some Ovid—that Everyman edition which has
Golding's trans/ from Metamorphoses, and Marlowe, Amores, etc.
When I damn well think of shit I DID read in latin (christly tacitus, et
al) damn well actual anger against the SHITS who never gave us any
of this: 10 pp/s per day was the limit of their considerations, etc. I
flunked the damn course finally, what else—impossible to take it on
any more.

Have written Rainer about possible deal there—things so bleak for
them in germany, it does sound the best deal they can get, and finally
excellent no matter such comparison. Many thanks again, to you, for
figuring it. Damn, damn kind. Hope to god he does take it up. Only
thing which might be a block: I don't see how they would dare try it,

unless they were somehow sure of, say, a year's employment, two kids and all force that as a condition—no immediate thing I guess but once I hear how he takes the idea—could perhaps the thing be tried as such, i.e., a year? With either Laubies, or myself, no such condition necessary—I am sure now we'll be there, or *I* will, no matter. I think Laubies will be also agreeable if he can figure out how to get there & then back. Well, you said you were trying it, anyhow, keeping it in their heads as "permanent replacements"—with the G/s that would probably have to be the condition, at least say for one year's time. Anyhow I'll write you what he answers, hope to god he will take the chance, he won't get another very soon, and life such a mess now.

Another issue of INTRO here, mostly poems by William Hull had seen two by him in GG/ one of which was ok.[229] Man Elath was talking about. [*Adds*: He worries me, i.e. Hull—I get it but I don't really damn well like it. I see what E/ means but hate the sprawl. Can you get a copy? INTRO—Vol.] And while I remember, some of E/s letter:

(This was in answer to my suggestion he take on the German thing Rainer has in mind, antho/ of americans, etc.)

"Cd throw a thematic outline ... show develp from what Whitman meant (societally also!), the development through Crane towards totality—the dingansich[230] to 4th dimension—and the comment of Hull which is a demonic issuing from lack of social totality to match creative totality of science—lyric gone sour-demonic ... with sideoffs at the regionals ... showing alienation from mainstream—tates [*i.e., tastes*] ... etc. . Pr ... outside of the worldhistoricbasic internationalism of whitmen's [*sic*] (seeing the dinge an sich (social) of the species in the U.S.A. ... totality and internationalism hand in hand ... (not a "people" in U.S.A. but *many*, leading thus not to be nation but an international force ... and *not* to classes ... but every individual in a *class of their own*. . leading to a *whole* species totality and *not* a national totality that cant [*sic*] help but failing since internationalism thus becomes hierarchic of secondary peoples. .leading to human struggles and basic instability and downright wast [*sic*] of potential . . . . etc . . . . thus regionalism is victorian etc....)"

A vocabulary is damn well the instrument needed. Our own, say, SI, or what is honestly your formulation, and my acceptance of sd formulation, is what he points at with *"in a class of their own"*; and his "totality" is the context necessary to your formulation in the first place. Much of the surface confusion, of the above, etc., is the result of an inadequate vocabulary, or one too much got from already well-limited "sciences"—I should think primarily the usual sociologist's, with the addition of key terms from other sources: Korzybski, et al.

Space is the root. Both physics & the terms inhering in culture-morphology, as you have suggested (both poems & prose), seem better able to handle it. Totality is a word in the process of stating a condition, but not yet itself the containment of the condition. That's one of the present headaches in any case—as you say, the goddamn vocabulary.

To change it: one damn thing done, anyhow,[*Added*: I *won't* I guess—anyhow to hell with it], I sent it to Brigante, for now—simply to give some sign of interest, which I wish to god could be more substantial:

THE QUESTION

A description of the sensuous
is its own answer : a multiple love is
mine.
            These Women.

Who in their beds, their
beds or buttocks bared for the nocturnal
revels, agh!

Or if her tits be rose, or roses, or any
flower, with what, say, to water this
garden of a particular
intent?

Signing off, the sexual abberation, etc.
all our LOVE to you all, Bob

[Encloses clipping, press photo of tribal bow and arrow marksmen, which Creeley heads "THE ORIGIN GROUP," and identifies: "Left to right: Creeley, Blackburn, Corman, Olson, friend."*]*

[The following survives only as a carbon copy among Olson's papers: the first two pages on a single sheet among water-damaged papers, with lacunae throughout; the final two pages, on heavier bond, found elsewhere among Olson's papers.]

[Black Mountain, N.C.]

Robt: Sun June 15 52—So damned happy to have [your] letter in. Have been flat, myself, and had known what a stimulat[*ion? ing?*] [*torn*], but had not gauged what a form of artificial respiration answering th[*torn*] me when I am not self-engaged, like I suppose they say, don't they.

Have lost, again, the thrust—that is, from anywhere where it really gets me in (am cursed with an ability to get something done—am unable to fall down properly—and so abhor myself when the issue is not from below). And then get despondent, & uneasily inactive—haven't for months, for example, taken care of any of those little businesses which keep a man alive by way of outlets, say (so admire your cracking through there with Elath, who is, certainly, the sharpest lad seems to me to have come along in these two years: I am full of admiration for his prose. What delights me is that true flatness, that picking up at the lowest (Glicksberg, say)[231] and keeping it there, leaving his insights to come in and up only as they damn well do, out of the welter—that management of welter, there: that is something to throw the steer, and turn him over on his back, climax done in, polled. And the correlations achieved are glistening: that moment, there, where Trotsky and Ez are suddenly alongside each other, but with none of that plugging I, say, would give such a jointure—I couldn't resist to go on with the thing, to see what more there is in it, to say that. And that Elath, is cool: he moves right away, and on. It makes for a circularity I, of course, take the maximum pleasure in.

And you are quite exact about his totality biz: this I have grabbed and ridden away with, for it is most most valuable to have it layed home in that word (that, and that one we have won over, methodology, they make a pair to open stuff that Zander, say, is prevented from by just not taking the totalitarian and the technological this live step further.

It is all damn freeing, in this sense that i[t gets] everything in (there isn't a damn factor of the reality we have which [is not] covered by totality. It is the character of the reality. Period.

I have not yet exhausted the returns from his piece, but what I did get on to, yesterday (going after Cid,[232] trying again to get him forward as editor), was this thing, methodology, which, as a word, I had been at before but had fallen off it, not then seeing what it contained, even though, as you know, I have never been able to keep it from coming into my mouth. What kept me sh[ort] was, -logy. This I balked at until, suddenly, this week the import of [the] principle as a force now and anew broke in on me. It came by way of being pushed to say what is the revolution I find myself believing is in progress (you will know how most everyone is somehow down at the mouth [torn] what is ahead—and how wholly dismal and boring that is, that they [torn] know, or that they move by nature instead of by their active self, g[torn] in some sort of species fatuity ((which leaveth me wholly cold, aside [torn] them—again, that crack of the Old Man's: Greek art, coital[233]

((([torn] "progress" is something underneath humanism, this going on, even [torn] of people—and it has come to fascinate me in what I now take permanence (painters, for example, all seem to me—that is, those [I have] known—to be of this school, though, from what I discover the word [*torn*] to mean, leads me to think I have been poor in my acquaintances

[*Approximately six lines lost.*]

w[*torn*] this was, as I say, that I said, art is the only morality, and t[*torn*] just the making abundantly clear again that the principle of art is revolutionary—is something all human beings could be raised by, the point being that the only valid communication conceivable as justifying any act toward any other is expression, not all those others which have glutted the business, business, wants, guile, power, impression, etc

the context is totality: i put it that there are three things the Eisenhowers, the traffic managers, rob by:[234] (1) organization, the technique of
(2) efficiency, the characteristic of the machine (on which they base their manipulation of us, not, notice, on our or their own efficiency)
& (3) quantity, that factor (which Elath's totality gives me the proper word to indicate its essentiality)

As you'd know, I take it the revolution afoot is to turn these three aside, to wear these aspects of the reality outside in (for I am not one to ignore that these creatures have power, and that they take up what power they have from the same source we do, that, reality)

In other words, that the rev is the identity of a person and his expression, that these are not separable, and that this is why art is the only principle left
yet, saying that, is not much compared to coming to grips with how that identity is now accomplished

At which point, *methodos*, which turns out to be a meta hodos, better, meta hodos[235]—and look!
"with a way, with a via, with a path (weg, that which died, and does not die, which is

any man's job—and now the more so when der
weg stirbt,[236] long live the methodology
in other words, the science of (-logy,
the principle of—PATH

What could be more exactly what we are: method is not the path but it
is the way the path is known
So, current usage, definition 2, look:

"orderly arrangement, elucidation, development, or
classification; more generally, orderliness and regularity or
habitual practice of them in action" (it says it, there!)[237]

gets me to this qed:[238]
I. TOTALITY is the reality
& II. METHODOLOGY is the discipline to
express it

[*rest of page torn*]

has, now, to include one hell of a lot—can)

and II, the methodology is
1. to have a path
2. that such a path is only
accomplishable by hab...prac...
order....and regularity in act...

Hope this doesn't drive you nuts; just the way it comes out, these
days. Not important, merely to get it straight, this way—don't mean a
damn thing another way, that is, for any of us who are stuck beyond
this point. Its only use, conceivably, as preaching to those who might
want to know. You don't, any more than I do. Its only use in its
application—and how it applies to oneself I never could figure. One
just goes on using one's head, that's about it—for the use of it. To
make this sort of structure. It is one sort, not, for me, any where near
the kind of structure I care most about. For example, found Boulez
saying this:[239]

"All my attention this past year has been given to widening the scope of the series and making it homogenous. With the thought that music has entered into a new form of its activity: *serial form,* I have tried to generalize the notion of series.

> ((note: ordre
> seriel,[240] i had to find out, is the French way of
> talking about the twelve-tone scale))

A series is a succession of n sounds, of which no tone as regards frequency is like any other, giving rise to series of n-1 intervals. The serial production from this initial series is made by the transpositions $b, c \ldots n$ of the entire series, starting from all the pitches of this series. Which gives then: n series. The inversion also yields n transpositions. The total number of series is equal, therefore, to 2n.

((note: he goes on for several pages, with illustrations, graphs, etc. But what I wanted to offer you was his conclusions:))

We may then conceive of musical structure from a dual viewpoint: On the one hand the activities of serial combination where the structures are generated by *automatism* of the numerical relations. On the other, directed and interchangeable combinations where the arbitrary plays a much larger role. The two ways of viewing musical structure can clearly furnish a dialectical and extremely efficacious means of musical development.

(((note: don't know that I take him right, but I see this automatism as covering that thing I meant above, p. 1. about inert progress, that one can grant hits from chance, in fact I take it that the John Cage school of music-making—the music of changes—is just this automatism, and that Boulez means to cover it with this alternative to the *arbitrary* (Cage even backs his composing by unpredictability up to the use of the method established in the I-Ching (Book of Changes) for the obtaining of oracles, that of tossing 3 coins 6 times![241]

CHARLES OLSON & ROBERT CREELEY

You will imagine where I stand in this choice of these two
methods!

Boulez goes on directly: "Furthermore, serial structure of notes
tends to destroy the horizontal-vertical dualism, for 'composing'
amounts to arranging sound phenomena along 2 coordinates:
duration and pitch. We are thus freed from all melody, all
harmony and all counterpoint, since serial structure has
caused all these (essentially modal and tonal) notions to
disappear.
((nota: isn't that cool, &
familiar—wow)) i love it!

"I think that the mechanical recording means (the magnetophone
in particular) we will be able to realize structures which no
longer depend on instrumental difficulties and we will be able to
work with any frequencies using the serial method of generation.
*And thus each work will have its own structure and its own mode of
generation on all levels.*
((and how abt that—jesus, it's crazy, how
this boy is of the Company!

He ends: "We will be able, within a serial space, to multiply the
series by itself. That is, if between *a* and *b* of an initial series we
can express the series in reduction, this would give a great
expansion of the sonorous material to be used in relation with
the other serial functions."

[G]oddam it, ain't it beautiful—and if we had out own goddamned
mag (just, [f]rom where i sit, you, Elath, Boulez, and say
me......
christ, Robt, when I think of what is kicking around, and
could—put together—be made available
(this chicken-shit, of having
to have Elath come on us by
chance—the time has come
for all men ...

(((what finally struck me as the true way to pull off the deal
here, is for us to constitute such a venture, and Laubies, Gerhardt
and you be the bosses and BMC the place—if, now, i could find
someone to back such a proposition with some dough, then I am
sure BMC would be damned glad to get you all, to get it, such, a
mag)))

Anyhow, fuck mags—the point is, isn't it beautiful what's around,
who there are who are at work!

Will get this off. Please write, and keep me on all things, mostly,
please, yrself, how ye be. Very damned jealous to have the full details
on yr book with the goose (had seen the ad on back of his #3, and was
green with it)—but willy that, very happy: christ, jesus, and me with
no fucking book in existence. jesus. and you in there with all those
beautiful things. Can't stand it. hold my hand. pleased as hell, and
unhappy as same. christ. (take it yr order, and contents, just damn well
perfect—take yr word for it plus my own impression in course—(can't
bear to look em all other [*over?*], simply, that i am not in strength just
now on my own things—am sick of everyone of them—and so excuse
me for a funk. Doesn't matter: know for sure you are on the right
track—those late poems are absolute beauties, starting with SONG—
no question at all: you are punching, perfectly. Is such a damn straight
go of a man, going *thru* the poetic, and coming out the other end. Will
read em, will—just the thought of several of them. Go back to, "what
the hell can i teach you." They are beautiful. I wish I had the same.

Ok. Feel—if I do get on the other side of the present—will have
something. But am fucking nervous about that I will get on that other
side. It is so fucking huge a heave for the likes of, me. But shit. There it
is. I have to. No choice. (Damn well think my lust for principle must be
that I wasn't given any when they might have settled in, deep.) Ok ok
ok. All love & faith.   O Charles

[*Probably encloses the following:*]
Did want to spell out a little more clearly how I take it my removal
from Black Mt (if I go through with it: I am still puzzled on the

finance question, how to make a living, for a year, without going to
Guatemala & the Yucatan!) affects our other plans, yrs, specifically,
of coming there with Rainer and Laubies

(crazy thought: what wld I
do if—the luck running—I shld get that damned Fulbright to go
to Mesopotamia![242] That wld be some upheaval, eh? Then I
could at least get together with you—*there*!

Ok. With what is. That is, I don't see why removal would disturb the
thing (only practical is, that, once even this removed I lose some of
my "tyranny"—as Dehn[243] described it, in a moment of anger, over a
push I was making about leaves of absence seeming to me properly
to include a leave of presence proposition!)

Main point is, that I follow you absolutely on yr analysis of a MAG:
that we will be without outlet of my primacy, soon. And that the time
has come to make one we run—that some common minds do exist:

for me they are, say, you, and more Elath and a Zander
than Paul B[*lackburn*]
I follow you on Seymour-Smith[244] (allowing
my innate suspicion than no Englishman can
dispose of kultur sufficiently to engage himself
with kinetic)

And Rainer, of course (he provoked me, didn't
he? and so much else,
that, translating

I want you to be able to include Twombly (who goes Sept 1st
to Spain, Africa, Greece, Egypt, to Aden: for a look at the
caves, & the past)
Otherwise? (And ain't that crazy: I'd
guess—if we conceived a thing as non-aesthetic—that a lot of printable
stuff (say, Sauer, Hawkes—his book for you to get [*from*] England is
his Prehistoric Foundations of Europe—Barlow, Anderson on
maize,[245] etc etc Frobenius … ok, you know my biases, in this direction

If I can manage to swing that visit in down there [*i.e., Mexico and*

Guatemala], then I'd be in touch with the sit., and able to swing what weight—on top of that free to stay for periods, etc. Well, I 'll watch things, and seek to work them in the most favorable ways.

I just want you to know any such disengagement as the present one comes from the most severe personal necessity—and is no setting aside of what use I may be there to you all.

(Remark above on English jumps from reading right now a new book on Melville by a Ronald Mason (Lehman, London): fantastic, how clear.[246] and thoro, the climax of all those rational men on HM[247] from John Freeman (Englishman) down: Mumford, Matthiessen, Sedgwick, Leyda, Chase, Arvin, even Auden.

As against the "others": Weaver, Lawrence, Dahlberg, self

Thing is, Mason, excepting DHL, is more onto the spirit of the man (the book's title is from CLAREL: Spirit Above the Dust) than any of those others. Yet, the *statement* is removing of the force: is so adjectival (jesus, the english are shakespearian) ...

Blake, e.g., is his true master (more than HM) and it is his love for Blake which informs this book with a character.[248] Yet (again) what abt this Blake? What abt him? I am twice now given him as bible, and by god I must soon find out why I don't pick up from him. Never did give him a true run. Shy off. Yet things quoted from him make such sense. Figure he's just a man of the old reality, and whatever he does have, it ain't usable as Rimbaud, Dostoevsky, Melville and Lawrence are, that's all

OK. To say   Write.   Love, Olson

[Olson's undated marginal comments, in pencil on a copy he retyped from Creeley's 17 June letter are incorporated within brackets below:]

[Lambesc, Bouches-du-Rhône]
June 17, 1952

Dear Charles,
          I heard from Laubies, and he's very excited about the
chance to come there, and also realizes it won't pay well, etc. Anyhow,
you can count him in pretty certainly, if it's still ok at that end. I
haven't got any answer from Rainer yet, but should pretty soon. Hope
they both can make it, honestly think it would be worth it.

I was banging my head on this thing, see what you think:

The Festival

Death makes his
obeisance:
              to the two
first, children. The wall
falling, to catch them and then
another, the aunt aged 6
also.

It's hard to think through it. Having just written that thing about
Hull,[249] or irony—what to say of myself. More, a damn complex to the
whole incident, of which the poem can be too little in any case. The
story not of that importance, or here not, but what had happened:
yesterday the woman who comes to help Ann, etc., told her about two
little kids who had got caught by a wall falling, pulling at it with a
piece of wire or something, and it all let go. There were three there, in
fact—the "aunt," the oldest, not killed outright but badly hurt and
died I think this morning. I was sitting in this car, waiting for Ann, just
before noon; Dave & T/ with me, all these kids going by, teachers with
them, etc. Just a little earlier, across the street, little group of people,
three women, two or so men. One of the women, blonde, not too old—
mannered kind of stiffness, really an awkwardness. Hair sort of
straight, but combed hard to make it neat—I meant a hardness to the
actual texture. Face very tight. Weird grief of a country people in any

place; they were standing very awkward—people going by, looked at them, etc. Hard high sun by that time. Clothes, an old black. Nothing fitting well—square on the women. Tight and awkward. Finally old car comes up out of the side street, a hill there and parks sort of crossways, by the sidewalk. They all moved over to it, some slowness in getting it—car very old, big one, doors opened with difficulty, and some further awkwardness as to where each would sit. They were the family, live some distance from the town. Later, the kids going by on my side of the street, all dressed up—a gesture to the deaths. It made that split, the town, those out on the edge of it, very clear. They were so much better dressed, all of them, than the family—also a lot of flowers they had with them. One of the women, with the family, had a big rectangular shaped bunch of flowers, sort of a form to it, a white stripe made by white flowers, against a darker backing, almost black, of the rest. [*Creeley adds in margin*: All they had was this one thing.] This was fixed onto a rough and thick board of sorts, sort of in the center, and the bunch of flowers seemed wired to it—this to hold them firm. They had all gone in the car, when the kids came. A holiday for them, the kids, because of the accident.

Charles/ forget the damn poem, will send letter anyhow for what else is there.

Am not very good these days—just now in this biz of W/ Hull, poems, etc. If you can look at them, would very much like your comment. In fact I should wait till you have seen them, hardly fair to bang in before but am so christly disturbed by them—for me they are very ugly & can't myself acknowledge that that is how it has to be. One poem not in this INTRO (was in GG/) somewhat of a definition of all that goes on in the longer ones (INTRO group (8) mostly long ones—etc.):

EX TEMPORE[250]

This nook I am
wanders a parabola
on graph my bent invents:
this disc I abstract brutely

from shimmer-obscured complexity,
renovate, classic, to referrant,
a gyroscopic mean.

Whatever I am to me
is through grossness a gross disparity.

As close as any say
I am excursion of roses
scarlet-lurching, worming to black.

Or say
I am passion clipped from a mandarin's nail,
or vertigo in a peanut shell.

Or some such random say
no more profane:
as any as close.

To hell, for the moment, with any question of "good or bad" means,
etc., I am after what is the position, and I hate it frankly, I go sick to it.
Defining comment is: Whatever I am to me / is through grossness a
gross disparity. And means, or position to be got by: Or some such
random say / no more profane: / as any as close.

In the longer poems, irony [*Olson comments*: Crazy that this word
utterly balks me—had, even, to look in dict.—& found (as ever) the
clue: that the root is *Eirōn*, a *dissembler in speech*!] is constant, as Elath
says H/ uses phrase as "symbol," you get clotted & compulsive
surface. Structure is loose, intentionally—poems ride out on any detail,
description is, in this sense a via for the energy. Elath further makes it:
"absolutism of scream—lyric gone sour-demonic."[251] [*Olson*: How
about E finding out—lyric, *gone, gone*]

I can't shake my own belief that irony is *not* the instrument for any
despair. Is this a too damn simple revulsion. I know, say, that Lawrence
thought of Joyce as writing "obscene" books, etc.,[252] I think, more, I
know why—it is frightful to have this kind of writing present in the

VOICI

what it don't take is
style, inverted or uninverted

commas (which I never damn well
understood anyhow:

get a load of Tough Shit
before the Book Store Window!

Concerns honest or otherwise,
what is the import

(not to bother no one, but
likewise, perhaps of the issue, what

is it all about

You tell me

thinking that David will be 5 in Oct and of
school age? Am wondering if both French and
English will be taught in French schools.

concerns no one but
who wrote it, and if, say, they DON'T?

That wasn't the point, - which comes to,

alors:

the Greek fishmonger.

Section of Robert Creeley's 19 May 1952 letter to Charles Olson, with newspaper cartoons and unpublished poem "Voici." *Charles Olson Collection. Literary Archives, University of Connecticut Library.*

VIA AIR MAIL

Robt Creeley, Esq

Bouches du Rhone
FRANCE

Pavillon Les Magnolia

route de Caire

Lambesc

A

P.S May 5th: after
enclosed, *Origin* 5. came
in. — + I have just
written you a letter
abt Stevens, etc.
But just because I
am in such a rage,

Errata:

if They can 9 ... now sooner

very nasty thing

19th (1918) —

A CREELEY FOR SPR-ING

(by way of —) on his way in ending up such shit. d

and will not want
to bother with it
again, I think you'll
get it if I send the
letter off to you via Connan-
just to give him my answer

Photos A & B
Envelope of Charles Olson's 5 May 1952 letter to Robert Creeley, with unpublished poem "A Creeley For Spring" and postscript on *Origin*, 5. *Creeley papers, Stanford University Libraries.*

The painter and translator René Laubiès. *Creeley papers, Stanford University Libraries.*

face of a reality god knows I *also* have part of, and in. I think it a
frightful giving-over, an irresponsibility—and how the hell to judge
any man like that. His horror is god knows real, any line of the poems
is clear in that.

I feel here I am doing, very actually, what you had called me on in that
letter,[253]—I wish to god I could see a means past it, some way to
demonstrate, coldly, [*Olson marks rest of paragraph and the next with bars
in margin:*] that this means, in Hull, is of necessity defective, that a man
can't, *must not* literally, giggle at the end of his own damn rope. [*Olson:*
Don't know that this is true—another matter.]

I think I told you, earlier, about Slater & Crane, how C/ wrote him a
letter shortly before his suicide, or before he got on the boat, about his
own work and the fear he had he was not making it, that the change in
his style became an impotence, and that he was through. The poem he
was talking about, in this fear, was THE BROKEN TOWER[254]—for me
it is impossibly close, or this fact, knowing it, is Crane as much as I
will ever have any man. Incredible wish, of that—what he took as
necessary, demanded, of himself. How the hell to eulogize, anyhow,
any of this so simply.

Elath writes he thinks Hull is "major," that this complex of a literal
and common despair, and the demonic, the issuance as scream in
extremis, in hate, [*Olson comments*: SHIT] "sexual torment of mature
flesh," is, even of necessity, the phase now reached—through
Whitman, through then Crane, and now to this position in Hull. I deny
it absolutely, I deny that even this relevance, [*Olson marks remainder of
paragraph with bars in margin:*] of an entire world, can effect this
disintegration without another *kind* of protest.

It brings me to Melville, and your own statement, of him, in your own
work, the placement there in the LETTER, the hall,[255] and what I know
of my own experience he had been led to in the writing of PIERRE.
What else can any man do. What is to be got out of, that this, at least, is
of the place, quite literal, one walks into no matter, and has to. What is
any relief, not facing that. I can't get it coherently, I hate the slop I get
here. I mean, *one is there* [*Olson underlines and marks with bar in margin.*],

how else to say it—Hull's "world" is hardly unknown to me, it is much of my own. [*Olson marks next lines (down to "think of") with bar:*] But dignity is a man more than anything else—his way of holding himself, his intentional grip on what he has of himself, what he has been given. The horror of that fracture, grotesque beyond anything I can think of, of the concentration camps, the destruction of presence, of the will to presence—what Hull hands over without a single damn cry. Irony is that loss, and irony, in despair, seems to me the ugliest of all human acts, even though the most human of all acts. To me it is an obscenity, and I stick there.

Irony in rage, an anger which is the issue of a man's misuse, and how he has been misused, and knows it, is what I can take as my own, or what could be. Williams' essay on Poe, Poe himself—what W/ makes there so clear.[256] But Hull depends on the horror of his "poetry," it is all he now has. For a man to base himself on his own disintegration is, to me, a literal outrage of himself, and if anything is—contra naturam. Literally, deeply that—killing, taking the weapon to oneself.

I don't honestly know, I trust Elath or do from that article, I am damn well bewildered by Hull, I don't like him, in fact I hate what he does, I think it is utterly negative, admits impotence, gives over what very damn little is left to begin with. I hate that. I'll hate myself when I do it.

I hardly get all that in ["The Festival"], I know. I don't try to. Mainly myself. The rhythms, not goddamn well to go at it, like this, but in them some indication of my own feelings. I can only give them—I don't here see the use of making a "description"—people so badly, badly treated as it is. And no one ever means to. Nothing of it would be clear from the poem I guess—nothing damn well clear to me, just now, in any case. I don't at all mean an irony—I wanted simply its statement, of them so caught. And only that one incongruity, of the "aunt," because that is how it had been told to me, of this last girl's death—referred to as the "aunt."

One sees a lot of funerals here. I don't ever remember having ever before seen so many. As the custom is—hearse goes in front, usually a car, the usual, but sometimes a wagon, with black box, and a white cross going up just in front of it, behind the driver. People walk after it. Usually they just make their way down the street, there isn't any interruption to, say, traffic, or anything else. Few members of the family, etc., in a little knot at the front—then rest following at a slight distance. One time I was in Aix, in the car again, and raining a little. Saw procession going by, just one man at the front, a midget—forced step to keep up with the hearse. Behind him, usual group.

Forget it I guess. Say what you think of the poem when you can get to it. In any case, I wish I were now writing prose, I feel that damn need but I can't yet. I am so goddamn disturbed somewhere, nothing at all happens, or nothing I can get hold of. To hell with it for now anyhow.

I can get books now from England, I think I said that. Anyhow could you note me titles of Malinowski, Hawkes, etc., etc. I'd already written them about Waddell, Frobenius, and Strzygowski—no answer on that yet. They sent me a book-list, though very random one. Anyhow, they list two by Hawkes: Guide to Prehistoric & Roman Monuments in Eng/ & Wales (18/-), and A Land (21/-); and one by Malinowski: Freedom & Civilisation (16/-).[257] The thing is, that seems cheap, etc. Books are, of course, very damn cheap there; I was trying to take some damn advantage of that fact while we're still here, and can get them quickly & simply.
(Also Jung & Kerenyi: Intro/ to a Science of Mythology,   : 1951. (25/-)[258] which I thought I'd get anyhow.)

Also heard again from Seymour-Smith, I guess he's going to make that pamphlet biz—anyhow he has your address, etc. Beyond poetry, & stories, he notes hope for something in "mythology," etc. Don't know quite what that comes to—but might be something—or some way to circulate your own notes.

I forgot to tell you Buddy has now got a camera, etc., and is doing some filming at least. Was planning to bring it along, what he has done & projector—hopes to come in July—anyhow something moving, and may damn well work out yet. Will keep you on in any case.

  This to get back, hope it's all ok. Write soon.

All our love to you all, Bob

[Lambesc, Bouches-du-Rhône]
June 20, 1952

Dear Charles,

    Terrific stuff on Boulez, and what you quote from him. This coincidence at least—it must have been even the same damn day I'd had the idea of a thing, to be called: Charlie Parker & The Prose Sequence.[259] Anyhow it makes an incredible amount of sense to me, it is so damn, damn close.

    (I do think that CP/ is a lot of it, in his own practice; it's only in sd practice he can anyhow articulate. I heard him, on a radio program once, say he listened to Schoenberg,[260] in reply to some question about what "classical" music he liked, etc. Not too simply 12 tone scale, etc. That could be anything.

    More close is what Buddy had told me, and he is also a musician, etc. That "bop" in Bird's hands, at least, was very close to Spanish BULL FIGHT music, and you'll remember your own pick-up on that, or what comes off in the poem. I think, even, Bird et al have listened specifically to such—or it is that closeness.

    Likewise, there is *no* music than can more literally illustrate my own, say, sense of what *kind* of progression is possible, than that like Bird's, or the bull fights (which I can hear now & again on the radio we've got at this point) and *flamenco*. Last is probably the most incredible—when good.

At least CP/ had cut through the vertical-horizontal dualism noted by Boulez as long ago as I can remember hearing him. At best, or what, only, he would allow, was group's continuity, behind him, in that older way, and then his own fracture of it, on top. One is not damn well silly saying it, one damn well should take time & listen.

Anyhow many, many thanks for these quotes—I damn well see what you mean.

Nothing more from Elath; if ok with you, would like to forward him some of your present letter—I'd written him about your own closeness to the context he is after—this is quicker. Would that be ok? Certainly we have to get him, I mean he is of that sense, I hate to see it split off from what is yours, or mine. (I am still bugged by the Hull, I cannot make that connection—perhaps E/s own wish to be poet, say, and is not one—I don't know. Hull is so much the underside of what Elath is the top. That disparity is a little damn hard to account for; I don't mean any criticism of what H/ calls "the reality," I just don't see its use in this fashion.)

Things pretty good here. Moving some with the Englishman; his plans for a series of pamphlets seem pretty well set, though not exciting at this point. But I like him, he writes straight—no damn jamming, or any need to be sly, etc. His plan is this: to issue 4 pamphlets as a first "series." To be 3 English, and 1 Am/—probably Blackburn's Provencal trans/. I can't get him beyond that now. Not that I damn well mean to slight B/s work. Just that other things would be more pertinent in such an exchange. Anyhow that's the door. Next spring, 4 more: this time reverse balance, or 3 Am/ and 1 Brit/, and where I shall damn well need your help. Can you figure a ms/ for that—will need it when the time comes; tho there's enough to do it in any case. I'm arguing at present with him, on my own work—it's going ok. He's the first, at that, who'd ever listen from that place.

I'll tell you how it comes, he's also planning a magazine, and I have the job of Am/ editor. That one's loaded, or I hope so. Obviously the effect cannot be homogeneity, etc. Would be dull at that. (Perhaps to give over this job to Paul B/ if he'll take it—I don't damn well know how to do it very well at this distance, postage & all gets christly expensive, and hardly anyone ever answers a letter anyhow. Damn them.)

I'd like to get to Mallorca, where he is, and see him. That would make it go quicker. He has it lined up very coherently, he seems to know how to go about it. It will be the material that will get us fighting I guess—he can do what he likes with Brit/ but hard to be too damn passive an "advisor" on Am/ work. I just don't see it. Well, will try it and tell you what, if anything, comes of it.

Granting we do damn well get there, I mean Laubies, the G/s, and us—couldn't we make a magazine somehow? I had your own excitement, reading just that wish, in your letter. It's always seemed to me the obvious place, and time, etc., granting I know very little of how it literally goes there. But I would damn well like it, it makes a hell of a lot of sense. With G/ printing, etc.—why not. Cid will fold, he keeps saying he will anyhow, at the end of this year. That leaves us without very much in the way of space, or any place we can then shift to. The kind of outlet any of these other magazines might mean won't ever be the like of that—hate him as I often do. The move seems directly to our own issue, and hence the doing away of that perhaps only slight, but goddamn well irritating, displacement I've felt with him.

It isn't so much this damn little booklet, say, E[merson]/ will print—I know him as well as anyone, and feel even sick it took all this patience, etc. Or to hold myself in, that way, comes to a hypocrisy, and I don't like it. Even though the book gets out, etc. Either the clean place, where it is straight—or the other kind affects an eventual dirtiness, and that kills too much. I'm not damn sure, at all, I haven't that to deal with, with E/, right now. At least I've kept clean with him, I tell him what I think of any issue, etc. But it's hardly the same.

Too your saying what you do about it, it's very damn kind. I know what you mean. Myself, it makes no sense, or not enough. Or as Ann says, I don't write your poems yet by any means. It is a question of how much—not that too simple quantity, but of what, and of what kind, and how completely. Areas in poems you've even put down—I wish I had got to it, even that much of it. I can't read, literally, poem like THE CAUSE, THE CAUSE—without knowing in what degree, put it, I have slipped back, or dropped, in trying a like place—only "place" I know. Simple enough to make it little—I don't mean that usual "size." Really what Ez put as, simple enough to "control" what has no energy[261], and any poem of yours that's gone down, never goes down on that; you can't nail the whole world every damn time. You do it as often as any man I ever read. I mean it.

Things are cool enough, but not much good. I wish I was there. The baby coming puts us off a little—usual nervousness, though nothing too tight. I was reading Dana, and letters of Crevecoeur, etc.[262] The first is a beautiful thing—I wish I had all of Prescott [*crosses out* Prescott *and adds in ink* PARKMAN!] here, I cd read it with a hell of a lot of pleasure. [*Types in margin*: But both D/ & C/ lean off, on their "positions"; I wish to god they wouldn't. Or I was thinking of M/s TYPEE. A different placing, weight.]
                                        Anyhow this to get back, write soon. All our dearest love to you all,   Bob

Whole thing of E/ and what it relates to, is a headache. How the hell does one work out of it. Either a) hold on, and swing him round to your own sense, no matter what, etc.; or b) fuck it, and go your own way.

But I have as much a damn difficulty keeping on with Cid, at times, as I've ever had with E/. Our one smash was on your book, I didn't see his letting go for anything—I think it hurt him more, as a publisher, than it did you. The book will come out, anyhow—delays are hellish, but it will come out. It won't be with E/s press, and that's where he loses—he loses you, and what you attract.

In the same sense, equal
hell, or one gets it, of such fracture as even reading Elath in INTRO
comes to. Look at the prose in the same issue; I'll bet $20 they
wouldn't print a story of mine. The best aspects of Hull are "devices"
very faintly reminiscent of your own—really juxtapositions, which are
not at all common to his method, and which I don't suppose he
realizes as a possible relevance, etc. That's it. What can we do?

One wants this: a) when he has the thing, either his own or another
man's, to have sufficient sympathy, from those professedly of his own
intent, etc., to get a hearing; b) to get it sans any pull, or pushing over
into his own ground, as, say, that lean of "corrections" which M/
Moore used to pull on Crane, the "friendly advice, etc."; c) to be able
to work, put it, in concert with others, but also to remains a damn clear
instrument, or like what they call "chamber music"—each his own, to
make it a whole thing, etc.

It's naive, like that. I have it now to hand because Laubies has finished
the lithos/s and I want the damn book printed.[263] I want it printed
more than the poems, if that's relevant. One thing to do it by
yourself—but if ever another man somehow sees it, and makes a like
thing to be his own acknowledgement, one loves that, and what else.
The book is 4 stories I wouldn't have put together, as 4; the litho/s
make that difference, in fact it is the litho/s in their juxtaposition to the
stories, that is what I can love.
                    Anyhow I've sent that too to
Emerson, saying I'd pay for paper, it can't go much over $30. It's 20
copies. More, it is this whole thing—what to do when this comes. I
hate being with nothing, I don't see it. I can't print it myself, someone
has to, it's Emerson who looks most likely.
                    Tho no assurance I guess
he'll do it, it is a risk, etc. No money, etc., and only work, and 20 copies
is damn few no matter what they are of.

IF we could get a unit, to free us from all this stuff, a place to print, a
means, a damn coherent attempt, etc.—free of any of what it now
comes to, or that I get printed by E/, and you are without any book—
can't we get that. Don't we kill ourselves, in time wasted, and all the

worry of it, lacking it? It makes sense to me. If BMC has any means at all, for such a thing—why not. It is minimal but only if it is there; it is absolute hell without it—it is not a vanity, one damn well does not address air. The wish to see what's done out is, I should think, as normal as taking a shit—backed up, it's hardly good in either case, granting both is too simply shit in many instances. Anyhow, how it goes.

[Lambesc, Bouches-du-Rhône]
June 23, 1952

Dear Charles,

Not much new. We scared hell out of ourselves with the current issue of CI, like they say—an article on chemicals in foods, etc.[264] Which brings together much of that I'd hit here & there before. Impact, so, is considerable. I damn well don't know if you shouldn't come here. And damn quick.

Also Larry Eigner, who I guess I'd written about before, i.e., man who lives in Swampscott, Mass. We had that battle about the stories but it never holds for very long. He is pretty sharp at that. A hell of a mess for him, finally—cerebral palsy—goddam wretched, though the damn "pity" is worse. He doesn't need it anyhow. He'd been sending poems in his letters for about a year and a half, and they get to be very good, some of them. Or this part from one in today:[265]

Life by eating and passing
solid and water
  parts are constantly changed
every two springs
          different man

How much bigger, for a while bigger   ⦚

    Fall leaves
alternate
Winter and summer, familiar
      two main seasons

But scarcely enough
This tree grown for   (right on through here)
the phone wires
    airy space
between the upright branches and the lower ones
it is scanty and rich too

when I see the branches which yet twist like trails
ride and making room
  and yet still standing after all

the sprays that survive me ...   (all through here)

(Part here is[*n't*] worked out yet—it goes on:

in the street quiet like safe buildings
a tame Africa with rose bushes
and even lilies flashing color
while above half the opposite, wind
bearing down
an autumn tunnel roaring

On the same day. Each forest
robins at some recesses
shouting or
holding with joy to
rollicking ground

    the flat islands float up high   ⦚

(Another rough part—goes on:

the abstract forces

hitherto abstract

Lower   and the sky's acts
    which somehow is forgotten
something against something
not seen....

Quality of his rhythms interests me very damn much, sometimes.
Likewise sharp images. A real kick, I mean slap to it, at at best. And
apparent looseness here—hardly fair so chopped up, and also one he
isn't done with. A very damn fantastic mind, at points:[266]

The children were frightened by crescendoes
cars coming forward in the movies

That is, before they found out love,
that is, Comedy

the cheeks blew
The music rises and continues   [*Adds*: nice.]

and the sea does

and there were no accidents today
the bombs showered us in the air

Like that—"the flat islands float up high"—which is something.

There was one I liked very much, quality of it, or what to say, if I can
damn well find it. Called PARTS OF SALEM.[267]

In fact, if you like it, why not think of it for the Broadside series—I
think it is that good. Everyone goes dumb to this rhythm he damn
well has—only mag to yet print anything is GOAD.[268] (Cid knows
him, and sees a lot of it I guess—but nothing doing to date. Poem like
this following I can't see why he doesn't print—or what he thinks he's
waiting for. E/ cuts him anyhow, it must be hard to swallow.)

I don't want to break it in the middle—why I'm farting around here:
damn damn beautiful things he makes often, or like this:[269]

… Or down the sizeable hill
    up which the common trucks pull junk
    with their irregular wooden bodies …

Another:
                (well, no room—let me copy this one I'm thinking of.

PARTS OF SALEM

                    down to the folds
I saw the upper halves of cars
without the wheels I knew to be
moving around my corner,   and
the action of those sitting there still
forward, drivers and children,   hands
a new hat on an old man
the street sudden smile at noise

last among the marble sites
and the brick exchanges
                    rises of earth
filled and massed with human stone
parking space alleviates
ancient commons which were lonely
and magnificent prairies breaking the heart

because it was five yards off
talkers at one curb   lost as
if forgotten   yet
what has there been, now, to speak of

Girls and mothers of one hour
in passing in tender hair
and men counting silently

It's a very odd & moving thing, or is to me. Certainly it's not done
with quickly. Just now reading it—I'd first wanted to move out some
of the middle, but not now—it has this odd, odd quiet, and space, to it.
Well, you say—tell me what you think of it anyhow.

Perhaps I grew up somewhere near there, etc. Salem, Malden, etc. It is
a particular feel, finally, or character of movement which he has hit
exactly on the nose. (His address is 23 Bates Road, Swampscott, Mass.
Name is Larry Eigner, etc. In case it's worth picking up.)

Otherwise it goes pretty slow. The other night, man who works the
garden, or most of it, talking about Casals[270], who I guess he knew,
and also Lorca who he grew up with. It was a wild thing. He was
telling this story about a fete there, a "Grand Concourse des Poetes,"
and Lorca at 17, poem, etc. I made a translation from his telling it, he
gave it in Spanish, and then in a sort of French—with real wild
movements of his hands. Anyhow, it was something to do, see what
you think.

AFTER LORCA

                    (who said this poem at a "Grand Concourse des Poetes"
                    somewhere in Spain when he was 17, and everyone was
                    pushing at him to go first, so he drank a bottle of
                    cognac, and said it with the guitar going behind him)

The church is a bizness, and the rich
are the bizness men.

              When they pull on the bells, the
poor come piling in and when a poor man dies he has a wooden
cross, and they rush through the ceremony.

But when a rich man dies, they
drag out the Sacrament
and a golden Cross, and go doucement, doucement
to the cemetery.

And the poor love it
and think it's crazy.

I may be too, eh? But I like it, and very much [*adds*: not like that
though]. It's a damn wild feel, to get anything like that. Mouth to
mouth. I have never had it before, or my part, too, in it. Though I may
be wrong there, thinking it can be like this. But for god's sake why not.
One gets too damn christly meek. Fuck it.

When I think of Vince I want to vomit, and the same with Cid. Just a
goddamn simple & hellishly inappropriate fact. Fuck it.

Listen to either one: or you read it anyhow, that GG#3. Cid & his
christly TITS.[271] I laughed, and I damn will laugh—at that.

But that don't make me anything else. Right now it's ok finally, I am
getting back together some at least. Wouldn't it be goofy to be
somewhere by that sea you wrote us of, the pools being so clear, and
that time, yet, of you & bridge & the bus.[272] I get too stiff here, I get all
fucked with how it looks to me, and I to it. Which is the ultimate
drag, any damn place.
              Anyhow I keep thinking of getting there, it
makes sense. It could be very damn great. At least I don't see why not.

Write soon, I'll do likewise.

All our dearest love to you all,
                    Bob

Last verse of Cid's maybe part of it—but MUFFLED. I don't know. All thru a bag, etc.

[Lambesc, Bouches-du-Rhône]
June 25, 1952

Dear Charles,

I was trying to tell Buddy about Boulez, etc. Could you tell me where to get the article, i.e., who published it, etc. I'd like to get it, very much. It made a hell of a lot of sense. Anyhow, when you can.

Crazy book I got inadvertently for Dave, ZOO ANIMALS—wild text:[273]

"Sloths live in jungles, where their long, shaggy, greenish-brown coats acquire vegetable growth which produces a most effective camouflage. They are quite helpless on the ground. In the ant-eaters the head is long and slender and ends in a powerful snout. The mouth is toothless and tubular and the tongue long and worm-like. The enormous fan-shaped tail serves as a parasol and can be folded over the animal's head and body when it is exposed to strong sun-shine. The Great ant-eater of the forests of South and Central America stands 2 feet high at the shoulders and may exceed 6 feet in length. Sloths, ant-eaters and armadillos have no front teeth, and are found only in South America."

Sound pretty mean, eh? Phew.

Also reading[274] Anson's Voyage, but in that Penguin abridged version;
I guess he cuts a lot of the descriptions, etc. Book moves very
"swiftly"—almost too "swiftly." Hardly begun, and there they are,
standing for England, etc. Wild in point of understatement. Style is
cool enough, though a bit stuffy. Not up to some of the others, same
time. Everyman has the whole of Hakluyt, but I don't think much of it
is in print. Cook, too—I haven't got it yet. What else is there? It is wild
reading.

(Also reading Xenophon in Rex Warner's translation; it's
ok. Some of it is too much.

In both books, odd disparities of the
moral frame, I mean against our own. Sometimes only a question of
assumption, etc. But interesting. One hits it most clearly in the Anson
book—and by "moral" I guess I get back to your sense of what
sanctions are in strength, to be found or got to, for a course of action,
etc.[275] Sometimes it's only a "weather" sign, though behind that is, of
course, a lot. (I found that out in NH, which is still, or where we were
was, a great web of it—just before Tom was born, it came out very
clearly in neighbor's suggestions, etc. Things one should or should not
do.) Anyhow in Anson, editor has put in footnotes here & there; of no
real purpose—brief explanations of what bending a sail means, etc.
Now & again he gets ruffled by weather, apparently Walter was very
much on this last thing—much of his attention given to it, and to
natural manifestations of any sort (which I guess is the bulk here cut,
sadly).

At one point (p/ 175) Walter says, "And as the new moon was
approaching, when we apprehended violent gales ..." and then
continues to relate the great precautions against storms they then
took, "lowering the main and fore-yard close down, that in case of
blowing weather the wind might have less power upon the ship ..."
Footnote here, "New moon gales: statistics have not shown that gales
are any more prevalent during time of new moon than at any other
phase of the moon. But the fancy that weather changes with the moon
is one which exists even in many minds today." What is so great—that
the text goes on utterly oblivious, as of course it would. And the next

paragraph, "... We flattered ourselves (for I was then on board) that the prudence of our measures had secured us from all accidents; but on the 22nd, the wind blew from the eastward with such fury that we soon despaired of riding out the storm." It's very damn nice!

Even better in Xenophon, which has no such notes, etc. At one point it is damn well black—though it is for most of the narrative as I figure you know anyhow. Anyhow, things are tough, and "he got a little sleep in the end and had a dream. He dreamed that there was a thunderstorm and that a thunderbolt fell on his father's house and then the whole house was on fire. He woke up immediately, feeling very frightened, and considered that in some respects the dream was a good one, because in the midst of his difficulties and dangers he had dreamed of a great light from Zeus; but in other respects ..." it wasn't so good. He goes to the divers chiefs and they talk it over, they then rouse the camp, and one of the leaders says, X/ will now tell you what he told me. And X/ does, and just then someone sneezes, and "when the soldiers heard it, they all with one accord fell on their knees and worshipped the god who had given this sign." And they win out, etc.[276]

Throughout, that sense of the moral a constant accompaniment to the action. Action, in fact, subsists on two levels—of the intention, of the mind's acts in accordance with its sense of sanctions & fitness, etc., and then the cold doing, the act so cast, etc. It is very beautiful at times.

[*Types in margin*: I see an edition of Pausanias, "transl. with a Commentary by *J. G. Frazer*," 6 vol/s.[277] Ok?]

Also reading Lucretius—some of it is good. There is a passage on what is close, certainly: "Or consider what happens when we have surrendered our limbs to soothing slumber and our body, replete and relaxed, lies insensible. At that very time there is something else in us that is awake to all sorts of stimuli—something that gives free admittance to all the motions of joy and to heart-burnings void of substance."[278]

(A side-issue, and perhaps smug too: "Often from fear of death mortals are gripped by such a hate of living and looking on the light that with anguished hearts they do themselves to death...."[279]

Lucretius is a very flat man, very level, etc. Coming from Xenophon, or any of these others, it is not so much reason as an utterly *resistless* intelligence; although I know it attempts cool 'logic,' etc.)

Passages in Dana, about what it's like when a man dies at sea—and how that loss is dealt with.[280] Dana, who has, I think, no real will for 'looking for it,' as, say, Conrad has in a narrative that might border D/s at many points. But the thrust, then, in, of the 'action'—very beautiful. Perhaps because it is in spite of him.

Anyhow, I had felt it last night—is this question possible, or better, since I think it is, at what does it point: how shall we differentiate between that which satisfies the needs of our "environment" and that which satisfies ourselves. Horribly put, there. Anyhow it makes room for me; it's the difference between Elath's formulations & those of Zander and the rest.

Hot as hell here—have to go down, etc. Write soon. All our dearest love to you all,

Bob

[*Enclosed*:]

I'll get that P[ausanias]/—not too damn much, and 6 vol/ will keep me cool for a while.

While I think of it: that J/Hawkes' noted in past letter is, I figure, C/Hawkes' wife, or near relation anyhow. I note a Penguin book: Prehistoric Britain, by Christopher & Jacquetta Hawkes.[281] And it wd/ seem that coincidence is too much to make either anyone else, etc.

Yr man's name CF H/s, and must be the same one? Seems so. And this wife must be in it too. You know that wd/ be very cool indeed for BMC, both of them pulling, etc. Two for the price of one, etc. Her gig seems to be monuments, etc. Literal signs, etc. He must do the correlating.

Anyhow I'll pick up the Penguin, 28¢ etc., "In this book the authors describe half a million years of Britain's pre-history. They tell us of the geological evolution of our country and of its earliest immigrants and invaders."

Hold yr breath/ we're going d o w n.

Have you seen this one? Will send you a copy if you say so. What is title of bk/ you had? Of CF Hawkes?

Ok.

I see he also did intro/ to book abt/ Lascaux Cave Paintings (Faber).[282]

———— ════════ ————

[Washington,D.C.]

wed june 25 52

lad: a note to let you know I MADE IT—much helped by my good wife, C, but, i made it. And from the feel of my own house, it will take some force to remove me therefrom, some damned attraction—in fact, from the accumulated sense of lost work now mostly a year, I shall probably resist attractions, if I at all turn out to be able to get back on the track, alone here, and doing financially risky things (like tapping into that Wnner*gren dough, to get me started again on my own)

The beautiful feeling is, that my own speech belongs to nobody—that I don't have to smile out a single sentence! (Not that such would be a problem to most other men but—as you'd guess—most of my trouble lies in such stupid areas!

[*Adds in ink, along margin of first two paragraphs:*

Write me here, of course—]

Yr last letter just came in forwarded by Con the one abt the deaths, there—and yr lines.[283] And by god it strikes me as sure sign I am in my own place that I am able—just like this—to respond (when i think of [strikes out all] so much of yr work, in the past year, which has got lost from my comment on it because of the nuisances of being broken off by meals, persons, and my own geometric entanglements as a result of the other interruptions!

I don't think The Festival works, and my guess is that it goes two ways: (1) that just such an incident is so very deeply the narrative in it that you wld have to give it that extension in order to achieve even yr own feeling, like you say—that is, it is not description you were avoiding but narrative which got left out ((might just be why, at the end of yr letter, you cry you wish you are back at story!))

but more important, (2), death as subject. It, too, in our time, has had its base moved so profoundly that to touch it (like to touch love, memory, life) involves major repairs—and such, in writing, ain't they always vocabulary questions?

That is, it is *chance* which you are grinding on—that loss if 3, and such 3, such 3 to which you will have 3 and I have 1, that thought (I am new to it, and you must tell me, but it does seem an angst a child brings, the thought of what damned accidents it is beholden to—that we slipped through this far, seems such a miracle, no? Anyhow, my damned heart yawns, sometimes, when I think of those things—and the years of my daughter

And I take it the reason why chance will not support that irony there, that word death, is that all of us have got tremendously exposed to death as chance in the increasingly invasive ubiquity of destruction—

that is, it wasn't so long ago that accident was as meaningful as it must be there, in that small town you are in. That was the law not so long ago: (what flashed into my mind was a story of Edith Wharton's I have never been able wholly to take my emotion away from—Ethan Frome: and just because that sliding accident[284] (even the purposefulness of it) speaks of chance at time at a time when it was still close to our intimate affairs, and not off there, in the sky or state, where it forces on us the necessity to think in the most difficult of all of the adjustments "totality" involves us in—survival, that the one law of the present horror is a thing which goes into the marrow of a man where courage as honor lies, that his calculation must be, survive, be able to crawl out of the ruins

My other thought is, that the deaths of the other sort, the living ones, are also so increased (organization has dealt this out, as well—the murders of poison and job and doctrines—also in such quantity that physical death is in as much need of res-toration as physical life ...

Ok. First thoughts, and for what they may be worth to you.

I come to that momentous letter I have carried with me here, to answer, containing THE QUESTION, those lines Con and I both think are very fine.
((in fact, Robt, this poem is one in which I take it yr linage is impeccable—and because it is, that force which a line now adds to a poem—that lustre—it is one of yr finest, is verse in its own kind of beauty (the beauty which goes beyond the man who made it, his fineness, his perception

the drop in that rides me big—i can't do more than tell you it is absolutely tops
sensuous/ is
mine/ women
their/their/bare-d/tur-nal
the agh!
(and the whole last four lines such knittings of these

Beautiful, thruout (look: settle an argument—how do you see yr

phrase, "a multiple love is/ mine"—do you mean it to apply to yrself
or another? Just for the hell of it, this once, let me ask such a stupid
question, just for kicks, between Con and me. OK?

Equally, to yr poem, was yr go on Hull—not so much on him, or on
Elath's palpable bad "taste" (this bothered me, in his piece, that I could
not convince myself such a perceptive system rested on the right side
of the bed of the present riz therefrom—how was it, it used to be, in
the old ballad, abt which side of bed you got out of? don't now
remember, but it will work as well to put it as it also is there, that a
woman's place is next i' the wall[285]—and i am afraid that that is where
Elath is

      ((i feel too much, even just there in that finest of things, him
      on the Cantos[286], that he lies more on the wall side, that he stems
      from thoughts not from sensations (to use Keats' distinction of
      the sort of life he said he chose to live, not that of Thoughts but
      that of Sensations[287]

      that is, it is true that Ep did comment on his combination of
      intelligence, but when he did (instead of when he put it into the
      metric of the Cantos and so made that metric forward from 1919)
      Ez wrote an epic of a society dates 1429–1919,[288] and so, no matter
      how incisive the idea is, did not write a primal thing
               (this can be seen another way, that Elath, like Ez
               himself, gets caught in an analogy (The Comedia)
               which falls to the ground if you have the audacity, as
               I have had to have, to think the Com is overrated)

Well, I could go on, but want to just say yr own words on irony
are as fine a moral essay as I have ever read, and I deeply
treasure it, in fact, if you would think of publishing it, let me
know, and I'll make you a copy of it. I'd encourage you to do it.
For this thing you are striking at is prevalent—and in some
relatively fine figures.

In fact, all this impedes me. For Con encouraged me to go so far
as not even return to BMC for the last 4 weeks of their summer

session. That means I shall have to find a substitute. For that was a commitment. You will know I'd think of Paul B, simply, that you encouraged me to. But I do wish he were someone whom I took more interest in than I do in him. In lieu of him, and in lieu of Lawrence Richardson (who is a combination of classicist and archaeologist I like),[289] I did think of Elath, so liking his mind, in that go. But his liking for Hull raises those doubts of his creative depth I felt, and I wonder. Wish to god you were the one. Well, will push this off, and love love love

[Adds, in ink, around margins on page:]
want to come back? the date is july 23rd! and you cld go straight on through the year! (By the way, I brought up the matter of a year's promise to Rainer with Huss (before the Board of Fellows), and he was delighted.[290] The only hitch, Robt—(& it made my leaving even a greater job than I'd thought)—is that Huss himself has decided to go back to acting Sept 1st! Which leaves me without my most important leverage there; and I tell you now, not to kill yr & Rainer & Laubies' hopes, but to keep you current. It may work out even better, though. For Huss & I decided to look for a successor for him before we, either of us, announced our desires. Will keep you on. [*No signature.*]

[Washington, D.C.]

Thurs June 26 [1952]   ROBT: Con shot me another of yr letters,[291] and damned helped by same—flatly, by yr statement of what you call those areas this person does strike. For just now, and just such a putting of it, is so goddamned crucial I can't think of what cld, this morning, have been of such use. You see, it's rocky, to be back here buried in this house with all the other work staring me in the face across the intermission of two years!

It came on me after I finished that note to you yesterday.
Figure it was helped by the heat. Anyhow, it pushed me finally into
the street, on the town, walking amongst people, and then unable to
sleep, and reading until dawn.

Filthy heat, anyhow: never knew its
like. Jesus. Sick with it. 98 degrees. But much worse than that sounds.
Like Sugar Ray Robinson, last night: lost his fight with Maxim in the
14th on a technical KO simply because he couldn't get off his feet from
heat exhaustion! He had won 10 of the 13, and lost his supper just
then: 104, in the ring![292]

You see, terribly self-screwed—have my thumb so hard on myself
can't squeeze out the work form under pressure. Crazy stupid trick I
always had, anyhow. And this is such a time—that sense, that I don't
know what to say. So, your saying, he has his areas, that was mighty
helpful, by god mighty …

OK. No more of that. Did get some thing
done yesterday, rewriting one thing, that go. "There are Sounds …"[293]
Long time ago. Has kept in my mind, simply, that the obscurities,
there—and in this instance they are just such, the thing is consciously
worked among them in itself"—*are* the poem, in this instance. And so
has kept me interested, how to reduce them and yet make the poem
work as of them

(strikes me you were engaging yrself with this sort of
problem in that one of yrs on the price of coal—was it THE
LIONS?)[294]

Anyhow, yr just saying, here, in this letter, you can't nail the whole
world every damn time, that quickens me. For it never occurred to me
that I tried! And what yr saying it does, is enlist my respect for
poems—for their own damned wonderful individuation, that they
make their own way. So this one, one which perhaps nobody cld ever
get much out of, yet, it contains, for me, several damn attractive
engagements as against, say, THE CAUSE, THE C, which is a rider for
me

I still got it on my mind. Maybe another run of it, for you, might improve it. Let's go: [*On verso, a version of "There Are Sounds ... ," with some markings in pencil.*]

[*Continued, from verso sheet, at bottom of letter:*]
Now I don't know a thing. Give me yr word (to some extent, I am preparing that volume, still, making towards it, but very crab-like— and whatever you think goes in—
  ((You see, I still think I ought to use those 64 pages, no?
    Granting you the right of such a selection as you proposed
      (*24 pp* approximately, let's continue & argue that—and tell
      me of anything which stands in your mind
(regard all lines hooked back *on right* as of one length))
                        [*No signature.*]

                        [Lambesc, Bouches-du-Rhône]
                        June 29, 1952

Dear Charles,
        Very goddamn wonderful to have you there—it sounds damn fine, & goddamn well gives you some leeway. Anyhow, very cool.

Let me clear that poem, first.[295] It's a very damn funny thing, if I have figured right, i.e., which side of the fence either, or any, of us fall to. Myself, it lands like this:

A description of the sensuous
is its own answer : a multiple love is
mine.

Not to be soupy, but juxtaposition is of two equivalent statements, & two, then, disparate stances. Only that character of each is, call it, "statement, of position." By that main stress, then, sentence reads, literally, that a "multiple love" is my answer to that need which the *description* might be thought to answer in some other's case.

I mean, in any case, that it's in the sense of an attention, one could hope a capacity—it's my being able, or hoping to be able, to have a "love" which can be "multiple"—not many women, so simply. A love, in any case, which allows a multiple instance not by virtue of there being a great many "things" to love—which fact I take as condition of any reality, simply to begin with, I mean, there they all are, etc.—but rather that an attention or capacity for such love, i.e., to be in the man, to be allowable there. Blocked—then the first statement holds, or it's what, I think here, one reverts to, in I suppose a frustration; not being allowed common touch, or relation—he can only describe, & get touch in that sense. I hope, anyhow, frame of the first statement makes clear it's a dead end, i.e., a circle altogether closed.

Broken down like that—I get scared. Anyhow that's the sense as I had it—and interesting (!) that Ann immediately read it as there being many women, and perhaps that's a fault. But damn well no—here one is hard against it, the two positions, man or woman—and *must be* different readings—or poem damn well does sink.

Subsequent stanzas, call them, play out on almost *just* this aspect. Or beginning, "Who in their beds …," you get damn well objective (!) statement of fix—to then come to "reason," in last.

Fuck it anyhow, i.e., impossible to work it out like that. Anyhow, not that there are so many ladies to love, etc., which there, of course, are. But that one can—and by virtue of being *one*, oneself, to begin with. I.e., one man—enough to allow *all* contact. If only because one is sexual, and what else.

I go with you on that death poem—no good.[296] No good for a damn good many reasons—and reading even that Lucretius—I couldn't answer him—or with no damn "poem" like that. Impossible to [be] interested in "death" in just that way—he has it: "you must understand that the *minds of living things and the light fabric of their spirits are neither birthless nor deathless."*[297] And wonder, just now, why that comforts me so much, i.e., it isn't an assurance, is it. But it is the sense I meant here, even so. He says later—"From all this follows that *death is nothing to us* and no concern of ours, since our tenure of the mind is mortal ..." By god, that's Lawrence. I like it. In fact, it is very interesting material, this man I think still bordered, very much so, on precisely that old phase, or present one we damn well *must* get to. In short, what you have told me of. Take this sentence, for one—it is damn well beautiful! "In fact, *nothing in our bodies was born in order that we might be able to use it, but the thing born creates the use ...*" Well, like Ann said—I can't believe that? This is damn well it—it is so christly well posed on just that brink, I now believe myself to get some sense of—between that world, or really that kind of attention, you have posited—and what we now have. I want to believe it. I know it is not "true" in any of the facile senses, etc. It is a beautiful damn sense—and also tosses poor ole L/ back into the damn wonder he's trying to crawl out of. Too much.

Also—what I wanted to get to: book I just read called INTRODUCTION TO A SCIENCE OF MYTHOLOGY, by Jung & Kerenyi. At the beginning, K/ quotes just that thing from Malinowski you had.[298] Damn good. And Jung, in a complementary piece, makes very damn clear utter uselessness of treating this material either as explanation, or something to be explained.[299] It is, in that sense, a damn valuable book. Jung's weight, here, is damn valuable. K/ is more collector, or statistician, but makes, even so, some hits. Anyhow, what does get out:

"The primitive mentality does not invent *myths*, it *experiences* them. Myths are original revelations of the pre-conscious psyche, involuntary statements about unconscious psychic happenings, and anything but allegories of physical processes...."

I.e., put that, which is familiar, alongside this later statement:

"Psychology therefore translates the archaic speech of myth into a modern mythologem—not yet, of course, recognized as such—which constitutes one element of the myth 'science'...."[300]

I.e., at this point, to damn well shout: you going to let them psychologists *get away with that*? Poets of the world unite, etc. Anyhow, it is very fine, it opens up science, call it, clearly as an attention, an attitude toward the "real" which is, in short, a methodology among divers. Here, or could be, we jump in with both feet—"literature," this act of writing, & why, to now assert itself—I think it can, or must.

Anyhow it's now very clearly a methodology which is called for; Jung's statement proves that, if nothing else. Also, earlier in this book, K/ talking: "We have found the exact expression for this ('This return to the origins and to primordiality is a basic feature of every mythology.'): behind the 'Why?' stands the 'Whence?,' behind the
         the   . More strictly still, there is no initial question at all in mythology ... nothing but ... a spontaneous regression to the 'ground.' It is not only the man who experiences a living mythology that draws back a pace like a toreador, or slips as into a diving-bell; the true teller of myths does likewise, the creator or re-creator of mythologems....."[301]

I figure a review of the book, i.e., just as an instance, to open some of this up. I don't damn well know if it will come off—I'll send you what I get. (I.e., figure it for Lash, if possible.)[302] Man called Northrop Frye in KENYON (same issue as the story) on some of this—but mainly old gag of archetypes in literature—and he used Yeats' Sailing to Byzantium as an "example."[303] That, will never do, etc., etc. All the same damn "description," etc. I mean, methodology, means, etc., is the emphasis; one don't say, now I'm going to write about the Primordial Child, etc. Not tonight!

I hope, very damn much, the gig there at BMC holds. I get, anyhow, the difficulties, and thanks for keeping us on. On Paul B/[*lackburn*], I'll enclose some stuff from letters, will show you quicker than blat, etc. Ok. And send them back when you can. Anyhow, think he would be excellent for the job; wish to god I could get there right off, it would be terrific, but baby probably coming just at that same time. Or we hope so!

Some damn way anyhow. Going there would mean two things: 1) literal way of getting a "place" for us all till we can get together; and

2) some damn means to work out what I now have to hand in an
equally literal "talk," etc. I am too off here, I am too cut from my own
damn tongue. I think I could take a year anyhow, on impetus from
being shut up here. It's hell, damn honestly—I hate it.

Otherwise, or if it doesn't work—I don't know, I think we would
probably stay on. If Rainer can get that press, that would be
something; but he wrote, recently, that they might take jobs in some
place like Karlsruhe, to get the money—and so would not come here,
to France, for at least another year. I can't wait honestly—too damn
killing. Laubies stays around Paris—question of keeping on, etc. We
can't bother with that either. Perhaps Mallorca—if this Seymour-Smith
makes out, etc. Might be it. Or, what might do too, Spain proper, or
some place near where Buddy is—I am damn sick of NO contact, etc. I
get it with Ashley, but we're too damn tight, kill too much in each
other. And with the exception of the Hellmans, there's no one else who
isn't damn actual drag.

Really this damn leeway, for us now—the hell. There's only one damn
place that would make ultimate sense, i.e., some place back in the US,
either close enough to such damn things as friends, etc., to allow
contact—or just a fit, some place that is good for us, etc. Here is not.
BMC would be it—I mean, could be, and certainly would be with the
G/s, Laubies—and who I would count most anywhere, yourself. I
want that very much—but I get it, I mean if it works, crazy—if it don't
we'll figure something else.

You should see me sailing Dave's boat, I overhauled it, and put on
bigger mast, & keel, etc. But I don't have tools! Too bad, eh. Anyhow I
like it—wind catches it, sails open way out, I have the jib almost like a
balloon, etc., very fine! Me & Leonardo,[304] only I buy mine at the store.

Also my sister wrote a very wonderful letter, about her & my mother
going to hear Williams read.[305] My mother never having gone to
anything like that in her life.

"Mother and I went to hear Dr. Williams, she will write you, too. —He

was up there with Karl Shapiro, Ludwig Lewissohn, & Peter
Viereck.[306] What do you know? Lewissohn is a fool—he kept trying to
make a lyricist out of Williams—uphill work—; the way he introduced
him—you would have thought he was dead—Williams, that is. —
Quoted that poem—'There is hunting in heaven—Sleep safe, etc.'[307]
He had to scratch to find one he could handle ... He (Williams) sat to
read, just turning the pages & looking at the people. Everybody I
could hear near me responded in a way that staggered me. —Dead
silence, tremendous applause—and the people who have money to go
to these things don't read poetry. Common speech, and he really got
to everyone. I was maudlin, with tears in my eyes—at the whole idea.
How he looks—a bit gray-faced—lot of dignity but not chilly. I got the
feeling he could hardly sit through Viereck quietly. Karl Shapiro like
you might expect—sort of good-looking, ties matching sox—a real
businessman. —Thought he might be better understood than Williams
as his poetry is nothing if not obvious—but not so ... Viereck is
hysterical. At first I thought he must be Shapiro because I knew he
wasn't Williams & he looked too dotty to be conservative. Really
weird. Spotty sort of youth—*young* he looks—pale—with a band-aid
on his chin and glancing wildly around. —He read his horrible stuff
horribly—screaming & whispering—sort of acted it out, suck in a gust
and go along on it till he needed another—which decimated his lines
in strange places sometimes ... Mother liked Williams. After it was
over—we rushed up—already there a young man telling him he was
more poet than doctor (shyly) and Williams saying he was simply
both & the manner of his life affected his poetry very much he
thought. Then I moved in & said why we were up there—and he said
he was glad we got there while he was still alive. He shaves like a
doctor. Wouldn't seem out of character at all with a bag coming up the
front steps. He is quite deaf—will never be sure if he understood me at
all—really don't think so—but there were people crowding us out. He
shook hands with Mother anyway...."

I used to read her some of the stories, from Life Along The Passaic
River, she used to like what he said, though a little shocked now &
again at his frankness, i.e., like Use Of Force, etc.[308] Them's trade-
secrets! She tried to get the doctor in the office to read some—don't

think he ever wd/. Tant pis....[309]

So it goes. Hot as a son of a bitch—(Dave worrying about tant pis—thinks I'm fighting with you, etc., i.e., had murmured same to myself in writing it—often I'm singing along anyhow—he stands just close enough to get bumped everytime carriage goes back.) Anyhow hot. Overcast now, but don't help. Hotter.

Anxious to get that Pausanias, now, and was anyhow. Used as source many times in this book to hand, i.e., Jung & K/. Some damn breakthru on *sense* of "narrative prose" necessary, i.e., IF one cd/ make clear why either AM/GRAIN or yr ISHMAEL are "novels"—and NO cheap psychology—then we'd bee MOVING. I think this might be chance—i.e., it's why Jung's point, of psychology, is on it. I.e., that 2nd quote from him.

Or why "novels" ain't "novels"—same damn thing. Damn "division of labor" again. Too much.

Ok, I'll get back soon. Heat not too bad, to hell with it.

All our dearest love to you all, hope Con & Kate are ok—let's ALL go to Lerma!

Bob

[Lambesc, Bouches-du-Rhône]
June 29, 1952

Dear Charles,

Enclose thing on that book;[310] I got it done last night, all at one time, etc., and plagued by it when I went, finally, to bed & must have been awake almost till morning. And when I did sleep, damn confusion & toss of dreams, etc.

Reading it now—perhaps hardly that to another, etc. Just now reading
1st few [*Pisan*] Cantos, I have to stick by keeping him out there, i.e.,
where it says Williams & Lawrence. And yet whole structure strikes
me as almost literal attempt to duplicate that pattern, call it, by which
a myth comes to presence—or in the book, Jung, etc., this emphasis on
the submerging & then reassertion in a variety of guises, etc. Fantastic
writing, and yet I think wrong. Or "wrong" against Lawrence; I mean
we are present or we are damn well nothing. One can, if he wants to,
repeat, in hopes of something adhering—that (Clock tick pierces the
vision),[311] or like that. But what Lawrence writes, in that part of THE
PLUMED SERPENT, and also in the 1st part of MAN WHO DIED, is
not a mnemonic lean in any sense. Either here—or nowhere. It is as if
Williams were *correcting* Pound, in that final part of PATERSON, i.e.,
The sea is not our home ...,[312] and how he dates it, Pound fashion[313]
—it is hard to think he is not thinking, just then, of him.

Reading Pound pamphlets—hit that phrase, increment of
association—but *never* intentionally? In fact it *is* that we don't "catch
'myths' by going out some night with a bag, etc."[314]

I don't know, I put the damn book down, had been reading it with
Skeat's Etymological Dictionary, etc.[315] Those first few—the *words*. It is
incredible. But it is NOT it. How the hell to deal with it. I can't believe
it, and yet I learn more from him than any man I've ever had to do
with. Or I learn how, etc. Even so it is nothing I wouldn't see, even, go
because I am damn well otherwise. Those who count for me are, too.

Well, fuck it for now. But one has to deal with him—no game counts
unless he's dealt in, etc. Anyhow, most *exact* passage in all the damn
book is, for me—O white-chested martin goddamn it....[316] Joyce *dead*,
after that.

THE NEW ODYSSEY

C. J. Jung & C. Kerenyi, Introduction To A Science Of Mythology;
Routledge & Kegan Paul, London 1951, 25/-.

No one is going to catch "myths" by going out some night with a bag. A *reality* is difficult, and not ever simply pointed to. Communication has a constant content, no matter that its means be the time & place of its occurrence. It is not a "romanticism"—it is something literally primordial, if any of us have come from anywhere.

At least it is very hard to begin. The loss of the past years, judged in other terms than those now current (I mean even deaths), is hard on any man, and not to be got out of. On the one hand, simply that outcrop of "division of labor," the hell of a culture split, and cut up into fragments that cannot function so separated. On the other, nothing at root, the so-called modern *weltschmerz*, sickness, usually home-sickness, *angst*.[317] A time which considers its literature as a somewhat "formal" instance of entertainment is not so much to be despised, as destroyed. Anger makes that logic.

"The myth in a primitive society, i.e., in its original living form, is not a mere tale told but a reality lived. It is not in the nature of any invention such as we read in our novels today, but living reality, believed to have occurred in primordial times and to be influencing ever afterwards the world and the destinies of men...."[318]

We don't so much make the *real*, as we witness it, and in that act become its own testament. Of course what is "real" and what isn't can be brought to the tests of pragmatism—it burns me, therefore it is. It is a part of it, if only that. One makes no case for the general, or what is not there as opposed to what is.

A writer has, then, *what* to do; or in what place shall he suppose himself to act, and for what purpose. We need clarity god knows, we need at least that. I believe that one can effect, in practice, a *methodology*, a position which will allow him his own speech, particularly his own speech; and whatever is there, is there to be offered.

Clearly any man now stands in gain of an incredible amount of *means*, or how to do it—almost anything. Poetry, for one thing, has cleared itself since 1910, of the litter & wash of affectation, although it can be got back, certainly. At least to the contrary some men, I think Williams and Lawrence, have affected a content unmistakably common—and "common" in no sense usual. What to call it. There are parts of PATERSON that are of any continuum, it is *religious* in that way.[319]

This ground is dangerous, one assumes too much—and hoping to say one thing, says another. "Psychology therefore translates the archaic speech of myth into a modern mythologem—not yet, of course, recognized as such—which constitutes one element of the myth 'science.' "[320] That is the important sense—that it is *one* place.

Integrity, then, becomes of a final kind; it is what one faces into anything with, what one has for that. To say that literature has a diversity of means is relevant—but a literature is of use only in one character, *communication*. It is not "naive" to write of oneself, to make that the ground, but to go false there is to affect a *common* falseness. And one which works deep, and cannot be got out easily.

A criticism can say very little of this, finally, or it can say this or that *means* is faulty—it can't presuppose a "good" content.

To that end a writer says what is true for him, or even of him. In that he makes what is his own reality, his perception of it, perhaps actual for another. "The primitive mentality does not invent *myths*, it *experiences* them."[321] It is not a question of "good," or of anything else.

We work for that which will allow, in full character, the *reality* not granted by a partial, or disrupted, "literature."

(ok/ hot as hell up here—I'll write you in the next day or so—please do likewise!

All our love to you all,

Bob

Etc. I hate to end it damn well there, i.e., it sounds too much like bull-shit re Ez, etc. I think he puts the Cantos as *myth*—almost literally, if not just that. And it's the *last* damn thing they are.

Anyhow that biz of "tale of the tribe," etc.,[322] you'd noted it, and I think I got it from him straight, too, somewhere—I can't just now hit it.[323] "Myths never, in any sense, explain; they always set up some precedent as an ideal and as a guarantee of the continuance of that ideal...." It is his "method" in part. Particularly the last sense of *structure*.

"The myths ... are as a rule *tribal history* handed down from generation to generation by word of mouth...."

I.e., hardly new—but just now playing it back, against my sense of the Cantos—it would seem it. As though the conception were: a deliberately evolved *myth*. Obviously a great deal of the material is from this sense of source—and I don't think the rest, either the history, Chinese, etc., etc., represent any kind of deviation.

If a critic wanted to show structure, in the Cantos, he could lay them alongside the "history" of any mythologem; and I think he'd have it— or a damn good part. In some sense: the *reversal* of the "myth" process—assendto.[324]

It could be pernicious, and I hate, again, to get Puritan of all things. But Pound *covers* Lawrence, and I hate that. Lawrence, in something like SUN[325] even, is got by a fix demonstrably primal—that seems it to me. I don't see how there can be charts, etc., here—but one can damn well acknowledge even so.

Anyhow we damn well don't want "myths," or any such construction; I should think what ever could be of use, here, is absolute insistence on the SI—for these reasons Jung now makes even clearer. We goddamn well have our "myths," if we can find the means to give witness to them. And by that no damn willfulness—or "intention," etc. It isn't so simply that these archetypes are recurrent, now as well as 2000 years back, etc. What we damn well have, as confrontation, is our *use* of anything—this included. I think Lawrence is damn well impeccable, in something like THE CAPTAIN'S DOLL[326]—it is very damn beautiful USE of intelligence, and by that, even by definition—new & old together.

Look, I wanted to compliment you on that end of HU—not so damn much that it is a "success" (I now think it's that too) but because it is damn fine *conception*. It damn well *has* to be that way, I can see that now.[327]

If we could damn well fuck "history" and balance the works in one hand, I think Lawrence does, at times. But "history" is still Ez, it seems, even in the act of writing. Goddamn well to stay *literate*, and yet hold on—no damn relaxing from such points as are given, with or without the "past." You have to beat that damn biz of *memory*, I don't think he does; I think Lawrence does in almost every word—I wonder if [*he*] even knew it was a problem!

Ok. I don't feel very cool about it—but it seems the main line anyhow. Fuck it for now anyhow—boiling.

(Sorry to jump like that, hell of a day, Tom crying downstairs, Ann feels beat & hear her now calling to him, etc. Ok. Write soon, will do same.)

[*No signature.*]

[Lambesc, Bouches-du-Rhône]
[ca. 30 June 1952]

Chas/ Very grateful for what you say of the letter—if you think it could take that kind of use, then certainly ok with me. And damn good of you to offer to copy it, etc.[328] I haven't heard anything more from Elath, I wrote him some three letters, since that one—perhaps I get too damn pushing, etc. Anyhow, I wrote him more or less what the letter was, although, in writing him, I couldn't put it *out*, like that—or clearly into my own sense of it; I wanted to grant him fact of H/s energy, and also some of technical side (viz use of phrase, as symbol, etc.—tho it doesn't interest me very much).

I think they should get it,

i.e., INTRO—or to let them see it, in any case. The address is, Intro, Box 860, Grand Central Sta., NYC 17. Man's name is Louis Brigante. They probably won't touch it—but they might, at that.

Anyhow, whatever you think; but not Cid, I just don't want to go into this, with him around—I don't want to be used by him, in that way, any more— i.e., poems, or stories, are of a nature that they will stand anywhere— but statement of this kind is too open to use by an editor—and Cid *uses* us miserably in this context. I think so, anyhow. In the INTRO context, of course it would make a hell of a lot of sense—they printed 8 poems by Hull—if they want a comment, or at least one side of it, then this might be used for that. They can attack it as they will, etc.

I heard from this Souster—what do you think about that. The fact they reprinted from Origin #1, is damn good; I tried to get that, but they're sold out—goddamn Cid again wouldn't tell me the address till the fucking last minute, etc. Anyhow—is S/ worth pushing; I sent him this poem, i.e., The Question—was free, etc.[329]

Continue to think Lash could be ok—wonderful damn thing, i.e., with little form, for payment on that review of Jack's novel, etc.[330]—it says: "for 1 essay-review...." Very nice! Or they got me!

I think Paul B/ could do the Fenollosa, if you say so—the thing is, by reviews et al, we can make a context, or can indicate area we aim to inhabit. And to do it there, in context of university magazine, read by gink & genius, etc.,[331] it's cool—or very nicely out, and free, and cold, etc. Good feeling to it, in *this use*.

Anyhow figure it in: what with you there now, and clear, anything you want. I think L/s waiting in this case. I would like to damn well USE it while we can; can't say how long it would be open—or seeing ORIGIN drift like this, even when we were counted in at the start— who the hell knows.

When Cid writes: "The people involved will be, I hope, you, Charley, Paul [Blackburn], Dennie (that Raoul Dennie[*sic*]?—hmmm.), Duncan, Enslin, Vin, and myself. That should be fairly representative of

ORIGIN ..."—that's shit. That is fucking well Untermeyer. I.e., this gig
for the Brit/ mag, not SS/, but another—V/s baby.[332] I got no eyes,
anyhow. Fuck it. (Like Souster's reprint, now, of G/s 5th "montage," in
CONTACT #4[333]—1) they don't tell G/, and 2) G/ wasn't happy with
trans/ to begin with and 3) he's revised the poem anyhow. So what
does that make him. They print it anyhow & think they're being nice to
him. Ultimately, Cid's damn thinking too—the same.)

[*No signature.*]

[*Enclosed:*]

david   creeley

                    olson pggy (this is verbatim ...) mama is piggy
david creeley. we live outdoors and just in the street and dada wrote
that letter on the chimney. we have electricity and a sink and a tree for
me to climb on. we live in a little village, so little-so little house this big.
we got the garden too except it's all the time full of grass except the the
things that are growing in it aren't ours—. Mr. Marti who owns the
things in the   garden. Corn and beans are ours. We don't have almost
anything—piles of trees. We went to a fete and it was a nice fete with
lots of people dancing, piles of people watching the fete & nice pretty
girls dancing with pretty clothes. We don't have any windows ou
anything except we live on one porch. There's a tree all dead, doesn't
have any leaves on it. We have a *basin*. We go swimming it it.

                                                          Four.

(I.e., he's four, etc.)   Thomas one.

                                f ujtttedd
                                              dda

T*   *DA   DAVID

[Lambesc, Bouches-du-Rhône]
[ca. 1 July 1952]

Charles/ Can you help with me biz to hand, i.e., the letter re Hull &
all. I heard from Elath today—a note re some trans/ he'd made of
Trakl (I thought WAKE might use them) and that's all. I mean 3 damn
letters, etc. It didn't sit very well.

But to keep cool : I want to see if
he'll be willing to come out on this thing of Hull. Can you make 3
copies (or 1, & 2 carbons) of that part of the letter; send one to Brigante
(at address noted, etc.), one to *M. Elath, 139-33 Jamaica Ave., Jamaica 38,
N.Y.*, and one back to me. The last you can let go if it's a bug, I can
remember enough of it.

I want to see if either he or Hull will make
any comment, i.e., for use in INTRO. I'd felt sneaky anyhow—coming
out like that behind them—hence wanting to send it at least to
Brigante.

Now I'd like to see what either one says, it can be put like
that at this point. Not just anger, the snub is hardly that close—but to
ask it him where he can't kick he wasn't, etc. Ok.

(I wrote him you'd
forward copy—simply send it plain, etc. Cold. Likewise to Brigante, or
in letter to him, if it's ok with you—just say I asked you to forward it,
for possible use together with a reply from either M. Elath or W. Hull.

If they don't pick up—won't feel any damn reluctance to get it out
elsewhere. It burns me, ok. Hardly the first damn time, etc.

But
goddamn well to see what they say. As it is, I send off E/s mss/, etc. To
Wake, etc. But it's ok, so fuck that.

But damn well wasn't making
jokes when I wrote him about Hull.

Bob

Yr letter just in, let me get this off & will give you a decent answer
directly.

[Lambesc, Bouches-du-Rhône]
July 2, 1952

Dear Charles,

        Let me clear this one damn deck, and then get on with it. Briefly, I've laid out substantially what you note in this last letter, i.e., as what would interest you as a publishing program, etc., to Seymour-Smith for his pamphlets. I.e., he's been decent enough to count me in on it, as, specifically, Am/ editor, or simply contact, etc. He wants apparently to do something—so can hardly *not* say, at least, what I think he might.

        The problem is this: as the "series" is now planned, we'll have only that damn usual run of "poets," for as long as what very damn little money there is, I take it, holds out. Why bother. No one is that important right now; we can get out elsewhere, as witness, you with Cid, me with Emerson, and so on. Or I say it just to emphasize, another gig, "poetry," is not it, and is, further, even DULL.

My excitement about such things as Frobenius, who I can't yet find even a book of, any—about Boulez, and those notes sent—about Barlow as you'd noted him for me there in Lerma—that excitement is damn tenacious. And more, I think usable. In short, I gave him this:[334]

Robert Barlow, Mayan Notes
Pierre Boulez, Composition & The Law of Conjecture
Henri Cartier-Bresson, Journal

etc., etc.   I.e., I simply made a brief list, at random or apparently, interjecting such along with more usual list of poets & such now figured by him.

The length of each pamphlet is 16 pages, and the issue is planned as, roughly, a first series of three, Paul Blackburn's Provencal work, and two British poets—from then on is, in some sense, now wide open. The further series, to begin the first or so of next year—call it spring—"I shall make out a list of books (pamps, rather) to be published by Roebuck during the first six months of next year, and price them and ask for subscriptions. There should be, say, eight titles for that part of '53. I hope to get this list out to send out with the three pamps at present underway. Another eight for latter half of next year ...?"

Can you do this for me. Help me get enough of the above, i.e., of these things you've noted for me, *in hand* so that I can shove them straight at him. Otherwise shall look awfully damn vapid if he says yes. Can you get hold of, for example HC/s material. Or some of the Barlow. Just to show him what it could be—*literally*. Also that article of Boulez. Otherwise I'll have no damn pants, etc., when he takes a look.

Also, if you have it: to note Robt Duncan's address, I'd count him in. And anyone else you think could make it, or be of use here. In the event that material is simply too long for 16pp/ format, could either try to work longer spread, to 32pp/, or else break it as: I & II. Something like that. Get decent man for covers—make such ACTIVE, fine, etc.—and see what the hell happens. It makes sense that way, it does NOT any other. If we don't BREAK this base of "aesthetics," then no damn sense to it—i.e., pushing what is the old garbage, etc., no matter how "nice." Ok, and let me hear what you think; and also abt Barlow, HC/, Boulez, etc., when you can. [*Adds, around margin, concerning Olson's "The Praises" manuscript*: only forty pages off:! Goddamn well thot that bunch of poems noted came to MORE than 24pp/—I was worrying abt ROOM! Ok, and cool again—will pick up in next. Ok ... (My face is REAL red ... I was damn sure there were enough for 64/—or all those long ones? Anyhow, will pick up.]

Goddamn well good to see that poem again,[335]—let me figure it piece by piece, etc. Just to get moving.

Everything up to, "... the overwhelming shrine ...," I make, and very damn clearly. Only headache here might be this sense, of thing, as against very sharp *physical* quality of everything preceding.

Reading this 1st section then, hard against passage beginning—"We are ...," seeing how this last, i.e., I see how this last maintains a *physical* clearness, tho it is an extension, now, of that 1st context. The part between, i.e., that noted as the shrine, up to, "We are ...," or finally, what seems to come out, just lines, shrine, to, it was a rough night, i.e., I can't get them, as against clearness of preceding, sense of.

Ok then up to, *possible*. Hard to move up to, *to go forward*, following it, i.e., I almost want to jump:

of such pleasure, enough: enough
                    to make it

          to go forward, the waters up and down, this night, etc.

Which runs it too fast I know. But I have reluctance, on the word, *possible*.

Actually, or seeing it, now, am not sure if this isn't *only* place I get balked, right here. Or not earlier, to any damn importance—it is that impact of 1st lines, to that last point 1st noted, are damn fast & a damn wild play, etc. And run out, then, i.e., line moving longer, though of a now differing kind—have to come to it, i.e., what reading gets to, now.

Problem of section—"to go forward ...," and then section, "What is it makes us want to ...," i.e., one so after the other—of getting them not slowing each other—or the two, so, together—a real weight. It is damn hard to figure, just here. Line—"it matters more than any lust ..."— very heavy, i.e., is stopper, to some extent—and then, line following— "It is not easy ..."—one reads too much of this still thinking back, of lust, and of what that complex, there, is about. Or how, precisely, as it is to be found precise—communication does goddamn well matter, "more than any lust...." Can't I think "end" there, but it is swivel point, is the expansion I think. I mean, overtly, directly—here, you say it straight out/communication: lust—which side, etc. So that "light" passage is bucking a lot, a residue, now, that reader carries into it—he won't stop, i.e., he'll continue to think of it certainly. As against, say, ICH where movement is on basis of *just* such "residues," i.e., moves on them, expands, slides, so—here "light" is a "new" sense, or breaks, I think, line up to here—or does not directly follow on this impact— rather, put it, refers itself to poem's content overall, etc.

Anyhow, way it now sits: *possible*—drains a little on, *to go forward*: problem of "Question ..." section but *only*, I think, as this relates to one following, i.e., not, as first thot, one before—just that this goes OUT, i.e., is into something, and switch, or play-in then to "light" is a disappointment—or make it straight, it is, here, to me. This, I'd say, IS the crop-out, what, I think NOW gets added, and god knows with relevance. But is also why, light image can't now hold, or must be somehow brought into line with, precisely, this NEW development. Is that horseshit?

Ok, I want to get back—will write you damn soon. Forgive all this shit—i.e., SS/, Elath, etc. SS/ could be some-[*continues along margin:*]thing if we cd/ budge aesthetic base, etc. Anyhow to try it—and I can't do it without you, it's honestly yr gig anyhow; but that it makes incredible sense to me too. Ok. Elath I'm not at all cool abt, right now—suddenly shrunk to damn personal sense, etc. Big letter I thot—opened it to find 5 lines or so abt how I sd/ send Trakl, & the copies. Real pathetic I was. All our love to you,   Bob

[*Added at top of letter:*]
Can you get me DUNCAN'S address—i.e., sd/ be counted on poetry side, even if that's all it comes to.

[Lambesc, Bouches-du-Rhône]
July 4, 1952

Dear Charles,

A damn correction on Elath—fucking good I did NOT flip, etc. I enclose letter just in from him. I think there could be some collaboration. The letter, of yours, he notes, was a section from that one with the Boulez quotes, beginning at that point where you review "totality" up thru Boulez quotes.

What the hell do you know abt Kortzyski [*sic*]. I've got to get the book,[336] simply to read it; can't really make the context, with him, lacking that back of us. No matter what it is. Anyhow another man on Cid—that's damn cheering. Boat was getting awful damn sloped, etc.

I noted BMC gig, for him—is that ok. I asked him to write you quick about it, if he could figure it. Don't let Hull biz worry you, i.e., see what he does here on that subject. (Still think it would be good to work a double play on that biz anyhow; i.e., thing from the letter with either E/s or H/s comment, or answer. What might come out, in the going-round, etc., would be worth the time. Anyhow, trying to interest E/ —so send on the copy if it's not a headache—see what he can do.)

If he could get to Wash/ to see you in any case, that would be it. Save so goddamn much time, and bull-shit. Already he doesn't want to write much, i.e., "can't afford much letter-writing...." I can see that.

This goddamn christly DISTANCE!   SHIT.

Well, ok. I don't know—IF this Brit/ can be hauled in on pamphlet series—wd even make sense to move there, to Mallorca. And we would.

But BMC, if a mag/ were possible—rather more direct, like they say. Only myself to convince, etc. Right now necessary to hand SS/ the works whenever he wants it, i.e., to have examples *in hand*. What scares me, i.e., that he'll say, sure, just like that, and—where's the material. Goddamn well STAND BY—anyhow, have enough of that

B/[*oulez*] from yr letter, to outline what cd/ be done with that. Anything from Barlow. Also, other things noted. (May come to naught, etc.—well, to try it. Ok.)

When E/ talks of "organizing" Cid C/—ho ho ho. But let's see what happens. Would be cool at that. Like to organize that bastard right into the fucking ground. As Ann says—they don't know what he *means* to you! She's damn well right; he's my "competition," only such I've ever got hung with—I heard his goddamn program back one night in NH ... "I'll never be free...." Idea of that man dispensing ANY comment on ANY thing relating to the "arts" is for me, incentive to UNceasing ACTivity. Voila!

Look how dirty he is—writing POEMS to me—fucking below the belt ... Publishing bk/ he says, or trying to, this winter—only poem "you'll know" is "Poem for RC/,[337] etc., etc." Grrrrrrrrrrrrrrrrrrrrrrrrrrrrrrrrrrrrrr. You sd/ see items in Vince/s gig,[338] holy shit! Never in my life, etc.! It will take 20 years to *correct* him.......
                                        All our love to you all,   Bob

WRITE. You're keeping me AFLOAT. Ok.

I don't think I got it straight, re that poem, i.e., lines "a multiple love is / mine." I.e., "do you mean to apply it to yrself or another?"[339]

In one sense—to another, i.e., as the first statement would be one "answer," to another—this second one is also that. For that sense of use, or application. I speak of myself, put it—but wish by that, to make clear a possible means, or precisely what to call it, a way of attention, of how one might, etc.—for another. In that way—I wd mean into [*it to*] apply to another, or would hope it might.

Otherwise those first figurings wd hold—they make the main line at least. Well, ok, etc. Did you ever see that damn magazine, THE EXPLICATOR? Paige had a copy—I was struck dumb. I.e., one full page given to an argument as to whether or not Milton's statement—when I consider how my light is spent, ere *half my days*, etc., etc.—was

intended to refer to *working days*, or to simply *days*, etc.[340] Utterly
fantastic, I wouldn't have believed—without seeing, etc. Too much.

Elath's "taste" well beyond that at least. Incidentally, he notes a
Grossman, whom I'd run into in POINTS, magazine put out in Paris—
agh. Here's Grossman: "General objections seem to have been along
the lines that I'm over didactic and prone to make rash statements that
I don't justify. As to first charge, any essay is too didactical. As to
second, I presume an audience (putative) sufficiently intelligent to be
able to comprehend the conclusion of a syllogism without having to
spell out the axiomatic premises."[341]

It's reminiscent of Elath, and reading him, first, had thought of ole G/,
etc. But E/ soon damn well breaks that level. The prose is beautiful, no
matter what else. Anyhow G/ isn't very cool, or is in a kind of damn
rash & stupid & pompous way. Anything for a laugh, etc., about his
motto; as long as laugh is very close to sneer, etc. Not interesting.

Tone is so goddamn much. Man trying finally to say something, has to
figure that—or that if it is not himself, or for me what my wife can
read—no good. I almost distrust unmarried men, writing put it—or
feel uneasy, because nothing then obliges them to this kind of position,
of being laughed at when it is silly; and having no relief whatsoever. I
don't think I could write "unmarried"—or without the sight of
another human, this close. I depend on it in any case. Blackburn,
unmarried, has evolved one of the most complex systems of personal
check I've ever witnessed—once he *is* married, it should be incredible,
what he'll then do. Or put it, the time, perhaps literal, he's now
obliged to put in on getting the kind of perspective either Con or Ann
could hand us in *one* look, is considerable. (I wonder if Elath's
married! What do you think.)
                              At the G/s in Freiburg—one evening
talking about just this. I was a hell of a lot more serious, finally, than I
guess he was. Or he was too, but it was something else again. We both
got married young, same age even I think, i.e., 20. Both of us walking
down the St/ Germain de Pré, looking at all those ladies—phew. (And
he damn well *did* remember it, and mentioned it about 10 days later.)

In fact Rainer felt it to extent he gave us almost complete run-down on every damn liaison he apparently ever had. He's been around!

[Lambesc, Bouches-du-Rhône]
July 6, 1952

Dear Charles,

Continues very damn hot—apparently a heat wave, and someone told Ann, or the paper said, it hadn't been as hot as this for 20 years. All of which hardly good with her pregnant, but the house is pretty well set for heat—big cedar in the yard, and lots of shrubs, etc. Not too bad, and get fine evenings—moon almost full now, very very beautiful.

Reading Duncan over again the past week; I had him almost completely wrong. He is very cool, at points—I think of that section you had marked, i.e., 2nd part of the long one.[342] He has an incredibly firm structure—very simple & fine. In fact it is easy to read by it—picks up very finely when one is looking for it, etc. I am not too excited by content—in this sense, and though he just now begins to move it, Blackburn is the more interesting poet for me. He makes a structure equal to Duncan's, and has a finer sense of sounds I think. One line like this say—

... three days are one long dreaming on this shelf of land
    where the kelp lies black, inescapable, and the tides run
    back to the black deep center of the world ...[343]

Particularly word, inescapable. He can make things like that—it is a very damn sure ear. Often hauls him off into, perhaps, subtleties too fine for reader to register, etc. I don't think so, though.

Thinking of him—a lot isn't going to be clear, straight off. I talked with him for two days & nights—would hardly do that with many, or feel myself at all allowed, like that. He is very clear, and has a great deal on him—not so much the usual bulk of any damn mess, I mean what family can do to you, etc.—he has that, but he has, too, this deliberateness, bred of it. He and his sister were left to live with grandparents, or great aunt & uncle—uncle rail-roading man, so off— aunt psychotic. She used to beat him often—sadistic, sexual, etc. Horrible to hear even vague account, or not vague, but deliberate, account he gave of that part of his life. One time sent to the store, a nickel in change which he dropped in the snow, just coming up to the house—and spent over an hour on his hands & knees, digging in the snow, bare hands, to find it—with the woman sitting behind the curtain, just the edge, watching him, and when he couldn't find it, and went in, she beat him, saying he had stolen it. She used to use a cane, etc. Frightful to have it on you—all that on your mind.

His content can't come floating up, etc. He can't yet allow it, even if a thing could be like that. I remember once, when I was about 8 or so, my glass eye somehow fell out, at school, i.e., rolled under several desks and all the embarrassment, etc. I wouldn't wear one now, in fact I can't wear any damn thing but the socket.

Anyhow, Paul has it I think. No one excites me, other than yourself, like he can. Coldness of it—but no damn ice, etc. I mean, coldness of his stance—it is very beautiful. He means business.

I shouldn't like to confuse here sense of him, as, say, then those nights & two days, etc., in NYC. Cats & all, etc. I don't know, I think he's got it, and did to extent of fighting with Cid over that BIRDS, etc. To get him to print it, etc.[344] That was, of course, before I'd met him, and at that point I was making not much more with him than I was with Cid.

Damn beautiful things sometimes, even now—when, I think, content is coming up through a hell of a lot—i.e., is muffled in that sense, tho no argument against his intent to be conscious.

Part from that same one:

In the wet sand the shell glistens
hollowed of life
yet a potent singer stripped to the song,
perfect among tide-marks on a cool breast of sand
the outright gift of a tide rip, catching
                         the sun's first throw.

Etc., etc. I wanted to show you this one, I got it done this afternoon, in
spite of heat & kids, etc. Dave whirling off his masterpieces—he's
painting on stones these days ...   Goddamn well going to break into
that there art yet, etc.

COLLIURE

              Of what one
wants. The
fact of the
desire recapitulated & brought round to
superior sense

              (as at
the close of land, the
boats, close to the shore
wait for the tide or better, a
superior instinct to provide them with

motion.

Very sad I guess. I wish to god we'd got that place—someday you
ought to see it. I wish you might see all these places, or at least
Fontrousse. Very lovely there, in the evenings, moon & all. I get to
miss it here. But place there was horrible. voila.

I was trying to quote that Williams poem, The End of The Parade, i.e.,
"The sentence undulates/ raising no song, etc."[345] In quoting, found I
hit line breaks pretty exactly, i.e., as cadence demanded. In that poem it

is not one's first figuring—or doesn't look as though it would be exact in that particular. Williams' registering of this kind of *density* I was thinking about earlier, re your *verticalism*, is pretty damn acute at most points. It gets to help me just now.

Well, fuck it—trying to get goddamn corn to grow—soil here real new to me. Not clay, though it acts like that. With sun, you got a brick if you water directly, etc. Canals, etc. Phew. I got six rows of corn—and feel like Louis Bromfield.[346] Ok.

WRITE SOON. All our dearest love to you all,

Bob

Black Mt [N.C.
8 July 1952]

Robt; to get you on—am back here. But keep writing either place. For yr letters reach me both ways, quickly. Example, have in today David's letter, as well as yr following one on affairs SS & E. (Am sitting down now, actually, to make those copies of yr go on Hull, for Brigante, and Elath, and copy for you.)

Just felt pointless—after a certain point—there without Con and Kate. And so came back, at first to try to get Con to go off with me to Okracoke, on the coast[347] for a week. But she is geared into her work here, and so I stay around.

This is a crise[348] of some sort I am in, so please keep firing and permit me irregularities—if they should be. Don't know. Feel off the act of writing, and until I am on again, will not be much good, eh?

Tell Dave we are both very happy to have that sort of news his father don't give us—such things as corn & beans, basins, & fetes. Wow. Sure shows who & when such things ...! "We go swimming in it." Sure. Four. One.

On the matters for SS:

> (1) the Barlow stuff will take some long time: that is, Sauer never gave me an answer on his mss.   (figure, that the thing was still so close to him he couldn't even get to mention it—son-stuff. And so the limits of COS, but ...)

> and I don't know any of the other friends of Barlow. Was waiting myself until I got to Mex City. But will, now, try to start to round up others that wld know, for you

(2) Boulez:

> I was quoting from a go in TRANSFORMATIONS NOW GONE FROM my hand, but will give you the French references

(3) Cartier I will write to & ask him to write or see you (he & his Indonesian wife live not so far north of you—outside Paris, to South:

> a big job on him—a double issue of VERVE—is due out this fall[349]

But will try to get him to use words, too, for you. He'll need encouragement, being a damned modest man—almost blushing, he is, his skin is, yet tough when he has anything in his hand.

Yr own go on the Jung[350] *completely* holds me, yet it is mark of my present crisis (some going over to another base of action) that I pick out things, cannot take it all (which was my former capacity, we could allow, perhaps). And what catches me is these sentences of yrs on the constant and common:

"Communication has a constant content, no matter that its means be the time and place of its occurrence." "... something literally primordial, if any of us have come from anywhere"

"... W and L. have affected a content unmistakable common—and 'common' in no sense usual. What to call it."

(Tho, right there, reject even
you using even so *religious*,
simply, that I take it it
won't, as word, deliver

itself from all that it has been—and is so much, now, again)
And: "To say that literature has a diversity of means is relevant—but a literature is of use only in one character, communication."

These things hit me, now. They enter in where I am just now most baffled (what you will have sensed has been growing like a "culture" (mold) in me of late, this biz I have no words for, of innocence (how to use it) of straightness (how to make my acts as organized as words can come out for me occasionally:

that is, perhaps the most rewarding of all THE NEW ODYSSEY for me is that one sentence:

INTEGRITY, THEN, BECOMES OF A FINAL KIND; IT IS
WHAT ONE FACES INTO ANYTHING WITH, WHAT ONE
HAS FOR THAT

This hits me in the soft of the moment: I have lost my way. Just that flat, it seems to me. And no sadness about it. Just the present fact. In fact, I am leaving the future alone, refusing to use any of my old devices for projecting same. And am, as a result, sick, quite sick, weak: that is, when you give up yr own methods, you are weak, until new ones are found? (The terror is, will there be new ones, where are they?)

And the question, of course, is no question, the answer is so obvious. But I feel in some such place as I was at 17 when I walked down power.[351] Now I feel as tho I were walking down some other thing (exactly the opposite) with the same blindness.

But it is unendurable to do. That is why I say I am sick, and am, daily, nightly, weak. No attention, No concentration.

Forget it. It is all so stupid there is nothing to say. The point is: I faced in, with what I had. And I didn't like the result—or at least got a distaste for it. And now I am lost: beauty turned out to be not enough. And now I don't know what will come in its place.

What burns me is, that I take it this is all very damned unnecessary. Even if it is what is happening. I am wandering, that is all. And at such a time! Wandering. I don't know that I ever did. Now I am. And I have no means to deal with it, or so it seems.

(Of course the other horror is I feel I don't have any language left. This is the worst of it, the hardest thing of all not to pick myself up by—the ride.

And you see it was exactly on this point of the mythological in the content of my own reality that it all broke loose? I lost the means to maintain the sort of assurance ICH required, lost it, and don't know that it can—don't now believe it is—to be found. Bad business.

Not clear enough to say any of this: (the way you have it there, clarity, god knows, we need at least that: and that's what I have damn well so lost I resist even taking up any of it but all of it, the ultimate thing, real clarity, which is no such thing at all).

OK. Let this be got off, for what it is, just to tell you, and to keep you in. For any word from you is a godsend. Yr friend is in bad ceth.[352]

Love from us all,

O

[Lambesc, Bouches-du-Rhône]
July 9, 1952

Dear Charles,

Heat awful here now, and am told that it will carry thru the month, then August, etc. Perhaps they are too damn complacent, I hope so. As it is, waiting anyhow for the baby to come— every night Ann prays it will be it, etc., or at night since the damn day would make it that much harder, with the heat.

It's hard to get to much, I feel like working, or like I do it anyhow, but not very much. Blackburn said I was working too much in my head, I can see some of that, i.e., verse gets, I think, very pulled in. Very tight in not so damn happy a sense; a thing like that one, Question, is not the damn usual, etc. But I can't get interested, I have to follow this damn thing now as it orders itself.

Thinking again of what you had said of the other, i.e., Festival one— wish that I might go clearly into that thing, it gets, now, close. I had heard two radio programs, usual bilge, but these two had an effect beyond, I think, their intention—i.e., one I had noted (?) about man marrying his brother's wife, after brother dies, and then breaking down, responsibility, then murdering them all. Another one—the same even tone—of man hitch-hiking, running from robbery, etc., gets in car with family travelling from some city down in the South West to some place like Detroit. He makes them keep driving for about 2 and a half days—only stops long enough for husband, who is driving, to get what little sleep can keep him driving. Mother and three children, oldest about 7, sitting in back, nothing to eat or drink. Finally woman gets hysterical, children crying, and he tells man to pull off the road at a point about 2 miles from where they then are. Story then breaks to tracking man, suspense as they know how to work it, of whether or not family is still alive—they have located car with bloodstains & several bullet holes in the frame—finally get man in Mexico, locate family, all of them, in bottom of a mine-shaft, murdered.

I am trying to *think* of that possibility, but I honestly can't. Last night Mr. Marti having dinner with us (his family over in Fontrousse with mother, she had a heart attack from the heat) and some brief mention of "Inquisition" in Spain, during Civil War, i.e., Catholic Church's acts on those who were against gov't. He said, that following brief Republican victory, i.e., taking of power, a lot of them went into churches, the catacombs, to look for their relatives, and he found his grandmother half buried, i.e., they had buried them alive, nailing their hands to the wall behind them. He could recognize her by a ring she wore. His daughter was also tortured in a like manner; he himself spent four years in a concentration camp in Germany, having been sent there from Spain by Spanish authorities.

It is that *discrepancy* of experience, although I cannot believe that the mind is to find itself in these acts which must outlaw it, must kill it if only temporary. That is, then quite literally eating alongside a man whose experience of what extremities are possible, to the body and the mind, were that precise distance beyond my own. I had the same thing with Rainer—then it was more articulate. Last night it was so damned actual, being so familiar, that speaking of it, then, it was in the order of explanation, i.e., he had wanted to tell us, or to explain to us, why he didn't like the Catholic Church and why he thought it an evil influence in that country.

At least I feel that loneliness very terribly now. If I ever thought that communication was difficult, and that all things one said must be said of oneself—it's now. All I can act is this—to hear, and by that to acknowledge, and by acknowledgement, to witness the necessary displacement. Not of myself, but in. I mean that accumulation—one is *not* compiling a "sottisier," etc.[353]

I wonder how much, literally, I could take, at what point myself would be nothing more in my own hands—what, of the kids, and Ann. How to show strength against these acts possible. It is obviously of no damn use to anticipate, I believe that more horror will be present, in the next ten years; I've felt as condition I had, not so much to tolerate, as to prepare for, in the sense of a conceivable experience—anything that might happen.

It confuses me, I guess it must do that. I know of so very damn few writers who have ever allowed this area, in the sense I get to have of it. There is part in Dostoyevsky, even something like scene outside the tavern—where the Captain has the fight with one of the brothers, and has his beard pulled—what he then says to Aloysha, how he makes his sense of it, with the money, throwing it into the air.[354] It is a content utterly unconceived in a writer like Joyce; or any of those idiots. But the same thing is present in Lawrence—the cold & incredible *anger* with which he writes that part of Kangaroo, where he tells of being "examined," the other man, the collier made to squat down, and being confused, forced to make himself a fool in that act.[355]

I don't see much else, that is, I hate the record "afterwards" (which is *NOT* Lawrence). No amount of comment would then make the least difference. One should fight every damn *inch* of the way, even if it's just dragging your heels. I go with magazines like GOAD, and others, because I want this speech, I want it in whatever form is offered to me. To break, here, generalities—to make clear it is all *flesh* that is abandoned, or that it is just this part is affected. Clear mind, saneness, etc., is bilge if the body be lost. It is trespass against the damn literal *flesh* that I get hold of—and want to make fight against. Some damn way—the horror is that so much must be a coercion, into *any* token of resistance.

Well, I don't know—it's damn clear just now, it's been coming on & off the past weeks.

A poem I wanted to show you. Get it in here.

HISTORY

At the corner of
this room there is a

marble fireplace dating I
think to when

someone took oils and
painted it. The Inquisition

is a remnant only to the
ones no one killed.

Write soon. All our love to you all,

Bob

(I.e. [*sic*], "reading list" only for narrative prose,[356] or better, senses I
have of it. I think I could demonstrate almost all of my own concerns,
by working thru such a list—making contacts as I went. Sequence wd/
be the hinge.)

Read: Miss Lonelyhearts

one story by F. Scott Fitzgerald
one poem by T. S. Eliot

James M. Cain
one story by Henry Miller

D. H. Lawrence, a novel
Herman Melville, Typee
Stendhal, The Charterhouse of Parma

Dostoyevsky, The Brothers Karamazov
a poem by D. H. Lawrence

Kafka
Delmore Schwartz

The Day of the Locust

Incidental reading as related to above sequence:

> J/ Hawkes, Beetle Leg
> R/ Dana, Two Years Before The Mast
> Homer, The Odyssey

(Mainly impacts of content, and lines of intention. I would put Joyce, for one example, between Eliot and Miller, or define him by that juxtaposition.

Sequence to show variations on "content" possible—not stylistic innovation, etc. Or even "like themes."

What I wanted was a "list" making 1) use of sequence, i.e., juxtapositions resulting—also in terms of material not so goddamn chewed or "related" that all comment concerning it was, of that necessity, a question of clearing all damn manner of preconceptions.

I figure man could read such a series, and get it, in spite of any overt comment—or better, without any overt comment.

Maybe just goddamn game—only for yrs truly anyhow.

(I mean "incidental" reading to be *further* aspect, i.e, in sense of, if, completing list, man then reads those 3 books, in that order—he will have three new, & further, senses of what's gone before. I.e., each will develop a sense of the material gone through. (As Hawkes/ the one of means; as Dana/ the one of a literal record, or speech; as Homer/ a kind of center, or even sun for all such effort, in the first place.)

I put Typee in, rather than others, because it is unique instance of such a man, put it, that kind of an intelligence, making a record of that kind of experience. It seems to me useful in that way. Or it is useful here.

[*On verso envelope:*] Laubies has found Greek boat to US for $140—now off to Marseille to see friend who works for ship's chandler ... to get it cheaper ... How does it look?!

[*Arrow continues the note onto recto envelope:*] We'll come live with *you*!! Only 10 of us ... (5 kids 5 adults—can all do *nothing*!)

══════════

[Black Mountain, N.C.]

Lad: (July 9) [1952]
  forget that fucking stupid letter of yestiddy

Enclose copy for you of that go of yrs (have sent off the other two). Still am firmly deeply moved by it—think it is a major thing (strikes me the *continuum* of the prose is mark of the solidity of the feeling & position—note para on Crane, how, the prose is)   Love it, and take up from it: think yr statement of *dignity* there (let me, just between us, mark the things which catch me now)

Duncan address:
1724 Baker St
SF 15, Cal

(((I shld be obliged if you wld teach me more abt how you take it irony is—an example, perhaps, I finding Hull more of sarcasm (at least the context of society forces his mandarin nails, etc., in this direction, inevitably: that is, we reject any such giggling.[357] Or I take it irony (as you put it, from anger) has more size? An example?)

Not at all impressed by E[*lath*]'s letter (returned)—sounds like another of those mechanics (as Ez, so often, in his businesses: "get on with it"—that tone). "Organizational problems." Shit. We won't lick the

enemy that way. Or what I mean is, we have to do that too, but it
cannot be allowed to exclude the courtesies (I shld say these are a part
of the dignities)

Don't know, that Korzybski had enough pull for me to go to him: (&
christ, tell Elath to get off the pot, on boulez reading mann's faustus:
mann, I am sure, has a gold of nothing, nithing [*sic*] at all

(again, the
German in Elath: Lubeck deutsch, what I have always seen Mann to be,
knowing these things, my grandmother being a Lybeck,[358]
and so....)
          'Course he's right abt me & what he calls philos: as you
know, it is exactly that which I have had to kick in the face here (as well,
as Lerma) that tendency of my scrutiny to get phrased so. (Do, of course,
figure, that this, like all things else in the totality time, is resolved not by
avoidance but by prosecution:
                    we have no course but to go all the way
through to the Other side of everything, once we are sucked,
launched, led, or whatever—in
                    This seems to me a clue to
methodology (and i learned it from one man, one, Arthur Rimbaud,
one statement, that, the other side of, despair,[359] that dignity

    (tho I am damned curious as to what E thinks I'd get out of K ((this
    crazy fact—3 yrs ago, here, when the place was first offering me a
    chance to define curriculum, I sd, gimme the dough, I'll go call K,
    and I swear he'll accept invitation to come do lectures here! Out of
    the blue, my only sense being, this guy bulks! And on this point
    you are pushing, in the Jung thing, where, the work now is being
    done, no matter that now, 3 yrs later, it's too late for me with this
    K (he is a holy man, by the way—or gets that sort of suck-in from
    his admirers
              what i have read of him seems not at all
    post-modern, but stuck (like I think E is) in between the modern
    and the motion

Blackburn's letter—returned—pleases me damn much—tho the
quiet of him, is, a little like Morse's, for me, that funny damned
tandem of the local and the Wordsworthian, or, the vernal—shoot it,
Keats, the Egotistical Sublime—ah, to be alive among live things
instead of, that DHL, that, negative capabilitarian,[360] those
goddamned things raging APART—

> how he damned well knew
that business of, that, those things, are, no matter how much they
are, NOT OURS

> > god i love him, how fine he was abt this thing, that it
> > is our selfs which is the form of the content, and that
> > that form is individual, and so, even another is to
> > that degree apart, is raging in their own
> > phenomenon, not mine

that is, it is here i take it yr common-uncommon is borne out, that,
what we have is what others have—i mean the human thing, and am
asserting its separateness from all those ambiences, spring,
satisfaction, etc—but that they have it—or even the recognition—is
impossible without the uncommonness of me, eh, yay, bang, ok,
yessir, whatdoyadoaboutit

There down goes all generality—and up goes preoccupation,
conjecture, & ex-press-shun (communication being—if some one
gets it, you, e.g., or who, where, that citizen, also raging, apart

(Did read DHL a couple days ago in which the said fellow was off!
Called WE NEED EACH OTHER.[361] Damn feeling thing but the
doctrine all thumbs! Funny, to see him missing just where I'd miss,
too, that that I can't get beyond CUIR ET CHAIR—and that, I figure
now, not good enough

S. Crew.

> (Curiously, that letter I wrote to Zander was—at a further point—

> where i take it Elath too leaves it out—what you put there, that

ONE IS THERE—these birds—German?—bring that old width of sight,

but also leave out that thing it seems a German has one hell of a time

keeping in: the openness of modesty which only makes arrogance support-

able   (DHL—Frieda, say: or guy like Holderlin, how, he does have it

(wld like to know more abt that Diotima, that woman of his—how come

he went off, and went mad after it?)[362]

                         (it's their women, I'd bet ya:
what abt Rainer's Renate—how do you find the texture, there. Shld be
interested to have you on that thing.
                         (God damn it, just now, the only
thing which interests me!))   (((Maybe I shld read some nuvvels!)))

Ok look sharp, be sharp, feel sharp[363]—or whatever. Sharp. And so many
of these good guys ain't, just where the razor and the beard meet   (when
the Razor and the Beard … how they—MET)

                         meet me, miss (a white
daisy   [*Adds, in pencil, in margin*:
      And the red   Made this into something—is in
rasp-   back of 2nd paper of you on Hull—
berry, for   tell me if it works, will ya?]
breakfast
         I fly
heavily, as
that snow heron who (here they call em fish cranes)
is terrific only
feeding, scared
goes like a pelican, and lands
in trees an awkward
ghost. Or has no fight
against the domestic

red-winged blackbird dive-
bombing
him

*[Enclosed with letter, the following note in pencil and two poems in
typescript:]*[364]

Sat. July 12

Robt—

To make enclosures—
① PB's letter
② E's
+ ③ reverse [*i.e., Olson's poem "Idle Idyll" is typed verso.*]

Things look sharp—but you know illusion.   Most on my mind is
the sense that realism & romanticism are one (that classicism is the
only desirable final result, & not, therefore, anything to do with
content.
                Love to you all—& special good business for Him—
who? And do you need [*baby*] clothes or anything? —there? Let us
know.

(Am more & more of a mind to ask PB to come here for the 2nd 4
weeks, even if I am here—so that I can keep at my own biz.

Am   O

Notes

[References to pages and notes in previous volumes begin with Roman numerals designating the volume number, e.g., I.110, II.53, etc. References to Olson poems outside *The Maximus Poems* are now to the University of California Press edition, *The Collected Poems of Charles Olson*, ed. George F. Butterick (Berkeley, 1987) or the supplemental poems collected in the Black Sparrow *A Nation of Nothing But Poetry*, ed. Butterick (Santa Rosa, 1989). References to prose works by Creeley are to the University of California Press edition, *The Collected Essays of Robert Creeley* (Berkeley and Los Angeles, 1989). And references in this volume to the Olson/Corman correspondence are to the National Poetry Foundation edition, *Charles Olson & Cid Corman: Complete Correspondence*, Vol. I, ed. George Evans (Orono, Maine, 1987).]

1 Volume IX of the correspondence ends with Creeley's plans to move to the United States at Olson's invitation of a teaching job at Black Mountain College.

2 Douglas D. Paige, who Creeley reports trilled his *r*'s after the manner of Pound's speech, was the editor of Pound's letters; Dallam Simpson was the Texas publisher of the Poundian organ *Four Pages*.

3 Edgar Wallace (1875–1932), prolific British author and popularizer of mystery formulas. The "King of Thrillers" published 175 books and sequels, half of them mystery novels, beginning with his most well-known title, *The Four Just Men* (London, 1905). Around the time of Creeley's letter, German films adapted from Wallace's books generated a fad called "Wallace mania."

4 *Lyrismos*, Greek for playing on a lyre; hence "lyricism." Olson rails against what he calls "lyric soullessnesses" in his "Introduction to Robert Creeley," which first appeared in *New Directions 13*, ed. James Laughlin (New York, 1951), 92–93, with Creeley's "Mr Blue and Other Stories," pp. 94–116.

Single Intelligence, a term coined by Creeley and used by both Olson and Creeley throughout the correspondence. See, e.g., Creeley's definition in his 7 August 1950 letter to Olson (II.99–100), and Olson's usage in "The Materials and Weights of Herman Melville," *Human Universe*, p. 112.

5 Still to be identified.

6 Paige's edition of *The Letters of Ezra Pound 1907–1941* (New York, 1950)

225

was published by Harcourt, Brace, with a Preface by Mark Van Doren (pp. v–ix).

[7] Creeley's review of John Hawkes' *The Beetle Leg*, "How to Write a Novel," appeared in Kenneth Lash's *New Mexico Quarterly*, XXII, no. 2 (Summer 1952), 239–41. Translations by Cid Corman and Edgar Lohner of poems by Gottfried Benn; translations also appeared in Vincent Ferrini's *Four Winds*, no. 1 (Summer 1952), *Origin*, no. 7 (Autumn 1952) and *Origin*, no. 10 (Summer 1953).

[8] Creeley had proposed that Olson review Hugh Kenner's *The Poetry of Ezra Pound* (London and New York, 1951) as early as his 4 April 1952 letter to Olson (see IX.226). Apparently, Olson never wrote the review, in part due to his reconsideration of Pound's work (see Olson's 5 May [1952] letter to Creeley, etc.).

[9] See passages on Ernest Fenollosa's *Chinese Written Character* from Olson's 30 March 1952 letter to Creeley, as Creeley retypes them in his [5 May 1952] letter to Olson (IX.229–31). Apparently, Olson never wrote the review.

[10] "The Surf" and "The Ball Game" are probably the poems Creeley refers to as "these last 2" (see IX.267–68 and 271–72). Corman would print "The Innocence" in *Origin*, no. 6 (Summer 1952), 117, but "The Cantos" and "The Rhyme" would have to wait until Richard Wirtz Emerson published them in *Golden Goose*, series 4, no. 5 (October 1952), 22, 25.

[11] Rainer Gerhardt's proposed anthology of American poetry after Whitman (see IX.201).

[12] *New Directions* anthology did not print the stories.

[13] Kenneth Rexroth wrote: "...Rapallo— / Far worse than treason or dementia, / Pound endured this Atlantic City / Of Czechoslovak yachtsmen and / Swiss gamblers for twenty-five years!" in *The Dragon and the Unicorn* (Norfolk, 1952). (Rexroth was appointed to teach creative writing and criticism at Black Mountain College for the 1949–1950 academic year but accepted, instead, the renewal of his Guggenheim Grant and wrote this poem during his travels in Italy in 1949.)

[14] From November 1925 to April 1926, D. H. Lawrence rented the Villa Bernardo at Spotorno, near Genoa. During this period, Lawrence's health was failing due to tuberculosis and his long-time friendship with John Middleton Murry was broken. Spotorno would be Lawrence's last permanent residence.

[15] The poet Basil Bunting (1900–1985) and his wife lived in Rapallo from 1930 to 1933 in order to be near Pound. During this period, Pound helped

Bunting publish his first book, *Redimiculum Matellarum* (1930), and edited a lengthy selection of Bunting's poems for *The Active Anthology* (1933).

[16] In Olson's 26 April [1952] letter to Creeley, he promises to offer to Paul Blackburn his teaching position at Black Mountain College (see IX.279).

[17] Olson's offer to back Creeley for a teaching position at Black Mountain College for summer session 1952 (see note IX.293).

[18] Marguerite Caetani, editor of *Botteghe Oscure* (see note IX.4).

[19] Reference to the pre-publication history of Creeley's story "The Unsuccessful Husband," which appeared in *Kenyon Review*, no. 13 (Winter 1951) only after editor John Crowe Ransom's vacillation. See note II.125.

[20] Creeley's use of "wopping" may owe something to Olson's poem "A Discrete Gloss" and its "wops red red red and why," a word choice which Corman questioned before printing in *Origin*, 6; see *Olson & Corman*, p. 233.

[21] "The Song of the Border-Guard," design by Cy Twombly, printed by Nicola Cernovich (with the assistance of Joel Oppenheimer), was second in the Black Mountain College Broadside Series.

[22] A proposed American number of *Fragmente*, to be edited by Creeley. See note IX.47.

[23] *Pic'd*: Berlin's friend served as a picador, or mounted man with a lance, in bullfighting. Belmonte, the famed Spanish bullfighter; see note IX.12. For "the bull biz," see Olson's 2 February 1952 letter (IX.81–82).

[24] Creeley's check for stamps; see X.21 above and X.28 below.

[25] Creeley had typed his poem "The Surf" (later called "The Surf: An Elegy") at the top of his 18 April [1952] letter to Olson and included the new poem "The Ball Game." That letter concludes with a lengthy reminiscence of Creeley's days as an 18-year-old copyboy at the *Boston Globe*. Douglas D. Paige may have sent Creeley photographs of Rapallo (now lost), as Creeley's 16 April [1952] letter to Olson suggests. The proposed book by Olson is *The Praises*.

[26] *Spang*, colloquial: "to leap, directly." Wesley Huss served as business manager and instructor of drama at Black Mountain College.

[27] The "Roadside" was a house on the Black Mountain campus owned by the college and divided into two apartments for faculty residence. Joel Oppenheimer, who was a student at Black Mountain in 1952, remembered the Roadside as more an outbuilding than a house.

[28] The college bulletin for "Spring Semester February 11–June 7, 1952" lists Creeley among the faculty to be teaching during the second semester.

[29] See Creeley's letter to Olson, 12 April 1952, below, concerning Olson's poem "The Cause, the Cause" (*Collected Poems*, pp. 190–93).

[30] Pound's racist epithet for Olson; see I.147 and VIII.184.

[31] The Englishman, identified later in the letter, is Martin Seymour-Smith, who will be Robert Graves' biographer and the character Artie in Creeley's novel *The Island*. Two poems by Seymour-Smith, "La Foradada" and "All Devils Fading," appeared in John Sankey's London-based magazine *The Window*, no. 4 (February 1952), on pp. 2–3, 4. Creeley's Divers Press would publish a volume of Seymour-Smith's poetry called *All Devils Fading* in 1953.

[32] German: "frightful, dreadful."

[33] Middle stanza from "Elegy," later published in *All Devils Fading* ([Mallorca], 1953), pp. [10–11].

[34] Lines from an uncollected early poem by Martin Seymour-Smith.

[35] Pierre Boulez was among a host of composers whose music was performed that month in Paris. See note IX.312. René Laubiès adds the following postscript on the envelope of his letter to Creeley, postmarked 30 April 1952: "I'll go to the concert of Boulez, in May, may I speak of Olson to him?"

[36] Samuel French Morse, "The Motive for Metaphor," in *Origin*, 5. Corman devoted the number to "Long And Sluggish Lines," a new poem by Wallace Stevens, and Morse's essay on Stevens.

[37] Wallace Stevens, as quoted by Morse in "The Motive for Metaphor," *Origin*, 5, p. 14.

[38] Morse mentions Verlaine as a source on p. 16, "The Motive for Metaphor," and he uses the French phrase—literally "amaze the does"; translatable as "scandalize the gallery"—on p. 21 following.

[39] Echoes Pound's phrase, "His true Penelope was Flaubert," in "Hugh Selwyn Mauberley," line 13. Verlaine's lover is Arthur Rimbaud.

[40] Paraphrases a stanza from Creeley's "The Painters," an unpublished poem Olson read in typescript: "Or Lawrence said so, and I / believe him. I have always / believed him" (note IX.292).

[41] From the opening line of Olson's "The Kingfishers," *Collected Poems*, p. 86, after Heraclitus' Fragment 83.

[42] See Olson's stories about his father, Charles (Karl) Joseph Olson — "Stocking Cap," "Mr. Meyer," and "The Post Office"—collected as *The Post Office: A Memoir of His Father* (Bolinas, 1975). Olson writes about his mother, Mary Theresa (Hines) Olson, in "The Present Is Prologue,"

Additional Prose, p. 39: "It was rough on my mother ... my father and I never let her forget the fall from grace, that she was only the most beautiful woman in South Worcester, Mass." In "My Father," Olson had written: "My father was my father / but my mother was the moon / She I have but he / died too soon ..." (*A Nation of Nothing But Poetry*, p. 29).

43 "This Is Yeats Speaking," *Partisan Review*, XIII, no. 1 (1946), pp. 139ff., collected in *Human Universe and Other Essays* (New York, 1967), p. 102: "Lawrence among us alone had the true mask, he lacked the critical intelligence, and was prospective."

44 Reference to Marianne Moore (here, in Olson's ironic metaphor of the spinster ("spinner"), appearing as the faithful wife of Odysseus, who in *The Odyssey* unwove her daily work in a scheme to put off the Suitors) and her long-time project to translate *The Fables of La Fontaine*, finally collected in 1954. (Is Pound her Odysseus, setting sail in Canto I, and receiving her at St. Elizabeths to discuss her translations?) The "cult of M. Moore" might be a reference to her supporters who had recently awarded her the Pulitzer Prize, the National Book Award, and the Bollingen Award for her *Collected Poems* (1951). Also, La Fontaine is mentioned by Morse in "The Motive for Metaphor," on p. 9. (Miss Moore would return Olson's objections with some of her own, writing about the "Projective Verse" essay, in "The Way Our Poets Have Taken Since the War," *New York Herald Tribune*, 23 April 1961, and *A Marianne Moore Reader*, New York, 1965, p. 241: "Inherited non-projective form can be projective, I would say, and projective form may be weedy and colorless like suckers from an un-sunned tuber.")

45 Perhaps the axolotl? A salamander that does not metamorphose into an adult, even though it reaches sexual maturity at about six months; found in Mexico and Colorado. Perhaps Olson is making a parody of spinsterly Miss Moore's fondness for the exotic biological reference, versus clarity, in her poems. While a bird would naturally eat an axolotl, Olson argues, only Miss Moore would "ornithologize" one. Olson's reference to ornithology suggests that he is playfully associating "axolotl" with "archeopteryx," the flying dinosaur Olson compares with Hart Crane in the poem "Birth's Obituary," *A Nation of Nothing But Poetry*, p. 17. Crane and Miss Moore are easily associated, as Creeley will do in his 13 May letter to come.

46 A complex of references, resulting from Olson's conjectures on Christ the Son, the Mayan sun, Gilgamesh's bull of heaven, the Mithraic cults, and Mexican bullfights. Perhaps most broadly a reference to Lawrence's *The Plumed Serpent*, a formative work for Olson, which opens with a Mithraic bullfight scene under a cruel Mexican sun and evolves around the native myth that the Mexico which Jesus Christ abandoned shall one day be saved by the return of Quetzalcoatl. Walter W. Skeat's *An*

Etymological Dictionary of the English Language (Oxford, 1882), p. 214, shows the word "fire" to be derived from the Sanskrit root *pu-*, meaning "to purify." Also, cf. VI.143, where Olson writes about the Crucifixion of Christ: "that blood, not the Sun, is where they think life is." From October 1951, when he purchased and read the book at Black Mountain, Laurence A. Waddell's *The Indo-Sumerian Seals Deciphered* is a source for Olson's theories of the sun. Pound, in "Terra Italica," *Selected Prose*, ed. Cookson, pp. 56–58, linked the Mithraic cult and Roman Christianity. He also refers to bullfighting in the same essay, a favorite topic in the Olson-Creeley letters.

But Joseph Campbell, in *The Hero with a Thousand Faces*, Bollingen Series 17 (Princeton, 1949), pp. 138–39, offers perhaps the best gloss on Olson's phrase, especially within the context of Olson's letters to Creeley about the phallic hero: "the sound of the bull-roarers [of the Arunta tribe, Australia] is heard from all sides when the moment has arrived for [the boy initiate's] decisive break from the past. It is night, and in the weird light of the fire suddenly appear the circumciser and his assistant. The noise of the bull-roarers is the voice of the great demon of the ceremony...." Campbell also would have appealed to Olson as a source for conjectures on the significance of cannibalism. Campbell continues, p. 140: "the rites provide also for the cannibal, patricidal impulse of the younger, rising group of males.... 'The natives,' we are told, 'are particularly interested in the Christian communion rite, and having heard about it from missionaries they compare it to the blood-drinking rituals of their own.'" (Olson, in his Lectures in the New Sciences of Man, *OLSON*, no. 10, Fall 1978, p. 42, refers to "a noise of [Cro-Magnon man's] bull-roarer.")

[47] *Cento*, Latin for a patchwork garment, is a standard literary term for a work made out of selections of other people's writings. Used here as a criticism of the plan of Pound's *Cantos*. Olson calls Pound "Cento Man" in his 8 March [1951] letter to Creeley, a sobriquet which he first employs in the correspondence in I.141. In the geography of contemporary poets, Hartford, Connecticut is home to Wallace Stevens; Brooklyn, New York to Marianne Moore; and Rapallo, Italy to Pound.

[48] Stock pantomime characters. Harlequin, the buffoon, is masked and dressed in motley; the dove-like Columbine, daughter of Pantaloon, plays Harlequin's sweetheart. Morse, in "The Motive for Metaphor," p. 8, quotes from Stevens' "The Comedian as the Letter C," *The Collected Poems* (New York, 1961), p. 41: "The plum survives its poems. It may hang / In the sunshine ... / Harlequined...." Cf. Williams' "This Is Just To Say," *The Collected Poems* (New York, 1986), I, 372 ("I have eaten / the plums...."). (Stevens' uses of Yucatan and Socrates in his poem would have further displeased Olson.)

[49] Olson encloses his 5 May 1952 reactions to Samuel French Morse's "The Motive for Metaphor" in his 3 May 1952 letter to Corman, asking Corman to airmail the original letter to Creeley after he has read it. Olson, only recently returned to Black Mountain from Washington, D.C. and New York, finds himself behind in his correspondence in the era before the advent of the photocopy. See also Olson's 13 [June 1952] letter to Corman concerning Stevens, *Olson & Corman*, pp. 266–67.

[50] French, meaning "to swear under one's breath" but translated literally by Olson, below and passim, as "to rail between skin and flesh."

[51] The anecdote is recounted in Olson's poem "The Morning News"; see note IX.206.

[52] Probably "Poetry is a means of redemption," quoted in Morse's note for "The Motive for Metaphor" on p. 6. Crispin is the character in Stevens' "The Comedian as the Letter C"; Prufrock is Eliot's central narrator in the poem "The Love Song of J. Alfred Prufrock."

[53] Final couplet of "Popular Song," an unpublished poem by Creeley, included in his 15 [April 1952] letter to Olson; see IX.256.

[54] The 6 May 1952 minutes of the Black Mountain College Board of Fellows show that Constance Olson was to be made Registrar. She was officially appointed at the Board meeting of 3 June 1952.

[55] Olson is poking fun at the Creeleys' new address at Pavillon les Magnolias, a place name as displaced as the camellia, named after 18th-century Moravian Jesuit missionary G. J. Kamel, who brought the shrub to London from Japan.

[56] For "father." "Phar" is the sound of "father" in Swedish.

[57] Probably Olson's 20 May 1952 letter to Creeley, and not a reference to Chapter 14, "Sleep and Dreams," in Lawrence's *Fantasia of the Unconscious*.

[58] I.e., Hermes Trismegistus, or "Thrice-Greatest." The ancient Greek name for Thoth, Egyptian scribe to the gods and legendary author of Hermetic texts (see Walter Scott, *Hermetica*, 4 vols., Oxford, 1924–1936). Mentioned in *The Maximus Poems*, p. 594. For Gnosticism, see also *Additional Prose*, p. 26, and *OLSON*, no. 2 (Fall 1974), p. 2.

[59] Olson reveals the insight into the character of Herman Melville which came to "center" his thinking in *Call Me Ishmael*. Between the writing of *Moby-Dick* and *Pierre*, Olson explains, "Melville became unsure of the center. It had been strong, a backward and downward in him like Ahab's, like a pyramid's ..." (*Call Me Ishmael*, p. 99). In Chapter 41 of *Moby-Dick*, Melville's white whale is "pyramidical" and Ahab is a "proud, sad king" or pharo, whose "larger, darker, deeper part" is as complex and grand as

the Roman baths at the Hotel de Cluny Melville visited and admired on 2 December 1849. By Book 21 of *Pierre*, Melville's metaphor of the descent into the interior has become the bitter passage Olson cites in *Call Me Ishmael* (p. 100): "By vast pains we mine into the pyramid; by horrible gropings we come to the central room; with joy we espy the sarcophagus; but we lift the lid—and no body is there!—appallingly vacant as vast is the soul of man!"

60 Cro-Magnon statues of goddesses, found outside European cave sites; discussed by Olson in the Institute in the New Sciences of Man lectures (*OLSON*, 10, pp, 43–59). See also VIII.30, 79, 172, and note 44.

61 Perhaps Edward Dahlberg and Ben Shahn, respectively, in a continuation of the inflammatory line of thought first advanced in Olson's unsent letter to Creeley of 15 July 1951, in which he complains "that great Jews have always dogged my tail..."; see VI.135–48. See also Tom Clark, *Charles Olson: The Allegory of a Poet's Life* (New York and London, 1991), 206–07.

62 Dioce, the Medean city named after Deïoces (d. 656 B.C.), traditional first king of the capital described by Herodotus. Dioce, along with Wagadu, represented to Pound the earthly paradise that would eventuate from Social Credit and cultural reforms. See James Laughlin's *Pound As Wuz* (St. Paul, 1987), pp. 122–23. "The Old Man" Pound, in Canto 74, announces his goal "To build the city of Dioce whose terraces are the colour of stars." However, Pound's ideal cities were nothing like Olson's polis. Olson complains to Creeley (I.92) that Pound "goes literary with lynxes, Dioces, and fuckings" in *The Pisan Cantos*, "but WE WANT SCOURINGS / where the right is, is, that he goeth by language: this we must do, and do, and do, otherwise we better go into, say, politics." In this way, Pound's Dioce "stuck in [Olson's] craw."

The "Jim X" who defuses the Dioce reference for Olson (*takes it out of his craw*, as he says, by rendering the literary in profane terms) may be James Laughlin in a statement unknown to me. Olson did carry the corrected typescript of Canto 74 from Pound, at St. Elizabeths, to Laughlin on 14 February 1946 (Seelye, *Olson & Pound*, pp. 72–75); perhaps Olson is remembering his conversation with Laughlin? Although Laughlin's New Directions faithfully published Pound (who Olson calls "Ex" in letters to Creeley), the publisher would come to criticize the poet's creation of the *paradiso terrestre*: "In Herodotus's account, the city of Dioce had its battlements plated with silver and gold. Why did Pound turn silver and gold into the 'color of stars'? Was it because 'colour of stars' is so beautiful, as image and as language, or because, without realizing it, he did not wish to signify the sovereignty of money in his sacred city?" (*Pound As Wuz*, p. 166).

However, Olson uses "X" variously in the correspondence. Olson wrote to Creeley in a [13 November 1950] letter, unavailable for publication in Volume IV, that "Jim X was JOHN QUINN—& what a guy! (in Ez's hands!" Clearly, in Pound's Canto 12, the banker Jim X is Quinn.

63 Olson discussed the relationship between these two Lawrence novels in his essay "The Escaped Cock: Notes on Lawrence & the Real," which had been published in *Origin*, no. 2 (Summer 1951), p. 78. See also VIII.189, where Olson tells Creeley that "DHL, in COCK, [*Part*] I, was farther ahead than any of us *yet*...."

64 From the Greek *charassein*, meaning "to engrave," according to Olson's copy of *Webster's Dictionary*, 5th edition (Springfield, Mass, 1942), p. 170.

65 Apparently *viva voce*. Recalled, variously, by Olson; e.g., he has Pound say "psychoses" for "psychology" in VIII.168.

66 Ernst Curtius (1814–1896), better known as the excavator of Olympia, secured the Troy site in 1874 for exclusive study by a German team which included Wilhelm Dörpfeld, an architect and head of the German Archaeological Institute at Athens. Earlier diggings at Troy, from 1870–1874, by the amateur Heinrich Schliemann (1822–1890) had established the importance of the site. It was Dörpfeld who identified Troy 6 from among the layers of ruins as Homer's Troy; Schliemann's bet had been Troy 2c. (Dörpfeld was to work with Schliemann, at Tiryns and at Orchomenos, a decade later.) Olson dates the beginning of "the new sciences of man" from Dörpfeld's application of scientific method at the Olympic site in 1875 (see *OLSON*, 10, pp. 3–5 and 107; also *OLSON*, 2, p. 54). Leo Deuel, the editor of *Memoirs of Heinrich Schliemann* (New York, 1977), corroborates Olson's view: "In truth, Schliemann's work only began to approximate scientific standards after he had learned to depend on men like [Rudolf] Virchow and above all the gifted young architect-archaeologist Dörpfeld, who had won his spurs at Olympia. Without these 'assistants' Schliemann by himself would have been unable to approach the detached analytic attitude of the scholar. It is equally doubtful whether without Dörpfeld Schliemann would have made any further progress at Troy," p. 16.

67 Ernst Robert Curtius (1886–1956), German philologist who is credited with bringing modern French literature to his nation's readers, was the son of Ernst Curtius. Cid Corman's collaborator Edgar Lohner (see note X.7) did his doctoral work under Curtius; he first came to Olson's attention with his review of the first number of *Fragmente* (see IX.175 and note IX.207). *Black Mountain Review*, no. 2 (Summer 1954) would feature a review of Willard R. Trask's translation of Curtius' *European Literature and the Latin Middle Ages*, Bollingen Series XXXVI (New York, 1953). See also Olson's essay, "'Ernst Robert Curtius," collected in *Human Universe*.

68 From Emil Ludwig, *Schliemann: The Story of a Gold-Seeker*, trans. D. F. Tait (Boston, 1931), p. 226.

69 Following is Olson's outline for what would become known as The Institute in the New Sciences of Man, a conference held at Black Mountain College in March 1953. Previously, it had been thought that Olson's first draft was set down in early 1953. Cf. closely the "1st [*sic*] Draft of Possibilities for THE INSTITUTE OF THE SCIENCES OF MAN" printed in *OLSON*, 10, pp. 3–5.

70 The following names make either their first appearance in the correspondence, or require fresh context.

Émile-Valère Rivière de Précourt (1835–1922). Starting in 1870, he explored nine limestone caves of the Baousse-Rousse region in France, from which he excavated over the next five years a number of skeletons which he dated from the Pleistocene Era. See his *Paléontologie: De l'antiquité de l'homme dans les Alpes-Maritimes* (Paris, 1887). Olson elaborates in his 1953 draft, "… 1895, Rivière's proof that these [prehistoric cave paintings] were of the Ice Age, 200th century BC" (see *OLSON*, 10, p. 3 and note 1 on p. 110). Douglas Fox and Leo Frobenius, in *African Genesis* (New York, 1937) and *Prehistoric Rock Pictures in Europe and Africa* (New York, 1937), do not use Rivière's christian name; a practice Olson follows.

Adolf Bastian (1826–1905), German ethnologist and adventurer. His observations from trips around the world are '*istorin*-style. Editor of *Zeitschrift für Ethnologie* from 1869.

Henri Breuil, whose discovery in 1901 of cave paintings near Les Eyzies dispelled official doubts as to the authenticity of the findings at Altamira. See note X.105 below. In the same year, his investigation helped to authenticate the dating of cave paintings discovered in 1887 by Rivière.

71 James Henry Breasted (1865–1935), U.S. orientalist and egyptologist. Organized, in 1919, the University of Chicago's Oriental Institute for the study of early man and ancient civilizations; subsequently led five expeditions to Egypt, Palestine, and Asia Minor. Olson read Breasted's *Oriental Forerunners of Byzantine Painting* (Chicago, 1924) in the late 1940s at the Library of Congress; Freud cites his *History of Egypt* (1906) and *The Dawn of Conscience* (New York, 1934) in *Moses and Monotheism*, a source for *Call Me Ishmael*. In Olson's copy of *Guide To Kulchur* (London, 1938), Pound mentions Breasted on page 62.

Flinders Petrie (see VIII.32) was dropped by Olson from the 1953 draft.

72 John Wesley Powell (1834–1902), U.S. geologist, explorer, ethnologist, founder of both the Smithsonian and the U.S. Bureau of American Ethnology, and a director of the U.S. Geological Survey. Having lost an arm during action in the Civil War, Powell makes a striking figure in the history of the American Far West, especially as the leader and recorder of

the first boat expedition to navigate the Colorado River the length of the Grand Canyon (1869).

Clarence King (1842–1901), U.S. geologist, mining engineer, and Western writer. Organized and for a decade led the first U.S. Geological Survey in the American Far West. His *Mountaineering in the Sierra Nevada* is a formative text of Western stories. Among Olson's papers is a letter written by King, and his library contains a copy of *Clarence King Memoirs: The Helmet of Mambrino* (New York, 1904).

John George Nicolay (1832–1901), co-author with John Hay of *Abraham Lincoln* (New York, 1890) in 10 volumes. Author of a study of the U.S. Civil War, *The Outbreak of Rebellion* (New York, 1881).

Powell submitted the *First Annual Report of the Bureau of Ethnology to the Secretary of The Smithsonian Institution, 1879–80* (Washington, D.C., 1881). Its contents include the Director's Report by Powell, with a note on his Grand Canyon expedition, and papers by Powell: "On the Evolution of Language," "Sketch of the Mythology of the North American Indians," "Wyandot Government," "On Limitations to the Use of Some Anthropologic Data."

[73] Vilhjalmur Stefansson (see note II.51, and "The Gate and the Center," in *Human Universe*, p. 17) and Owen Lattimore (see II.80, and *OLSON*, 10, p. 11).

[74] Perhaps Creeley's 4 July [1950] letter to Olson (II.46–50), a source for Olson's essay "The Escaped Cock: Notes on Lawrence & the Real," *Origin*, 2, pp. 77–80. However, the specific letter Olson seems to be quoting from—along with several that must have contained Creeley's comments to Olson during the writing of "Notes on Lawrence & the Real"—may be lost. In Olson's [22 August] 1951 letter, he thanks Creeley for providing, in a now lost letter, the essay's subtitle: "It was you who made it, 'Lawrence, or Notes on the real'—and jesus, how proud a subtitle it is, how proud I was, that you could take it … should find it possible to see anything I had to say to do with the REAL!" (VII.120).

[75] Seymour Lawrence printed D. H. Lawrence's poem "The Resurrection of the Flesh," written ca. 1915 but previously unpublished, in his magazine *Wake*, no. 7 (Fall 1948). See also Creeley on Lawrence's motif of the touch in his 6 October 1950 letter to Jake Leed, cited in note III.1.

[76] Last five lines of William Carlos Williams' "Tract," *The Collected Poems*, I, 74.

[77] Actually, Creeley quotes lines two and three from William Carlos Williams' poem "Turkey in the Straw," *The Collected Poems*, II, 231.

[78] Marianne Moore took it upon herself to rewrite both Hart Crane's "The Wine Menagerie" and his "Repose of Rivers" before printing them in *The Dial*.

[79] See Olson's 3 May 1952 letter to Creeley above, and note X.28.

[80] Lines 13–17 from Friedrich Hölderlin's poem "Von Abgrund Nämlich ..." ("For From The Abyss ..."):

> Frankfurt aber, nach der Gestalt, die
>
> Abdruk ist der Natur zu reden
>
> Des Menschen nämlich, ist der Nabel
>
> Dieser Erde, diese Zeit auch
>
> Ist Zeit,...

("Frankfurt, though to speak according to the shape / Of nature's imprint, human nature, I mean, / Is the navel of this earth, our time too / Is time ...") *Friedrich Hölderlin: Poems and Fragments*, trans. Michael Hamburger (Ann Arbor, 1967), pp. 552–53.

[81] Heffer's, the Cambridge, England book shop.

Olson mentions two books by L. A. Waddell in his 27 July 1951 letter to Creeley: *The British Edda* (1930) and *The Phoenician Origins of Britons, Scots & Anglo-Saxons* (1924). See VI.213 and notes VI.213, 214.

Olson's last reference in the correspondence to Joseph Strzygowski's *Origins of Christian Church Art* (1923) is in his essay "Culture"; see IX.146. Also see I.147 and note I.131.

Creeley is remembering the title Olson recommends in his 9 October 1951 letter to Creeley: Leo Frobenius' *Erythraa: Länder und Zeiten des heiligen Königsmordes*. See VIII.36 and note VIII.14.

[82] *Intro*, I, nos. 3/4 (1951), edited by Louis Brigante. See note 84 below.

[83] The quotation is praise of Olson from Cid Corman's Contributor's Notes to *Origin*, no. 4 (Winter 1951–1952), p. [ii]. Corman's poem "Insurance for Wallace Stevens" is found on p. 232 of the same issue.

[84] The citations which follow in Creeley's letter are from M. Elath, "In Another Direction: Commentary and Review of Three Anthologies," in *Intro*, I, 3/4, pp. 112–36 (especially pp. 126, 128, 130, and 116, as cited by Creeley), in which the books *The American Vanguard*, *New Italian Writers*, and *New Directions 12* are reviewed. The identity of Elath, a resident of Jamaica, New York in 1952, remains obscure: even then, Corman was reduced to circulating speculation that Elath might be a pseudonym for Gil Orlovitz or even Ezra Pound (*Olson & Corman*, p. 263). However, Olson will cite Elath prominently in his essay "The Methodology is the Form," sent to Louis Brigante on 18 August 1952 for possible publication in *Intro* (see below in this volume); and the mysterious Elath is noted by Creeley in "Hart Crane and the Private Judgment," *Collected Essays*, p. 17 and no. 9.

Alfred Korzybski (1879–1950), U.S. semanticist.

[85] From Gerhardt's "Rundschau der Fragmente (moderne dichtung in

deutschland)," a supplement to *Fragmente*, no. 1; probably the prose piece Creeley received in the Spring of 1951 (V.141–42).

[86] Kasper and Horton published Eustace C. Mullins' *A Study of the Federal Reserve* in the Square $ Series, in 1952. Mullins, who would write a biography of Pound (*This Difficult Individual*, 1961), was the notorious Director of the Aryan League of America and believed that a Jewish "conspiracy" was overwhelming national economies. See note VIII.76.

[87] Article by Nathan Davidson, appearing in *Contemporary Issues*, II, no. 3 (Summer 1952); the citation is from p. 166. Olson, who also subscribed to the journal, subsequently underlined the passage in his own copy.

[88] Creeley's generalizations seem to be derived from the article "Federal Reserve Banking System" in the 12th edition (1922) of *Encyclopaedia Britannica*, pp. 60–64; e.g., "many American enterprises [after World War I] had fallen into the habit of financing their own foreign trade by extending long credits to buyers, while borrowing heavily from their own banks on domestic account in order to get the funds they needed to carry on trade elsewhere" (p. 64). Creeley reasons that a big corporation—which is no more a "bank" than is the Federal Reserve Board—taps its own money supply. Creeley might as well have cited Nathan Davidson's article "America's Garrison Economy," in *Contemporary Issues*, II, 3, p. 166, which declares that "internal financing by industry has grown to such an extent that already seven large corporations behave as banks...."

[89] Acronym for the formal close "Yours Very Truly."

[90] T. L. Berger, in his review "Ideology And Literature," *Intro*, I, 3/4, pp. 169–71. In the final section of "Notes for a New Prose," *Origin*, 2, pp. 96–97 and *Collected Essays*, p. 467, Creeley writes: "We can note, perhaps, that while poetry may have combined itself in several, to mean, one thing worked in the hands of several men, at certain times with success, prose has never been effectual so taken, as a job, or so treated.... Certainly, the novelist hates his neighbor, hates him for writing, to begin with, and hates him doubly, for writing prose." By the time of Creeley's review of Williams' *The Desert Music and Other Poems* for *Black Mountain Review*, Summer 1954, the Poe of Williams' *In the American Grain* had come to represent the American writer in splendid isolation.

[91] Olson writes, in "The Necessary Propositions" (*OLSON*, 8, p. 44): "I had a dream recently in which I heard Merce [Cunningham] say, Dance is an object and an action." Olson reports his dream to Cunningham in a 15 May 1952 letter. See also "Merce of Egypt," *Collected Poems*, pp. 269–71.

[92] *"The Unwobbling Pivot" & "The Great Digest"* of Confucius, translation and commentary by Ezra Pound, with the Chinese "Stone Classics" text included (New York, 1951). Also disparaged by Olson in the previously

unpublished essay "The Attack, Now, In Painting & Writing" (enclosed in his 24 May letter below).

93 I.e., Masaccio (Tommaso Giovanni Di Mone, 1401–1428), Florentine painter. Olson perhaps refers to Masaccio's 1426 polyptych for the Carmelite Church in Pisa, many of its original panels either lost or sold.

94 In "The Gate and the Center," *Human Universe*, p. 18, Olson writes: "... the problem now is not what things are so much as it is what happens BETWEEN things, in other words: COMMUNICATION...." Cf. Pound's declaration that "Peace comes of communication" cited in Creeley's 11 July letter to Olson below.

95 Olson wrote "Theatre Institute Lecture on Language," left in holographic notes (*OLSON*, 8, pp. 50–55), for a theatre arts institute that he hoped scenic designer Boris Aronson would direct at Black Mountain College in Fall, 1952. (Aronson's ties with Black Mountain art were not new, though he was new to the campus. Aronson's wife, Lisa Jalowetz Aronson, had first come to the college in 1939 with her father Heinrich Jalowetz, the Viennese conductor.)

96 Praised by T.S. Eliot in his influential 1927 essay on the Elizabethan playwright Thomas Middleton (1580–1627). Olson reports to Creeley, in his 22 May letter below, that he has read the play and found it boring.

97 Olson had recently mailed Creeley copies of two poems: "A Discrete Gloss," titled "A Gloss" on the carbon copy, would appear in *Origin*, no. 6 (Summer 1952); and "The Thing Was Moving," the carbon copy dated "May 11, '52," which Olson mailed in his letter of 10 May above.

98 After Ernst Haeckel's law, "ontogeny recapitulates phylogeny" (*History of Creation*, 1867; English trans., 1892). Haeckel coined the term *phylogeny*, meaning the evolution of an animal or plant, in his *General Morphology* (1866). See also Butterick's note to Olson's poem "Have Them Naked Instead," in *A Nation of Nothing But Poetry*, p. 215. See note IX.214.

99 Olson, in "The Cave," *OLSON*, 10, p. 23 passim, speaks of The Plateau as man's archetypal experience of "EXTERIOR," while The Cave is "the interior." He glosses the term for Creeley on p. 70 below.

100 Olson declares himself "a post-modern and so a post-Darwinian" (see, e.g., *Olson & Corman*, p. 270), perhaps echoing Lawrence's "...nothing will ever quench humanity and the human potentiality to evolve something magnificent out of a renewed chaos. I do not believe in evolution, but in the strangeness and rainbow-change of ever-renewed creative civilizations" (Introduction to *Fantasia of the Unconscious*).

101 Probably C. F. Hawkes' *The Prehistoric Foundations of Europe to the*

Mycenean Age (London and New York, 1940), which Olson quotes below in his 25 May 1952 letter to Creeley.

[102] German words for "poetry" and "poet." Perhaps recalling Pound's equation, after Basil Bunting, "dichten = CONDENSARE" (*ABC of Reading*, passim, and again in The Money Pamphlets; quoted by Creeley in his letter to Raymond Souster printed as "A Note on Poetry" in *Contact*, 6, 1953, and collected in *A Quick Graph*, p. 28).

[103] In "The Cave," OLSON, 10, pp. 25–26, Olson warns: "… I ought to let you moderns know how conservative (or reactionary, if you choose) I am. For I think so far as *substances* go … that there are like significant curiosities: I think *stone*, for example, and *wood*, and *clay* are more interesting, again, than brick, or steel, or glass, or iron, or copper, or plastics—that these givens (rather than transformations of men) are solids to habituate ourselves with more fruitful, in their issue, than (as above, airplanes, any motors, than buildings, than mountains or their urban equivalents like such building as Manhattan's…. And not by orneriness, or by such faddisms as localism or regionalism (Madison Avenue, or Modern Design…). Not at all these pseudos…." In "MAXIMUS, Part II," written in August, 1957, Olson is unrelenting in his distaste for Fuller. "You see, I take it," Olson writes, "there are only two forms of mind about how it is human beings live on the earth. They either do, or they build nine chains to the moon / (as that devil in pants Fuller called his book, whose very name Fuller—full a ____ / Geodesic Horshit [sic]" (OLSON, no. 6, Fall 1976, p. 61).

[104] Olson's paragraph might be read as a preliminary start for his poem "He / in the dark stall…," dated 17 May 1952 (*Collected Poems*, pp. 265–68).

[105] Site of paleolithic cave paintings near Santillana del Mar in northern Spain. It was the first example of cave art to be discovered (1879). Henri Breuil's discoveries of paintings at La Mouthe in 1901 finally verified the authenticity of the Altamira rock paintings as Ice Age art. See note 57 above, and VIII.45–48.

[106] A pun of an oath, associating artist Ben Shahn and visionary painter Hieronymus Bosch (1450?–1516).

[107] Reference to Creeley's prosody for the word "is" in his new poem "The Surf," in an 18 April [1952] letter to Olson (IX.269–70). (See also Olson's advice, in 1950, that Creeley write his proposal for a Guggenheim grant with a winning " 'THIS IS IT' " style, III.61.)

[108] *De vulgari eloquentia*, Dante Alighieri's multi-volume Latin treatise (ca. 1305), in which he sought to establish his own Italian, "the vulgar tongue," as a literary language. In our own century, Williams would argue for an "American idiom," and Pound says, e.g., in his "Treatise on Metre," *ABC*

of Reading, p. 197: "Apart from Dante's *De Vulgari Eloquio* I have en-
countered only one treatise on metric [unnamed by Pound] which has the
slightest value." Pound implicitly compares Whitman's poetry with the
"reason" behind Dante's argument, in his 1909 essay "What I feel about
Walt Whitman" (*Selected Prose*, ed. Cookson, p. 116). Olson, in his 10
December 1954 letter to Creeley, will write that "the vernacular [in poetry]
came back into birth in the US sometime about 1910...."; see also
Muthologos, I, 183–84. See also Olson's essay "Quantity In Verse, And
Shakespeare's Late Plays," in *Selected Writings*, pp. 36–37.

109 In Olson's 22 June 1950 letter to Creeley, he pinpoints the development
of "a new language, for USE, made USA" after "WHITMAN, WHITMAN,
WHITMAN, date, between, directly between, [the publication of Pound's
books] 'Ripostes' and 'Lustra,' what 1912–13?" (I.140).

The cover of the first number of *Poetry*, which appeared in October 1912
with Pound as Foreign Correspondent, displays this motto from Whitman:
"To have great poets there must be great audiences too." Earlier, in 1909,
Pound wrote in a manuscript published years later under the title of
"What I feel about Walt Whitman" (*Selected Prose*, ed. Cookson, p. 115):
"... I see him America's poet.... He *is* America. His crudity is an
exceedingly great stench, but it *is* America.... He *does* 'chant the crucial
stage' and he is the 'voice triumphant.' ... Entirely free from the
renaissance humanist ideal of the complete man or from the Greek
idealism, he is content to be what he is, and he is his time and his people."
See also Pound's poem "A Pact," *Selected Poems*, p. 27. In *Autobiography*, p.
107, Williams dismisses his own first book, *Poems* (1909), as "bad Keats ...
bad Whitman too." Mariani, in his biography of Williams (*A New World
Naked*, New York, 1981, pp. 107–08), claims that "what Whitman had
learned [about rhythm] looking out at the breakers coming along the New
Jersey shore ... Williams would later call the single most important
moment for the history of American poetry" (Williams' comments in a
manuscript, version of January 1950, of *Paterson* 4). See also Williams'
poem "The Wanderer: A Rococo Study," *The Collected Poems*, I, 27, its
second stanza built from Whitman's "Crossing Brooklyn Ferry."

However, Olson's evaluation here of Whitman's influence reads closest
to Lawrence's in *Studies in Classic American Literature*. See also Creeley's
"Introduction to Penguin *Selected Whitman*," reprinted in *Collected Prose*,
where he notes that Pound and Williams disliked Whitman whereas
Lawrence finally upheld him (p. 4).

110 Williams' 2 August 1951 letter to Corman (Humanities Research
Center, University of Texas); see note VII.64.

111 Olson has constructed a parody of the polytropic heroes of Pound's
Cantos. First, he compares Pound, whose desire to influence social,

economic, and cultural change in the United States was never realized, to Gemisthus Plethon, who influenced Cosimo de Medici in 1439 to establish the Platonic Academy of Florence and introduced western Europe to the geography of Strabo and the astronomy of Copernicus, and in these ways caused to be laid the groundwork for the Italian Renaissance. (The ashes of Gemisthus are entombed at Malatesta's Tempio, a place sacred to Pound; Fritz Schultze's *Georgios Gemistos Plethon und seine reformatorischen Bestrebungen,* Jena, 1874, is one of Pound's sources for the "Malatesta" Cantos. Pound writes in *Guide to Kulchur,* p. 224, that "Gemistus Plethon brought over a species of Platonism to Italy in the 1430s. I take it he is more known by his sarcophagus in Rimini than by his writings.") The date 1429 is significant here because is was in that year that the 13-year-old Malatesta proved his military stuff when he led troops at Rimini in a successful repulsion of Pope Martin V's superior invasion force. Furthermore, Olson mistakenly believed 1429 to be the year of Gemisthus' arrival in Italy, and he dated the Renaissance from that point in his bibliography for *Mayan Letters,* in *Selected Writings,* p. 129, and *The Maximus Poems,* p. 75.

[112] The magazine is *trans/formation,* no. 3 (1952).

[113] Olson wrote: "It is all tied up with what he [Pound] calls a truism, London, 1913: are you are or are you not, a serious character?" (*Olson & Pound,* p. 101)—after Pound's essay "The Serious Artist," first published serially in *New Freewoman* (15 October 1913, 1 November 1913, 15 November 1913), pp. 161–63, 194–95, 213–14, and collected in *Pavannes and Divagations* (New York, 1918).

[114] Rimini, city in Italy where Malatesta built his Tempio. Pound's Canto 9 opens with lines recalling events, beginning in 1429, that required Malatesta to defend his inheritance. (See also VII.119 and note 41.) In this passage (repeated from VII.65), Olson criticizes Pound for "backing up only to" 500 B.C. to find but two sources of culture and civilization; whereas Olson is most interested in pursuing facts (from civilizations as diverse as Mayan and Sumerian) pre-1500 B.C.

"Bill's error": Probably a comment on the limitations Williams set on history in *Paterson,* which prevent it from being a "tale of the race." According to the ancient Greeks, the Pelasgians were a prehistoric people who populated Greece. In the *Iliad,* the Pelasgians are allies of Troy. In VII.65ff., Olson uses the Pelasgians as a representative pre-Socratic culture, and criticizes Williams there for not expanding the methodology of *In the American Grain* to include the ancient and non-American. Earlier in the letter, Olson cites the by now familiar Poundean term "serious character," meaning a personal standard which he thinks Pound failed to live up to. Taken as a whole, then, this passage continues the argument

Olson tested in the unsent letter to Louis Martz; see VII.63–73.

115 From Pound's "Treatise on Metre," in *ABC of Reading*, p. 201: "Most arts attain their effects by using a fixed element and a variable. From the empiric angle: verse usually has some element roughly fixed and some other that varies, but which element is to be fixed and which vary, and to what degree, is the affair of the author. Some poets have chosen the bump, as the boundary. Some have chosen to mark out their course with repetition of consonants; some with similar terminations of words. All this is a matter of detail."

116 A review of *Fragmente*, 1, by Ernst Robert Curtius, appearing in *Der Tage*. See also note IX.207.

117 "This kind of literary merit we do not welcome. The author has not been seen, since 1814, on the second floor of the Tuileries Palace...."
The exact source for the citation from Stendhal has not been located. However, the year 1814, when Napoleon Bonaparte abdicated to the Bourbons, was a crisis year for Stendhal and he refers to it throughout his autobiographical writings. "I fell with Napoleon in April 1814," he writes in *The Life of Henri Brulard*, trans. Catherine Alison Phillips (New York, 1955), p. 13. See also *Memoirs of Egotism*, ed. Matthew Josephson and trans. Hannah and Matthew Josephson (New York, 1949), pp. 40–41, 115.

118 Italian: "a fine fellow." Quoted by Stephen Shorter in his article "Pound In Exile," *Intro*, 3/4, p. 165. The waiter probably worked in the restaurant of the Albergo Rapallo, where the Pounds liked to entertain. Pound's unorthodox games of tennis were a regular feature at Rapallo in the years before the Second War; see, e.g., a description of Pound's doubles game in Noel Stock's *The Life of Ezra Pound* (New York, 1970), p. 365, and a photograph of Pound's serve in James Laughlin's *Pound As Wuz*, p. 11.

119 Creeley's concerns proved prophetic. Duberman, in *Black Mountain: An Exploration*, pp. 393–94, reports that Creeley's first class at Black Mountain College (his very first attempt at classroom teaching) "was the worst. It met in the large conference room of the Studies Building, which had a huge table that took up most of the space. Six students bunched up at one end, and at the other sat Creeley, forlorn, alone, staring sideways at the wall, mopping at his eye with a handkerchief.... Creeley talked in a nonstop monotone so low and gravelly, that no one could understand what he was saying. After ten minutes or so, Karen Karnes asked him if he could speak up; he lifted his voice for a few minutes, but it soon sank back into a monotone."

120 Unnamed family, friends of Ashley Bryan. In a 24 December 1951 letter, Creeley tells Olson that he felt as if the wife were the character he had earlier created for his story "The Party."

121 Aged 14, Creeley attended Holderness School in Plymouth, New Hampshire, on scholarship.

122 Williams, "Author's Introduction (1944)" (formerly "Introduction to *The Wedge*"), in *Collected Later Poems*, p. 4 and *The Collected Poems*, II, 54.

123 The three quotations following are from poems found, respectively, in Williams' *Collected Later Poems*: "Venus over the Desert," p. 172; "The Words, the Words, the Words," p. 150; and " 'I Would Not Change for Thine,' " p. 175; also *The Collected Poems*, II, 183–85.

124 From *Paterson* (New York, 1948), p. [10].

125 See VII.43 for Olson's comments to Creeley about teaching the Poe essay from Williams' *In the American Grain*.

126 *IF means are faulty*: Creeley is recalling Williams' Preface to *Paterson*, Book I: "... rolling / up the sum, by defective means...."
   Following, Creeley quotes Section 2 of "The Lion," *Collected Later Poems*, p. 181, and below it Section 1, p. 180; *The Collected Poems*, II, 180–81.

127 Last line of Williams' "Aigeltinger," *Collected Later Poems*, p. 66 and *The Collected Poems*, II, 124. Often cited by Creeley in the correspondence.

128 See note IX.234.

129 Novik (*Was That a Real Poem*, p. 134) fixes Creeley's first reading of Williams in 1944, when he bought *The Wedge* sometime before leaving Harvard for the war. Note also that an Olson graduate paper for F. O. Matthiessen at Harvard was published as "Lear and Moby-Dick."

130 From the conclusion to Williams' "Author's Introduction (1944)," *Collected Later Poems*, p. 5 and *The Collected Poems*, II, 55.

131 The citation is from M. Elath's review "In Another Direction," *Intro*, 3/4, p. 113. "The old man" is Ezra Pound. Elath expounds: "The only legitimate 'claim' the Confederate Critics [Tate, Ransom, et al.] have on the N[ew] C[ritics] other than corn bread & butter avowals, is their embracing of 'classicism,' which also was Embraced by Ezra Pound for a different purpose.... All 20th century classicism means is that it takes more than feeling to be a writer—it takes brains.... In striking at the NC, or what is ascribed to the NC, [Charles I.] G[licksberg] lops off classicism as if one had to be a 'classicist' to have concrete structure and intensity. G connects classicism with totality, totality with fascism, but by implication—by not following out his own logic in clear statement since his literary cause wd be lost." Glicksberg was the editor of *The American Vanguard* (1950), an anthology of short stories, which Elath reviews in "In Another Direction."

132 Familiar Olson citations from Rimbaud. For "ordered derangement" see Rimbaud's famous 13 May 1871 letter to George Izambard (trans. Louise Varese, *Illuminations*, New York, 1957, p. xxvii): "I want to be a

poet, and I am working to make myself a *visionary*.... To arrive at the unknown through the disordering of *all the senses*, that's the point." For "the other side of, despair," see note IX.65. Rimbaud wrote "Credo In Unam," an early poem, ca. 1870 and later retitled it "Le Soleil et le Chair." Mentioned again in Olson's 29 May 1952 letter below. Cf. Olson's attention to the French word *chair*, or "flesh," in his letter of 6 May [1952] and note 37 above; and to *soleil*, or "sun," passim.

[133] Mary Theresa Olson died in Worcester, Massachusetts, at the home of Mr. and Mrs. John Sullivan, on Christmas Day 1950. Mrs. Olson lived in Gloucester, in the unheated family cottage "Oceanwood," during the warm months, and sought shelter during winters with the Sullivans and other friends in Charles Olson's hometown (Butterick, Introduction to *The Post Office*, Bolinas, 1975, p. viii).

[134] In his Beloit lecture of 27 March 1968 (*Poetry and Truth*, San Francisco, 1971, p. 44), Olson refers to "an experience of, say, twenty years ago, which was to me dogmatic, when I knew there was a sun, I mean a helio inside myself, so that everything, that every other human being, and every thing in creation, was something that I could see if I could keep that experience." Butterick's note to that lecture (p. 68) documents Olson's experience as having happened on a bus ride from Black Mountain to Washington: "In the margin of a xeroxed copy of Richard Payne Knight's *Worship of Priapus* among the poet's papers, there occurs the following note, alongside a passage concerning a Greek iconographical device of a radiated asterisk or sun used to indicate the presence of the Divinity: 'yes: the *sun inside* (cf experience on Trailways to Washington 1952.' "

[135] I.e., a tarot fatto or "done fate." Not a specific card in the Italian tarot, but what Cagli called "the layout," or judgment, for a life. Robert Duncan often remarked, as if to explain Olson's capacity for work, that the young Charles Olson was told at a reading of his tarot that he had only a few years left to live. Olson tells us that Cagli taught him the tarot (*Muthologos*, I, 222), and Olson's first book of poems, *Y & X*, was written in conjunction with Cagli's drawings of the tarot. See also note IV.59.

[136] In Olson's 26 April [1952] letter, he tells Creeley to write to Gallimard, "who stand by to send you something" (IX.278–79).

[137] *Shui Hu Chuan*, the classic from the Ming Dynasty, translated by Pearl S. Buck as *All Men Are Brothers*, 2 volumes (New York, 1933). Olson owned the second volume. See note VII.67, and *OLSON*, 8, pp. 25, 77, and n. 12 on p. 106.

[138] Samuel Barber (1910–1981), distinguished U.S. composer of concert music and opera in the romantic tradition.

[139] "The Four Gentlemen," unfinished and never published, was probably begun about the time Olson was writing "The Fiery Hunt" and the first part of the mask "Troilus," April to July 1948.

[140] Olson's 19 March 1952 letter to Bernard Leach, well-known potter who had worked in St. Ives, Cornwall since 1920, reprinted in *OLSON*, 8, on pp. 23–25. Olson had organized a 10-day ceramics institute for Fall term at Black Mountain. See also his 8 March 1952 letter to Marguerite Wildenhain, whose pottery was at Pond Farm, California, in *OLSON*, 8, pp. 21–23. The Japanese potters Shoji Hamada and Soetsu Yanagi included the Black Mountain institute as part of their American tour. Charles Eames was designer of the Eames chair, although Butterick identifies him as John Heagan Eames (b. 1900), etcher and painter (*OLSON*, 8, notes on p. 25).

[141] *Moxie*, American slang for "courage, pluck, daring." The phrase might be read as "make moxie with youth," facetiously spelt.

[142] I.e., Edgar Taschdjian (b. 1904), Austrian-born plant geneticist teaching at Loyola University, Chicago, and a visitor at Black Mountain College (see Butterick's note in *OLSON*, 9, Spring 1978, p. 87). Victor Sprague had taught biology at Black Mountain since 1951.

[143] Miriam Leivers, from Lawrence's novel *Sons and Lovers*, is drawn from Jessie Chambers Wood, who, under the initials E.T., published a memoir of her relationship with the young novelist, *D. H. Lawrence: A Personal Record* (New York, 1936). She remembers a walk at Flamborough, p. 128, when "Lawrence skipped from one white boulder to another in the vast amphitheatre of the bay until I could have doubted whether he was indeed a human being.... He created an atmosphere not of death ... but of an utter negation of life, as though he had become dehumanized." The walks Paul Morel took with Miriam in Part II of *Sons and Lovers* fall short of metamorphosis. The episode Olson remembers comes from Richard Aldington's *D. H. Lawrence: Portrait of a Genius, but ...*, pp. 61 and 152, and Lawrence's poem "Bavarian Gentians." See note V.21.

[144] Lycanthrophy, in folklore, is the power to transform a human into a wolf. The metamorphosis was worked *by* Endymion, according to Keats' "Endymion," in order to restore the lovers Glaucus (a sea monster) and Scylla (dead from drowning). In "Me-mo to Stefan & John," *OLSON*, 8, p. 41, Olson defines metamorphosis as "the multiple, or, if you will let me use my cliche (& Ovid's), the metamorphic—metamorphoses, or, changes of the most literal & physical kind, the series of our own and any possibilities (a possibility being that which will happen and an impossibility being that which is past)."

[145] The Sumerians initially wrote left to right; see VIII.36–37.

[146] Note the titles of Michelangelo's last sonnets: Sonnet 73, "At the Foot of the Cross"; 74, "A Prayer for Grace in Death"; 76, "The Death of Christ"; and 77, "The Blood of Christ." After his sixtieth year, Michelangelo characteristically addressed his sonnets to "dear Lord." See *The Sonnets of Michael Angelo Buonarroti*, trans. John Addington Symonds (New York, 1948).

[147] Edmund, in *King Lear*, Act V, Scene 3: "The wheel is come full circle; I am here." In the paragraph that follows, Olson the Melvillean presumes to teach Creeley the epistemology of *Moby-Dick*: the rightness of Ishmael's open vortex-think versus the wrongness of Mapple-Ahab's closed linear-think.

[148] Freud, in *Moses and Monotheism*, speculates that Moses was an Egyptian who made a gift of the monotheistic religion of Amenhotep IV (d. 1358 B.C.) to the Jewish people.

[149] Perhaps "a complaint of Blanc" is an allusion to Charles Blanc (1813–1882), influential French art critic and designer. Although Robert Rauschenberg (born in Texas, and educated at Kansas City, Paris, Black Mountain, and New York) was not "a Washington character," the passage may also be a veiled reference to a current show of all-white ("blanc") canvases by that artist at the Betty Parsons Gallery? At any rate, Olson's "answer" to the unnamed painter is the essay "The Attack, Now, in Painting & Writing." It is not found on verso, but composed immediately following, or coming "on the back of," this letter to Creeley.

[150] Olson draws the sign below in the letter and assigns it to the ancient Persian city of Erech (modern Warka), 3500 B.C. From notes on cylinder seals in Ignace J. Gelb, *A Study of Writing* (Chicago, 1952), p. 65. See Olson's worksheet "Logography," *Additional Prose*, p. 20.

[151] Charles Rau, "Observations on Cup-Shaped and Other Lapidarian Sculptures in the Old World and in America," in *Contributions to North American Ethnology*, Department of the Interior, 47th Congress, 1st Session, House of Representatives Miscellaneous Documents no. 66 (Washington, 1882), V, 1–112; plus figures 11–61. See also *OLSON*, 10, pp. 43ff.

[152] I.e., the Quipu, Peruvian knot-writing system mentioned in Ignace Gelb, *A Study of Writing*, pp. 4, 8, 19, 250.

[153] Here Olson confuses Gelb's reference to wampum and her discussion, in the following paragraph, of mnemonic aids among the Ewe Africans, *A Study of Writing*, p. 4.

[154] The Marshall Islanders fashioned primitive navigational charts in this manner, according to H. Lyons, "The Sailing Charts of the Marshall Islanders," in *Geographical Journal*, no. 72 (1928), pp. 325–28. Shells

represented islands; ribs of palm leaves formed a framework to support the shells but also to note areas of open sea (straight leaves) and wave fronts surrounding islands (curved). See also V.90 and note V.85.

[155] Lone Dog, a Dakota Sioux warrior, painted on a buffalo robe a calendar of the events of his tribe for the years 1800 to 1871. The eighth figure clearly represents a red-jacketed man struck by two arrows. (This Sioux Red Jacket is not to be confused with the celebrated Seneca orator Red Jacket, d. 1830.) See Garrick Mallery, "Picture Writing of the American Indians," in *Tenth Annual Report of the Bureau of American Ethnology, 1888–89* (Washington, DC, 1890), pp. 266–87. Cf. Ignace Gelb's related discussion of pictograph names, warrior signatures, and calendars from Sioux tribes, in *A Study of Writing*, pp. 38, 40–42. Olson's use of the word "photograph," meaning *light picture*, is his way to link this kind of drawing and the keeping of a calendar, whose basis is the differentiation of days and nights.

[156] Olson underlined the etymologies for arrow and wooden instrument in his copy of Gelb's *A Study of Writing*, p. 67. L. A. Waddell deciphers the sign for "earth" in *The Aryan Origin of the Alphabet...* (London, 1927), p. 36 and in *The Indo-Sumerian Seals Deciphered...* (London, 1925), p. 25; for diagrams of the signs for "earth" and "star," see Figure 5 on p. 35 of the latter book.

[157] Ogham (from the Irish, "ogam") was an alphabet of strokes and notches used by the Celts in Britain and Ireland as early as the 5th Century. It has been preserved in inscriptions on memorial stones. See Waddell, *The Aryan Origin of the Alphabet...*, pp. 21, 22, 25ff., and Gelb, *A Study of Writing*, p. 144. Olson marked the margin in his copy of the latter.

[158] In Olson's letter of 9 October 1951, he relates the story of the Seirite miners (VIII.32–34).

[159] Walter Perry ("Big Train") Johnson (1887–1946), Hall-of-Fame power pitcher for the Washington Senators, earned his nickname because his fastball was said to travel at the speed of an express train. Johnson was named the Most Valuable Player of the American League in 1924, when Olson was an impressionable 14 years old. Olson used the line about Johnson twice, in *Archaeologist of Morning*, p. 207 and *Maximus Poems*, I, 110.

[160] The reference is cryptic. Olson remembers bird imagery in Marsden Hartley's Gloucester painting in *The Maximus Poems*, p. 37 and, in a complex passage of free association, links the painter and birds in his letter to Creeley of 23 June 1950 (I.145). However, Hartley had died much earlier, in 1943, and Olson would not presume to call him a friend as he would Corado Cagli (e.g., *Muthologos*, II, 72) or Ben Shahn (*Olson &*

Corman, p. 114). In his [19] July [1951] letter, he had told Creeley that
"... Shahn is the only American painter who has ever interested me ..."
(VI.162). Also, before deciding upon the title of the essay at hand, Olson
had used the term "attack" in his "Cy Twombly" essay (*OLSON*, 8, p. 12).
The New York Times, for 28 April 1951, notes a "Birds in Art" show by
members of the M. Levitt Gallery (13:4).

161 *Hamlet*, Act II, Scene 2; see note IX.72.

162 Christ was a major subject throughout the career of Domenico Theotocopuli, the painter popularly known as "El Greco" (1541–1614), whose
astigmatism is believed to have contributed to the mannered dispropor-
tion of his signature figures. See, e.g., "Christ Stripped of His Garments"
(1579), and "Crucifixion" (1595).

163 Pound, after Ford, in "The Prose Tradition in Verse," *Literary Essays*
(New York, 1968), p. 373.

164 Paolo Uccello's "Battle of San Romano" (or "Rout of St. Romano"), ca.
1455–1460, in three panels (now dispersed). Thought to have been
influenced by the rectangular tapestries in the possession of the Medici,
Uccello's patrons.

165 Olson describes items from the Viking vessel which had been discovered in Oseberg, Norway in 1880. Mentioned in "Session #9," the
Lectures in the New Sciences of Man, *OLSON*, 10, p. 81.

166 Is Olson misremembering André Malraux's 1924 expedition to the
Khmer temples in Cambodia, and the blocks of stone he found there
belonging to the bas-reliefs of the temple of Banteay Srei? Or perhaps
Olson is remembering the illustrations of 3rd millennium B.C. Sumerian
and Mesopotamian art in Malraux's *Museum Without Walls*, trans. Stuart
Gilbert, Bollingen Series XXIV (New York, 1949), pp. 28–31.

167 For the Latin *modestia*, meaning "modesty, discretion," on the analogy
of *potestas*, "power"? Olson uses the term in "Beginning of 3rd Inst,"
OLSON, 10, p. 16.

168 In an unpublished essay "The Methodology is the Form," sent on 18
August 1952 to Louis Brigante for *Intro*, Olson will write: "Socrates put it
sharply when he explained his choice of suicide over exile to his afflicted
friends: he pointed out that in his suicide, Athens committed suicide.... He
was right ... the polis disappeared." And, in *OLSON*, 8, p. 72: "... we *know*
the condition of Athens under Socrates which led to his death. I mean he
was tried and found guilty by a city." Perhaps suggested by Socrates'
remark to the jury, concerning his status as Athens' "gad-fly," in the
"Apology" (Plato: *The Last Days of Socrates*, trans. Hugh Tredennick, London, 1987, p. 62): "I assure you that if I am what I claim to be, and you put
me to death, you will harm yourselves more than me"; or by his dialogue

from prison, "Crito" (Tredennick, p. 89), in which Socrates has the personified Laws of Athens say to him concerning a jail-break: "Now, Socrates, what are you proposing to do? Can you deny that by this act which you are contemplating you intend, so far as you have the power, to destroy us...?"

[169] From the final, dark sentence in C. F. Hawkes, *Prehistoric Foundations of Europe*, p. 384, published in 1940, during what were perhaps the darkest days of World War II for Hawkes' native England.

[170] C. F. Hawkes, *Prehistoric Foundations of Europe*, p. 356, where Theseus' slaying of the Minotaur, which "freed his country from the oppression of Minos' tribute ... symbolizes the winning of mastery in its own house for European civilization as against the Orient."

[171] Cp. "... I sit where I am, etc.," in Creeley's [7 December 1950] letter to Olson, IV.72.

[172] Freud's argument especially in Part 3 of *Moses and Monotheism*. However, Freud's Moses is only an Egyptian nobleman—perhaps as much as governor and/or priest—and Flavius Josephus' speculation that Moses was "an Egyptian field-marshall in a victorious campaign in Ethiopia" gets mention only in a footnote (p. 32).

[173] In *Prehistoric Foundations of Europe*, p. 356, Egypt's "especial relations with Crete [cease] at this time in the reign of King Amenhotep III...."

[174] See Olson's essay "Culture," IX.145–49. For Olson's tracing of the line of humanism, see, e.g.:

The Lectures in the New Sciences of Man, *OLSON*, 10, p. 86: "On this track back, the date [of our culture] is in the rear of Homer 600 years, but just as declarable a date now as his birth, & even the birthplace of that religion & sociology is fixable: it is 1500 BC.... God came from the Aryan invaders who, by 1500, had so penetrated all the Middle East that their concept of a Supreme Being... displaced Abraham.... You already know that China dates from this same 1500, & we shall have occasion to wonder more about that date 1500—for example, the fall of Knossos... is 1450 BC.... [The fact that Hawkes'] *Prehistoric Foundations of Europe* ends exactly with 1450, says ... that date is the birth date of historical Europe."

"The Gate and the Center," *Human Universe*, p. 19: "What Waddell gives me is this chronology: that, from 3378 BC (date man's 1st city, name and face of creator also known) in unbroken series first at Uruk, then from the seaport Lagash out into colonies in the Indus Valley and, circa 2500, the Nile, until date 1200 BC or thereabouts, civilization had ONE CENTER, Sumer, in all directions...." See especially L. A. Waddell, *The Makers of Civilization in Race & History* (London, 1929).

[175] In "The Gate and the Center," collected in *Human Universe*, p. 20, Olson

wrote: "But the thing goes farther, & deeper. What has been these last 700 years, is the inevitable consequence of a contrary will to that of Sumer, a will which overcame the old will approximately 1200 BC." Actually, Olson's comments in the correspondence (II.84 and 92) pre-date the actual writing of "The Gate and the Center."

[176] Repeated by Olson in the Lectures in the New Sciences of Man, *OLSON*, 10, pp. 83, 86.

[177] Socrates (born ca. 470 B.C.) fought with distinction against the Persians as a *hoplite*, a heavily armed Greek infantryman, seeing action in the battles of Samos (441–440), Potidaea (432–430), Delium (424), and Amphipolis (422? or 437–436? B.C.). Olson errs in placing him at the battle of Marathon, 12 September 490. Marathon is mentioned in the 8 March 1953 lecture in the New Sciences of Man, *OLSON*, 10, p. 87. Xenophon, in *The Persian Expedition*, recalls a Socrates from Miletus at the battle of Cunaxa.

[178] Olson characteristically links the martyrs Socrates and Christ, but see especially *Olson & Corman*, pp. 102 and 108.

[179] Ammonius' explanation of a saying by Heraclitus, familiar in Olson, found in Plutarch's essay "The E at Delphi," *Morals*.

[180] From Lawrence's Foreword to *Fantasia of the Unconscious*.

[181] Olson sent Creeley a copy of his poem "For Us" (previously unpublished) in his 22 May 1952 letter. See pp. 94–95 above.

[182] Lawrence writes, in his essay on Poe in *Studies in Classic American Literature*, p. 66: "The central law of all organic life is that each organism is intrinsically isolate and single in itself. The moment its isolation breaks down, and there comes an actual mixing and confusion, death sets in.... But the secondary law of all organic life is that each organism only lives through contact with other matter, assimilation, and contact with other life, which means assimilation of new vibrations, non-material. Each individual organism is vivified by intimate contact with fellow organisms: up to a certain point. So man.... Men live by love, but die, or cause death, if they love too much." See also his essay "We Need One Another," *Phoenix* (New York, 1936), passim. "I leave him to his own / devices," Creeley will write in a poem to his son David, "A Variation," *Collected Poems*, p. 38.

[183] See Chapter 2, "Benjamin Franklin," in *Studies in Classic American Literature*. Creeley would write, 27 December 1953, in his review "D. H. Lawrence: *Studies in Classic American Literature*" (*Origin*, no. 13, Summer 1954, pp. 61–62, and *Collected Essays*, p. 198), after mentioning Franklin: "At a time when so much 'revaluation' and 'revising' are the practice, Lawrence can serve the very actual function of showing how it might be done. We have valued, foolishly, the perspective of time alone."

[184] Williams' "An Eternity," in *Collected Later Poems*, pp. 182–83, ll. 1–2, 9–10, 36, and *The Collected Poems*, II, 218–19; and *Paterson*, Book 4, Part III, p. 187.

[185] Corman's 17 May 1952 letter to Creeley opens: "Things worsen financially for ORIGIN, though it seems otherwise to gain adherents. I hope, though I can do no more, that somewhere the wherewithal comes."

[186] Corman's letter does not survive; however, Corman does announce changes in format for *Origin* in a 30 May 1952 letter to Olson.

[187] Charlie ("Yardbird" or more commonly "Bird") Parker (1921–1955), legendary saxophonist whose playing freed up the jazz solo rhythmically as well as melodically and harmonically. Creeley refers to Parker throughout the correspondence, but Olson himself once told an interviewer that "Black Mountain Poetics" did not define postmodernism for the decade of the 1950s: "... there was no poetic. It was Charlie Parker," *Muthologos*, II, p. 71.

Gene Krupa (1909–1973), jazz drummer and band leader, famed for his rimshots and playing speed.

[188] Olson wrote "The Born Dancer," *The Fiery Hunt*, pp. 49–56, based on the life of Vaslav Nijinsky, in the summer of 1951, a year after the Russian dancer's death. See VI.211 and note VI.209.

[189] Pueblo Indian ceremonial dances at their village in northern New Mexico, near the artists' colony in Taos. (Olson's spelling may be a pun on Tao, or The Way.) No record of Millicent Rogers can be found in Olson's papers or address books; an Emelyn N. Rogers was a student at Black Mountain College.

[190] Asadata Dafora wrote and danced lead in "Kykunkor," a dance-drama which combined African ritual and improvisation. Its first performance was in a jury-rigged New York studio in 1934. The Dafora group performed in New York throughout the years of the Spanish Civil War; as late as summer 1938, Dafora's "Companion Piece to 'Kykunkor'" was produced at Davenport Theatre on East 27th Street. Ferry Terminal is located at 23rd Street. See Maurice Goldberg's photograph of Dafora in dance costume in *The New York Times*, 31 July 1938, Sec. X, p. 8, cols. 4–5.

Olson's interest in the staging of African myths was also long-running. As part of a program at Black Mountain called "Exercises in Theatre," for summer session 1949 he adapted, directed, and narrated "The King of the Wood" and "Wagadu" from Sudanese Soninke folktales he found in Frobenius and Fox's *African Genesis*, pp. 97ff. See, e.g., note II.13 and note VI.208.

[191] Olson tells us that he attended New York's Cafe Society Downtown in the company of two of the boogie-woogie revival's greatest artists. In 1939,

the Cafe Society featured The Boogie Woogie Trio, pianists Meade "Lux" Lewis (1905–1964), Albert C. Ammons (1907–1949), and Pete Johnson (1904–1967). Although the authorship of "Blueberry Boogie" is unknown to me, the third member of Olson's illustrious party that night was probably Ammons, who was known for his composition talents. See the lp record *Boogie Woogie Trio*, Storyville, 670.184. (Perhaps Olson is thinking of "Blueberry Hill," a hit co-written by Al Lewis ca. 1940?) Concerning sexual euphemisms in boogie, see Kenneth Rexroth, "Some Thoughts on Jazz as Music, as Revolt, as Mystique," in *Bird in the Bush* (New York, 1959), pp. 28–29.

192 Aristotle, in "The Poetics," XIII, 7 (Allan H. Gilbert, ed., *Literary Criticism: Plato to Dryden*, Detroit, 1962, p. 86), defines the proper tragic hero's error as *hamartia*, or "an error of judgement": "He is not extraordinary in virtue and righteousness, and yet does not fall into bad fortune because of evil and wickedness [*mochtheria*], but because of some error [*hamartia*] of the kind found in men of high reputation and good fortune, such as Oedipus and Thyestes...." And in the "Ethics," III, 2 (p. 86, n. 68): "Obviously every wicked [*mochtheros*] man does not know what he should do and what he should abstain from, and through an error [*hamartia*] of that sort (i.e., dependent on ignorance) men become unjust and wholly bad."

193 Olson is quoting Ruth Benedict, "Psychological Types in the Cultures of the Southwest," *Proceedings of the Twenty-Third International Congress of Americanists* (New York, 1930), p. 577. See I.27.

194 In Olson's 15 April 1953 letter to Jung, he will write that men of "art, much more than science, are your advancers" (*OLSON*, 8, p. 61).

195 Sigismunda Malatesta in the "Malatesta" Cantos, numbers 8 through 11; Ulysses in Cantos 1 (originally published in *Poetry*, August 1917, as latter part of Canto 3), 6 and 7; Confucius in the "Confucian" Cantos, starting with 13 and following nonconsecutively; John Adams in Cantos 62 through 71; the "Chinese history" Cantos, 53 through 61. See Creeley's 19 May letter for what Olson calls "this hot job of yrs."

196 E.g., Lawrence's "Edgar Allan Poe," in *Studies in Classic American Literature*, p. 72: "These terribly conscious birds, like Poe and his Ligeia, deny the very life that is in them; they want to turn it all into talk, into *knowing*. And so life, which will *not* be known, leaves them."

197 See note X.118 above.

198 Cf. V.184.

199 I.e., the Harriet character, Richard Somers' wife, in Lawrence's novel *Kangaroo*. Richard Aldington writes, in his Introduction to The Phoenix Edition (London, 1955), p. x: "This Somers-Harriet contest is one of the

major themes of the book, and marvellously true to the characters of Lawrence and his wife."

200 *Tortoises*, Lawrence's 1921 collection of poems. Lawrence himself classifies his poems according to the periods of influence by Miriam and Helen, two of his early muses (Foreword to *The Collected Poems of D. H. Lawrence*, in *Phoenix*, pp. 251–54); and Kenneth Rexroth's essay, "Poetry, Regeneration, and D. H. Lawrence," *Bird in the Bush*, pp. 181ff., discusses Lawrence's poems in relation to Frieda, Helen, Miriam, and his mother.

201 A scene from Chapter 10 of *Lady Chatterley's Lover* (1928; rpt. Garden City, p. 128), in which Constance Chatterley thinks about Mellors, the gamekeeper: "That thrust of the buttocks, surely it was a little ridiculous. If you were a woman, and apart in all the business, surely the thrusting of the man's buttocks was supremely ridiculous. Surely the man was intensely ridiculous in this posture and this act!"

202 Identifies these female characters from Dostoyevsky with Mary Magdalene, the reformed prostitute mentioned in Luke 8:2. Olson is remembering *The Brothers Karamazov* (1880)—Grushenka, the story's small-town and earthy love interest, and Katerina Ivanovna are rivals—and *Crime and Punishment* (1866)—Sonya is a prostitute of great religious faith who makes possible the protagonist's regeneration at the novel's end. One might also note the real-life tension between Dostoyevsky's first wife, Maria Isaeva (the sensual and crude) and his mistress, Pauline Suslova (the sensual and demoniac).

203 Male characters in *The Brothers Karamazov*. Alyosha is the third Karamazov son (ascetic, representing Christian love); Dimitri is the eldest son; Ivan, the second-born (intellectual, anarchist); Fyodor Pavlovitch, the father (lecher); Smerdyakov, a servant, commits suicide.

204 William Carlos Williams' *A Dream of Love: A Play in Three Acts and Eight Scenes* (New York, 1948; and performed in July 1949 by We Present, Hudson Guild Playhouse, New York), a psychodrama about married life. His wife of many years, Florence "Flossie" Williams.

205 "After the Pleasure Party: Lines Traced Under An Image Of Amor Threatening," the second poem in *Timoleon*. Melville's poem treats a sexual encounter as a metaphor for reality. Olson had read the poem in manuscript (see Butterick, *Guide to The Maximus Poems*, p. 599), and he quotes from the poem in *Call Me Ishmael*, p. 103. See also VIII.71.

206 Perhaps an echo of Lawrence's title for his 1917 collection of poems, *Look! We Have Come Through*.

207 Victor Berard, in *Did Homer Live?*, trans. Brian Rhys (New York, 1931), pp. 185–86, understands *The Odyssey's* Book 11 as part of what he calls a Poem of the Seven (Western) Sea Gates. Pound, for one, worked under the

assumption of conventional scholarship which holds that the Nekuia section, or Book of the Dead, pre-dates the rest of *The Odyssey*.

208 Episodes from *The Odyssey*, Books 6 and 5, respectively. In "Letter for Melville 1951" (*Collected Poems*, p. 239), Olson had written that Melville, a modern Odysseus, "has moved on from Calypso." See also Butterick, *Guide to The Maximus Poems*, pp. 118–19.

209 No handwritten letter survives. Olson's chiefly typed 28 June [1951] letter, which begins "It's a sad and bitter man, greets you, this mawnin," may be the letter he is referring to (VI.89–96).

210 Olson defends "For Us" by arguing that it is formally a poem, not a fragment or a statement, recognizable after Pound's ideogrammic poems. By 1957, Olson *would* develop a doctrine of the black chrysanthemum, the "golden flower" of Chinese (and Medieval) alchemy. His sources for the doctrine are Carl Jung and Richard Wilhelm, *The Secret of the Golden Flower*, and Jung's "Dream Symbolism in Relation to Alchemy." See Butterick, *Guide to The Maximus Poems*, pp. 257–58; OLSON, 3, Spring 1975, pp. 64–74; and the study by Charles Stein, *The Secret of the Black Chrysanthemum* (Barrytown, New York [1987]).

211 A grant from the Wenner-Gren Foundation for Anthropological Research; see note VI.44.

212 Inland river in Buncombe County, North Carolina, near the Black Mountain campus. The lightness of the occasion belies the seriousness of the exact place that the Swannanoa had in Olson's mental map. In an interview in April 1969 with Andrew S. Leinoff (*OLSON*, 8, p. 78), Olson thinks of a society of "fourteen people ... left alone on a mountain" and ponders: "What would have emerged from those fourteen people stuck there, stuck on that sheer rise from the floor of the Swannanoa, of the Swannanoa River, flowing into the French Broad, the French Broad flowing into what? But this is the waters flowing into the Gulf of Mexico, not into the Atlantic Ocean. Black Mountain sat just on the edge of the flow of the rivers the other way—that is, west, and north to the Ohio, and then down, Yeah, from the Broad to the Kanawha, the Kanawha to the Ohio, the Ohio to the Mississippi and down into the Gulf of Mexico. There was a funny thing, that the creek we used to swim in was itself turned the other way, turned inward towards the continent, then down through the middle and out."

213 Corman, in his 30 May 1952 letter to Olson (*Olson & Corman*, pp. 255–56), proposes to issue *Origin* every other month, like the publication schedule for the *Neue Literarische Welt*. Olson's 3 June reply to Corman's letter begins: "CID; *that* raises me! EVERY TWO MONTHS...." (*Olson & Corman*, p. 258).

214 See also *Olson & Corman*, p. 260, concerning M. Elath. A related unpublished essay by Olson, "The Area and the Discipline of Totality," dates from 1953.

215 A manager of Black Mountain College's farm, and brother of Dan Rice.

216 Creeley retyped Olson's letter of 30 March 1952, and probably copied out Olson's 18 March 1952 letter also. Both letters feature Olson's speculations on the noun.

217 German: "spirit of the age." Pound, e.g., explains, in "For a New Paideuma," *Selected Prose*, ed. Cookson, p. 254, that the term Zeitgeist is "passive," while Frobenius' Paideuma is"active." Elath does not use the term "Zeitgeist" in the article Olson is citing ("in Another Direction...," *Intro*, 3/4, pp. 112–36).

Elath on the fourth dimension: "With a person like Burke it is the use of totality which started in reading, developed in writing and which is part of the totality of our times of which Korzybski's use of the 4th dimension is instance" (pp. 112–13); "Methodology is all about us. 4th dimensional ramifications are to us what catholicism was to Dante" (p. 115); "We seem to forget that metaphor is a cross of thoughts not words, and that when the cross is presented in words we have poetry, when it is presented in numbers we have a mathematical correlation of the 4th dimension" (p. 116).

Elath on science: "... Hart Crane ... was moved by the pressure of the 20th century to find some creative integration in the byproducts of early 4th dimensional speculation. Crane tried to find integration in Ouspensky and Whitehead. A year after he died, Korzybski published his *Science and Sanity*, the 4th gut he was searching for" (p. 119); he criticizes Southern New Criticism for believing "The *scientific order is hell* ..." (p. 120). Olson recommends Elath to Cid Corman because "one thing right off the bat which makes ELATH fresh, is, that he is already far enough along to know that the old necessary quarrel with science is passé—that he knows, spang, that *methodology* has displaced 'technique,' that Korsibski [*sic*] is more use to a writer than any of his fellow writers, etc." (*Olson & Corman*, pp. 268–69).

See also Creeley's 13 June 1952 letter below.

217a Olson's metaphor, perhaps suggested by D. H. Lawrence's notion of the collier's instinctiveness in a materialistic age, compares teaching for Black Mountain College with a coal miner's working in the company-owned town typical of Appalachia at the time. Also echoes Williams' "The descent beckons / as the ascent beckoned," from *Paterson*, Book II.

218 Probably Mark Heddon.

219 At the residence of Harvey Breit, author of *There Falls Tom Fool*, the

only book published by the Capricorn Press of Robert Symmes (Duncan). During Olson's 1940 visit to New York, when he also met Cagli and Constance Wilcock (Olson). (A famous meeting of writers, including Williams, Faulkner, Steinbeck, and Saul Bellow, would later take place at Breit's a week after Thanksgiving, 1956—to discuss Pound's imprisonment without trial. See Mariani, *A New World Naked*, pp. 740–41.)

[220] See Olson's "Black Mt. College Has a Few Words for a Visitor" (*Collected Poems*, pp. 268–69), a poem from this period: "o Paul / who has a rougher thought, who knew he could corrupt an army / were it not he had his friends he owed a something to, a rose / perhaps or rose inopportunely on a cop, and there! right on the street / or in the middle of Grand Central Palace, look! he showed / what he did not admit he meant." See also Paul Goodman's "Memoirs of an Ancient Activist," *WIN*, 15 November 1969.

[221] See note IX.166 and VI.135–48.

[222] *Cricket*, an American slang term, meaning "lively at night," and *grillo*, Spanish, for cricket. Olson refers to Cagli as "my cricket" in "Maximus, To Gloucester, Letter #29" (*OLSON*, 6, p. 19).

[223] *Le Fou* would be published in October 1952 for Richard Wirtz Emerson's Golden Goose Press, Columbus, Ohio, in an edition of about 500 copies. Robert Creeley's first book.

[224] Ernst Zander's article "War As A Way Out?" in *Contemporary Issues*, II, no. 7 (Fall 1950) on pp. 155–76 is translated and reprinted from *Dinge der Zeit*, no. 6. (See note 227 below.) His unsigned "Documents of 'The Great Business Partnership' " also appears in translation on pp. 177–80. E. V. Swart's "A Reply To Jackson-Davidson And Cafferey" appears in the same number, on pp. 186–96.

Olson seems to have agreed with Creeley's judgment that Zander is "quite interesting." He writes Creeley years later, in a letter of 1 April 1957, that the editor of *Contemporary Issues*, Philip McDougal, tells him that Zander is Wilhelm Lunen. And Olson will cite Zander prominently in "The Methodology is the Form." See also Olson's references to Zander in *OLSON*, 8, p. 21 and *Charles Olson Reading at Berkeley*, ed. Zoe Brown (San Francisco, 1966), pp. 14–15.

[225] Creeley quotes Zander, "War As A Way Out?", p. 163.

[226] French: "*Let's go!*"

[227] *Dinge der Zeit*, anti-fascist emigre magazine—German version of *Contemporary Issues*—printed in London, starting in July 1947.

[228] E. V. Rieu, trans., Homer, *The Odyssey* (New York and Harmondsworth: Penguin, 1946); W. H. D. Rouse, trans., *The Odyssey* (New York: New American Library, 1937). Robert Graves' translation of *The Golden Ass*

(Harmondsworth: Penguin, 1950); Creeley recommends Book 5. Ovid: *Selected Works*, ed. J. C. and M. J. Thornton (London and New York: Dent and Dutton, 1948); the volume contains Christopher Marlowe's 1598 translation of *The Elegies*, pp. 1–26, Francis Wolferston's 1661 translation of *The Art of Love*, pp. 42–100, and Arthur Golding's 1565 translation of *The Metamorphoses*, pp. 130–391. (Pound recommends and cites the Golding and Marlowe English translations in *ABC of Reading*, pp. 58ff.)

[229] A back issue, *Intro*, no. 2 (1952), pp. 3–26, featured eight poems by William Hull (b. 1918): "The Pied Piper and the Wishing Well," "The Certain Heart," "Quem Quaeritis?," "Dandy In Paradise Bar," "Metamorphosis: or How Amanda Turned to Mabel," "Will the Match Wind Globeless Blow?," "Abbess Heloise To Abbott Abelard," and "Phoenix In Our Woodlessness." In fact, only one poem by Hull was printed in *Golden Goose*, series 3, no. 1 (1951)—"Variations on a Wellknown Theme," p. 46. Creeley continues his comments on Hull's poems in his 17 June 1952 letter below.

[230] *Ding an sich*: German, "the thing in itself"; a Kantian term.

[231] Passages on Charles I. Glicksberg, the New Critical anthologist, and Ezra Pound found in Elath's "In Another Direction…," *Intro*, 3/4, pp. 120 and 115–16, respectively.

[232] Olson's letter to Corman, 13 [and 14 June 1952], in *Olson & Corman*, pp. 265–76. Much of this paragraph is reworked from the Corman letter on p. 273.

[233] See, e.g., note VI.175; VII.240–41; note VIII.5; and "Tutorial: the Greeks," in *OLSON*, 2, p. 45.

[234] From this point to the passage "by hab[itual] … prac[tice] … [and] order[liness] and regularity in act[ion]," Olson is quoting from his letter to Corman (cf., *Olson & Corman*, pp. 274–76).

[235] I.e., Olson thinks "meta hodos" to better suit his philology than "methodos." Etymology from *Webster's Collegiate Dictionary*, 5th ed.; used by Olson in "Note on Methodology," *OLSON*, 8, p. 43, and in "A Bibliography on America," *Additional Prose*, p. 8.

[236] German: "the way dies." Olson adapts the phrase from Frobenius' *African Genesis* and uses it three times in his essay "Human Universe." In *The Special View of History*, ed. Ann Charters (Berkeley, 1970), Olson explains methodology "as the correct application of the old Western conception of *The Way* and the Eastern conception of *the Tao* (the Way is the path, follow me etc. of Christianity, the 'Law' literally in Judaism, etc.—the 'light,' say. Or, most excitingly for me, the African 'Der Weg,' as in the folk tale in which Der Weg stirbt—dies" (p. 54). Cf. Pound's Tao

(The Way, or The Process), and see *The Pound Era*, pp. 454–59.

[237] Olson quotes from the definition of the word "path" in his *Webster's Collegiate Dictionary*, 5th ed., p. 629.

[238] Cf., *Olson & Corman*, p. 276.

[239] The citations that follow in the letter are from Pierre Boulez's part in "4 musicians at work," *trans/formation*, I, no. 3 (1952), pp. 170ff. Olson previously quotes from the article in his 13 [and 14 June 1952] letter to Corman, *Olson & Corman*, pp. 271–72.

[240] French: "serial order." Olson would write to Donald Sutherland, 21 January 1968, that he was first interested in Boulez's "Second Sonata" because of its "formalization of the use of chance by a *series* of series into which the accidence was spilled, and *then* used...." See also Olson's "*Paris Review* Interview," in *Muthologos*, II, 122.

[241] See, e.g., Olson's poem "A Toss for John Cage," *Collected Poems*, pp. 271–73.

[242] Olson's desire to work in Mesopotamia led him, in October 1951, to apply for a Fulbright lectureship in American Studies to Istanbul or Tehran. His application was rejected on 30 March 1952, but he was reapplying for an opening in Iraq. Olson spoke of culminating his long studies of Sumerian and Mayan civilizations in a book he planned to call *The Transpositions*; see *Olson & Corman*, pp. 280–81.

[243] I.e., Max Dehn; see note VII.135.

[244] Mentioned in Creeley's 4 May 1952 letter to Olson, above.

[245] For Robert H. Barlow, see IV.134 and note 64 there. Edgar Anderson, then assistant director of The Missouri Botanical Garden, and author of "Maize in the Hills of Assam," in his *Plants, Man and Life* (Boston, 1952). Mentioned in "A Bibliography on America," *Additional Prose*, p. 13, and *The Maximus Poems*, p. 98 (reference to "the history of weeds").

[246] *Spirit Above the Dust* (London, 1951). Olson would review Mason's book in "The Materials and Weights of Herman Melville" (*Human Universe*, pp. 109–16), and send him an early copy of the poem "The Collected Poems Of" (*Collected Poems*, pp. 278–82) in a 10 May 1953 letter.

[247] See especially: John Freeman, *Herman Melville* (London, 1926); Lewis Mumford, *Herman Melville* (New York, 1929); F. O. Matthiessen, *American Renaissance* (New York, 1941), esp. p. xviii; William Ellery Sedgwich, *Herman Melville: The Tragedy of Mind* (Cambridge, Mass., 1944); Jay Leda, *The Melville Log*, 2 vols. (New York, 1951); Richard Chase, *Herman Melville: A Critical Study* (New York, 1949) and "Melville's Confidence Man," in *Kenyon Review*, no. 11 (Winter 1949), pp. 122–40; Newton Arvin, *Herman Melville* (New York, 1950); W. H. Auden, *The Enchafed Flood* (New York,

1950); Raymond M. Weaver, *Herman Melville, Mariner and Mystic* (New York, 1921); Lawrence, the two chapters on Melville in *Studies in Classic American Literature*; Edward Dahlberg, to whom Olson dedicated Part 4 of *Call Me Ishmael* (see also Ann Charters, *Olson/Melville: A Study in Affinity*, Berkeley, 1968, pp. 5 and 8). Cf. this list of Melville scholars with ones in Olson's "The Materials and Weights of Herman Melville," *Human Universe*, and note VIII.137.

248 Mason makes 10 references to William Blake in *Spirit Above the Dust*. E.g., on p. 48: "Like Blake, Melville had too little hold on tradition to find any comfort there. He had only his own irresponsible imagination out of which to build his defiance. Blake's *Prophetic Books* and Melville's *Mardi* share a common heroism and a common failure." Mason's Melville is "Blakean" as a poet of the Imagination, whereas Olson's Melville (to paraphrase Melville's review of "The Mosses") is an author of the Truth. Interestingly, Mason was not a professional Blake scholar but, at the time of his Melville study, a British cricket commentator.

249 In Creeley's 13 June 1952 letter to Olson above.

250 William Hull's poem "Ex Tempore" does not appear in *Golden Goose*.

251 Elath's comments on the poems of William Hull are probably from correspondence now lost. It is interesting to note that Elath, in spite of the light in which Creeley presents his criticisms of Hull's work here, would send poems by Hull to Olson in a letter of early March 1956.

252 E.g., Lawrence's comments on Joyce's serialized "Work in Progress," in letters from the time of the trial of *Lady Chatterley's Lover*: "What a stupid *olla podrida* of the Bible and so forth James Joyce is: just stewed-up fragments of quotation in the sauce of a would-be-dirty mind" and "My God, what a clumsy *olla putrida* James Joyce is! Nothing but old fags and cabbage-stumps of quotations from the Bible and the rest, stewed in the juice of deliberate, journalistic dirty-mindedness..." (*The Letters*, Vol. VI, Cambridge, pp. 507, 508).

253 Olson's 1 June 1952 letter to Creeley.

254 Events recounted in Creeley's poem "Hart Crane" (*Collected Poems*, pp. 109–10), dedicated to Slater Brown. In "The Broken Tower" (*The Poems*, ed. Marc Simon, New York, 1986, p. 160), Crane declares that as a younger poet he had "entered the broken world / to trace the visionary company of love, its voice"—certainly a theme and a disappointment that speaks through Creeley's poems in *For Love*. Creeley calls Brown, in "Hart Crane and the Private Judgment" (*The Collected Essays*, p. 21): "the best friend [Crane] ever had."

255 A passage in "Letter for Melville 1951," *Collected Poems*, p. 236:

> Was writing
>
> *Pierre*: the world
>
> had moved on, in that hallway, moved
>
> north north east, had moved him

256 Williams' Poe, *In the American Grain*, pp. 224–25, is the enraged author of "Longfellow and Other Plagiarisms," who feels he has been misused by establishment writers such as Henry Wadsworth Longfellow and James Russell Lowell.

257 Jacquetta Hawkes, *A Guide to Prehistoric and Roman Monuments in England and Wales* (London, 1951) and her *A Land; with drawings by Henry Moore* (London, 1951); and Bronislaw Malinowski, *Freedom and Civilization* (New York, 1944).

258 C. G. Jung and C[arl] Kerényi, *Introduction to a Science of Mythology: The Myth of the Divine Child and the Mysteries of Eleusis,* trans. R.F.C. Hull (London, 1951), reprinted from the Bollingen Series 22 edition (New York, 1949).

259 Creeley would later write about Charlie Parker, and especially on listening to Parker playing "I've got Rhythm," in relation to poetry, not prose, in "Notes Apropos 'Free Verse' " and "Form" (*The Collected Essays*, pp. 494, 591).

260 Ross Russell writes, in *Bird Lives!* (New York, 1973), that in 1946 "Charlie spoke of his future and frustrated ambitions. He had been told that Igor Stravinsky and Arnold Schoenberg had made their permanent home[s] in Southern California, and he now saw the area in a new light. He wanted a home of his own.... He wanted to listen to everything by Stravinsky and Schoenberg, and Hindemith, Bartok, Varese, and Alban Berg as well" (p. 209). And Russell quotes Louis Gottlieb, who was studying composition with Schoenberg at UCLA in the mid-1940s, as saying that Parker "'loved to discuss the merits of the two greatest musical minds of the century: Schoenberg and Charlie Parker' " (p. 207).

261 Probably an amalgam of Poundian sayings. E.g., in "Affirmations," Pound declares that "Superficial capability needs no invention whatsoever, but a great energy has, of necessity, its many attendant inventions" (*Selected Prose*, ed. Cookson, p. 347). In "I Gather the Limbs of Osiris," he counsels the would-be poet concerning his training in rhyme in this way: "If he is to learn it with the least waste of energy, he might well study it in the work not of its greatest master, but of the man who first considered it critically, tried and tested it, and controlled it from the most diverse angles of attack" (p. 42); in the same essay series, Pound gives us an allegory of the engineering lab where "The latent energy is made

dynamic or 'revealed' to the engineer in control, and placed at his disposal" (p. 25).

262 Richard Henry Dana, Jr., *Two Years Before the Mast* (1840). Dana sailed to California upon graduation from Harvard College and reported his adventures in a documentary style later employed by Francis Parkman in *The Oregon Trail*. J. Hector St. John Crèvecoeur, "The American Farmer" (1735–1813), French-born U.S. author of the 12 essays published in London as *Letters From an American Farmer* (1782); revised and expanded in *Lettres d'un Cultivateur Américain*, 2 vols. (Paris, 1784).

263 The book, with Laubiès' lithographs, was never printed. Creeley's [18 June 1952] typescript, collecting the stories "Mr Blue," "The Party," "3 Fate Tales," and "The Grace," is housed at Simon Fraser University.

264 "Our Civilized World," a standing column, in *Contemporary Issues*, IV, no. 11 (Summer 1952), p. 158, excerpts the following from *The Evening Standard* of 18 December 1951: "Gloom has reigned in the Camembert district of Normandy because it was discovered that a recent falling off in the standard of the world-famous cheese was due to penicillin injections being given to Normandy cows against certain infections.…"

265 Lines from an uncollected early poem by Eigner (1928–1996), who does not appear earlier in Creeley's surviving letters to Olson. Eigner's disease, which may be the necessity behind the broken rhythms of his poems and certainly made typing for him a difficult physical act, conspired with a facility for poetry, which was to produce over 3000 poems in his career, to enable him to arrive independently at a projective-like poetics of body and intellect.

266 "A Fete," which Donald Allen would publish in the breakthrough anthology *The New American Poetry* (New York and London, 1960), p. 90. Creeley originally published the poem, untitled, in *Black Mountain Review*, no. 1 (Spring 1954), p. 59.

267 In *From the Sustaining Air* (Eugene, Oregon, 1967), p. 10, reprint of the book Creeley first published at Divers Press in 1953. Eigner had sent "Parts of Salem" in his 2 May 1952 letter to Creeley. He had more recently enclosed carbon copies, in his 18 June 1952 letter to Creeley, of the following poems: "By-pass," "Day Crowd Weather," "Even," "[A] Fete," "Heart," "Midnight birds," and "Sunday." By November 1952, Creeley would ask Eigner for a book-length manuscript of poems to publish at Divers Press.

268 An untitled poem by Larry Eigner, beginning "in the blackout…," had appeared in *Goad*, no. 3 (Summer 1952), p. 21.

269 Lines from an uncollected early poem by Eigner.

270 Pablo Casals (1876–1973), renowned Spanish cellist and conductor. See also VIII.54 and note 32 there. The man is Creeley's gardener, Monsieur Marti, to whom the poet will dedicate "After Lorca."

271 Lines 2–3 of Corman's "Episodic Sonnet" read "… the plump / pressures of your breasts …" (*Golden Goose*, Series III, no. 3, April 1952, p. 125). It is Creeley who uses the word "tits" in his own poem "The Question," sent to Olson in the 13 June 1952 letter above.

272 Passage in Olson's [5 March 1951] letter to Creeley, from Lerma, Campeche (V.46).

273 Passage from Edward G. Boulenger, *Zoo Animals*, Puffin Picture Book no. 73 (West Drayton, England, 1948).

274 Creeley's reading list follows. *A Voyage Round the World in the Years 1740–4 by Lord Anson* (1748), Everyman's Library (London, 1942), an account by Richard Walter, who served as chaplain to British admiral George Anson (1697–1762) on a world voyage. *The Principal Navigations, Voyages, Traffiques and Discoveries of the English Nation* by Richard Hakluyt (ca. 1552–1616), British geographer and enthusiast for the exploration of "The Northwest Passage," ed. Ernest Rhys, Everyman's Library nos. 264–65, 313–14, 338–39, 388–898, in 8 vols. (London and New York, 1926–1936). Xenophon's *The Persian Expedition*, trans. Rex Warner (Harmondsworth, 1949).

275 Cf., Creeley's later Preface to *The Gold Diggers* (London, 1965), p. 7: "Had I lived some years ago, I think I would have been a moralist, i.e., one who lays down, so to speak, rules of behaviour with no small amount of self-satisfaction. But the writer isn't allowed that function anymore, or no man can take the job on very happily, being aware (as he must be) of what precisely that will make him."

276 *The Persian Expedition*, trans. Rex Warner, pp. 99 and 106–07.

277 *Pausanias's Description of Greece*, trans. J. G. Frazer, 6 vols., 2nd ed. (London, 1913). Copy in Olson's library a gift from Creeley ca. 1956.

278 Lucretius, *On the Nature of the Universe*, trans. Ronald Latham (Baltimore and London, 1951), p. 99.

279 *On the Nature of the Universe*, trans. Ronald Latham, p. 98.

280 Passages concerning the drowning of sailor George Ballmer in Chapter 6 of *Two Years Before the Mast*.

281 Jacquetta and C. F. Hawkes, *Prehistoric Britain* (rev. ed.: Harmondsworth and New York, 1949). Creeley's confusion here results from the British archaeologist's publication of books and articles under a variety of names, including C. F. Hawkes, C.F.C. Hawkes, Charles Francis Christopher Hawkes, and Christopher Hawkes. Jacquetta Hawkes (b. 1910) was

his first wife and early collaborator. Our own study is further confused by the appearance of a second wife and later collaborator, the Sonia Chadwich Hawkes who co-edited *Greeks, Celts, and Romans* (Totowa, New Jersey, 1973) and co-authored "The Finglesham Man," *Antiquity*, no. 39 (March 1965), pp. 17–32, an article to which Olson refers in "*Vinland Map* Review," *Additional Prose*, p. 61. See also Duberman, *Black Mountain*, p. 343.

[282] Preface to Fernand Windels, *The Lascaux Cave Paintings*, trans. C. F. Hawkes, with a Personal Note by Henry Breuil (London, 1949).

[283] Creeley's 17 June 1952 letter above and Creeley's poem "The Festival."

[284] In Edith Wharton's short novel *Ethan Frome* (New York, 1911). Her character Frome is bound to his severe New England farm life, and Mattie Silver appears as his only savior. Just before the book's epilogue, however, they suffer a nocturnal snow-sled accident, a turn of events which leaves Mattie a hopeless convalescent and Frome without hope. Creeley, after the experience of farm life in New Hampshire, could not have missed Olson's point.

[285] Perhaps the reference is to the Irish ballad "Brian O Linn"—see *The Faber Book of Ballads*, ed. Matthew Hodgart (London, 1965), p. 200—and its stanza: "Brian O Linn, his wife and wife's mother, / They all lay down in the bed together, / The sheets they were old and the blankets were thin, / 'Lie close to the wall,' says Brian O Linn."

[286] Creeley has already quoted the passage from Elath's review "In Another Direction...," in his 15 May 1952 letter above and note 70; see especially p. 116 of the *Intro* review.

[287] In Keats' famous 22 November 1817 letter to Benjamin Bailey: "... O for a Life of Sensations rather than of thoughts!" Olson quotes the passage in "Projective Verse," and *Poetry and Truth*, p. 48.

[288] Olson mistakes 1429, the year of the teenaged Sigismundo Malatesta's military defense of Rimini, for 1438, the actual date of Gemisthus' arrival in Italy and the start of the Renaissance. See note 97 above. By 1919, at the end of World War I, Pound had written Cantos 14 and 15, the "Hell" Cantos, which he explained were a portrait of London. See V.51 and Olson's well-known remarks on "why i don't think Ez's toucan works after 1917...."

[289] See VI.24 and note 16 there.

[290] Olson must mean that he talked to Black Mountain business manager Wesley Huss "before going to" the Board of Fellows; no mention of Olson on Gerhardt in the minutes for June 1952.

[291] Creeley's letter of 20 June 1952, which Constance Olson forwards from Black Mountain to Washington.

[292] The world light heavyweight title was retained, 25 June 1952, by Joey Maxim when "Sugar" Ray Robinson, the world's middleweight champion who was winning the fight on points, could not answer the bell for the fourteenth round. In 104-degree heat in Yankee Stadium, referee Ruby Goldstein left after the tenth round, suffering from heat prostration.

[293] Olson would never publish "There are Sounds ..." (*Collected Poems*, pp. 196–97). The original version was written ca. 24 August and 28 November 1950. See III.150–53, and the photograph following p. 81 there.

[294] Creeley's unpublished poem "The Lions" notes the price of post-war coal in Europe; see the poem in his 26 March 1952 letter to Olson, and his comment on coal in his letter of the following day (IX.194–96).

[295] Creeley's "The Question" (*Collected Poems*, p. 35); he quotes the first three lines below.

[296] I.e., "The Festival" (*Collected Poems*, p. 27). Creeley does decide to publish the poem—it appeared in *Goad*, I, no. 3 (Summer 1952), p 22—but collects it only later, in *The Charm: Early and Uncollected Poems* (San Francisco, 1969).

[297] In *On the Nature of the Universe*, trans. Ronald Latham, p. 108. The quotations following in the paragraph are from pp. 121 and 156.

[298] Carl Kerényi quotes from Bronislaw Malinowski's *Myth in Primitive Psychology* (London, 1926) in his "Prolegomena" to Jung and Kerényi, *Introduction to a Science of Mythology*, p. 7; Creeley quotes the passage in his 29 June 1952 letter to Olson below. Olson quotes Malinowski in his [25 October 1950] letter to Creeley (III.135–36), and in early versions of the "Human Universe" essay.

[299] In "The Psychology of the Child Archetype," in Jung and Kerényi, *Introduction to a Science of Mythology*, esp. p. 100, Jung writes that the child archetype can be rationally studied as myths and fairy tales, but as dreams and psychotic fantasy it presents us with "a generally unintelligible, irrational, not to say delirious sequence of images which nonetheless does not lack a certain hidden coherence." And on p. 109: "Not for a moment dare we succumb to the illusion that an archetype can be finally explained and disposed of. Even the best attempts at explanation are only more or less successful translations into another metaphorical language.... The most we can do is *dream the myth onwards* and give it a modern dress. And whatever explanation or interpretation does to it, we do to our own souls as well...."

[300] Jung in *Introduction to a Science of Mythology*, p. 101.

[301] Kerényi in *Introduction to a Science of Mythology*, p. 10; Creeley has left blanks for but neglected to transcribe the Greek words αἴτιον and ἀρχή,

which R.F.C. Hull has translated as "the 'Why?' " and "the 'Whence?' "

302 "The New Odyssey," Creeley's unpublished review of *Introduction to A Science of Mythology* (among Creeley's papers at Stanford University). Creeley copies out the essay for Olson in his 29 June 1952 letter below.

303 Northrop Frye, "The Archetypes of Literature," in *Kenyon Review*, XIII, no. 1 (Winter 1951), writes (p. 110) that "Yeats's 'Sailing to Byzantium,' to take a famous example of the comic vision at random, has [the archetypes of] the city, the tree, the bird, the community of sages, the geometrical gyre and the detachment from the cyclic world." It is worth noting that Creeley's story "The Unsuccessful Husband" is printed some pages earlier in the journal.

304 Fun reference to Da Vinci's voluminous drawings for hot-air balloons and flying machines. Cf., *Paterson*, Book 4, p. 190: "a whirring pterodactyl / of a contrivance, to remind me of Da Vinci"; or Marianne Moore's "The Pangolin," in *A Marianne Moore Reader* (New York, 1965), pp. 39–39, and its reference to "miniature artist engineer ... Leonardo," and the line: "A sailboat / was the first machine...."

305 Probably Williams' reading at Brandeis, in the third week of June, 1952. See also *Olson & Corman*, p. 257.

306 Creeley has written to Olson, at various times in the correspondence, about all three men. Ludwig Lewissohn (1882–1955), author of the study *Goethe, the Story of a Man* (New York, 1949), and books of poems including *Breathe Upon These* (Indianapolis and New York, 1944) and *For Ever Wilt Thou Love* (New York, 1939) is mentioned in III.156, and IV.14–16, 84. He refers to Shapiro in I.103 and III.17. Creeley would note, disapprovingly characterizing the false standards of the 1940s in his Introduction to *The New Writing in the U.S.A.* (Middlesex, England, 1967), that "it is Karl Shapiro's *Essay on Rime* (written in the South Pacific at a military base, 'without access to books,' in iambic pentameter) which is successful, and Auden is the measure of competence." Peter Viereck (b. 1916), author of "Beyond Revolt: The Education of a Poet," in *The Arts in Renewal* (New York, 1961), and books of poems including *Terror and Decorum* (New York, 1948) and *Strike Through the Mask!* (New York, 1950). See also II.55, and V.122, 124.

307 Refrain from "Peace On Earth," which Helen Creeley Axt says is a poem Lewissohn "could handle" because it opens Williams' modest first book, *The Tempers* (London, 1913); *The Collected Poems*, I, 3.

308 "The Use of Force," a story in *Life Along the Passaic River* (Norfolk, Connecticut, 1938), collected in *The Farmer's Daughters* (New York, 1961), pp. 131–35.

309 French: "Too bad; never mind."

[310] Creeley's unpublished review, below, of Jung and Kerényi's *A Science of Mythology*.

[311] Perhaps the passage on Kate's watch at the end of Chapter 7 of *The Plumed Serpent* (New York, 1966), p. 129, a novel otherwise dominated by the sound of drums.

[312] Williams' refrain, coming at the conclusion of *Paterson*, Book 4 (1951), which Creeley reads as a corrective to the opening Pound chose for his *Cantos*: "And then went down to the ship...." Here "final" because Williams meant it to be the last book of the "long poem in four parts," according to his original plan announced in "Author's Notes," p. [7].

[313] In *Paterson*, Book 4, Williams' concern for documenting experience spans the historical (a reference to a hanging of 30 April 1850 appears on p. 238) and the personal ("Turn back I warn you / (October 10, 1950)," on p. 234). Not to be confused with Pound's Fascist-style dating of the Money Pamphlets and his letters from Italy, starting from 1922 and Mussolini's March on Rome (e.g., "Anno X" for 1932, etc.).

[314] Six *Money Pamphlets by £* (London, 1950–52), were published by Peter Russell, editor of *Nine* magazine and founder of the Pound Society in England; the first four pamphlets are reprinted in Pound's *Selected Prose*, ed. William Cookson (London and New York, 1973). Pound's term "the increment of association," which Creeley explicates as "usage coheres value," appears passim. Creeley quotes it for publication in his essay "To Define," in *Nine American Poets* (Liverpool, 1953), p. 2 and *Collected Essays*, p. 473.

[315] Walter W. Skeat, comp., *An Etymological Dictionary of the English Language* (Oxford, 1882), which Creeley has been using as he reads *The Pisan Cantos*. See, e.g., Kenner's *The Pound Era*, pp. 99ff. on the influence of Skeat's *Dictionary* on the generation of Pound and Joyce.

[316] Not found in Pound's *Money Pamphlets*, but a line from Canto 76, *The Pisan Cantos* (New York, 1948) and *The Cantos*, p. 459.

[317] German: "world-sorrow," and "anxiety, fear."

[318] Malinowski as cited by Kerényi, in *Introduction to a Science of Mythology*, p. 7. See note X.298 above.

[319] Cf. Jung, in *Introduction to a Science of Mythology*, p. 102: "A tribe's mythology is its living religion, whose loss is always and everywhere, even among the civilized, a moral catastrophe. But religion is a vital link with psychic processes independent of and beyond consciousness, in the dark hinterland of the psyche."

[320] Jung, in *Introduction to a Science of Mythology*, p. 101.

[321] Jung, in *Introduction to a Science of Mythology*, p. 101.

322 Pound wrote, in *Guide to Kulchur*, p. 194: "There is no mystery about the Cantos, they are the tale of the tribe—give Rudyard credit for his use of the phrase." The phrase appears in Rudyard Kipling, "Literature," in *A Book of Words*, Vol. XXXII of *The Writings in Prose and Verse* (New York, 1928), pp. 3–4, 6. Pound further explained, in notes he dictated to James Laughlin (*Pound As Wuz*, p. 111): "*Cantares*—the Tale of the Tribe. To give the truth of history. Where Dante mentions a name, EP tries to give the gist of what the man was doing." See also Creeley, "Why Pound!?!", in *Collected Essays*, p. 29.

323 The following citations are from Kerényi's "Prolegomena" and Jung's "The Psychology of the Child Archetype" in *Introduction to A Science of Mythology*, pp. 8 and 100 respectively.

324 Obscure. A play on "ascend to"?

325 Lawrence's short story "Sun," in *The Short Stories of D. H. Lawrence*, II, 246–63.

326 The title story in Lawrence's *The Captain's Doll: Three Novelettes* (New York, 1923).

327 Apparently, Creeley here refers to Olson's laborious rewrite of the passages on the Mayan sun-moon myths that occupy the last pages of the "Human Universe" essay (see VII.215). Cf. Olson's broadside "Olson, Sex And/Or Gender; Distinctions of Sun and Moon, After Frobenius," *Matter/Fact Sheet* 2, n.d.p. The first draft of "Human Universe" (then called "The Human Universe") is reprinted as Appendix A in Albert Glover, "Charles Olson: Letters for *Origin*," Ph.D. diss., SUNY at Buffalo, 1968, pp. 258–90.

328 See Olson's 25 June letter to Creeley above.

329 Here Canadian poet and editor Raymond Souster (b. 1921) comes into the correspondence. *Contact*, the mimeographed magazine he edited out of Toronto from 1951 to 1954, would prove an important outlet for new writing by Olson and especially Creeley, starting with "A Note on Poetry" (which Souster culled from Creeley's letter to him of 15 July 1952) in *Contact*, no. 2 (February–April 1953), pp. 14–16. But Souster begins his printing of Olson and others by reprinting poems in *Contact*, no. 3 (May–July 1952). Reprinted from *Origin*, 1 are the following poems: Olson's "I, Maximus of Gloucester, To You," on pp. 9–12; William Bronk's "A Rain of Small Occurences" (original "The Rain...") and "A Winter Shrub," pp. 1, 5; and Samuel French Morse's "An Intervale" and "Midsummer," on pp. 5, 12. The number also contains an article by Corman, "A NOTE ON *ORIGIN*," which names Olson "the key figure" (pp. 15–16). Creeley's poem "The Question" would be published in *Origin*, no. 7

(Autumn 1952), p. 181. Souster, prompted by Creeley, first writes to Olson on 12 July 1952.

330 Royalties paid Creeley for "How to Write a Novel," a review of John Hawkes' *The Beetle Leg*, which appeared in Lash's *New Mexico Quarterly*, XXII, no. 2 (Summer 1952), pp. 239–41.

331 *Gink*: slang for an odd boy, from Scots "ginkie," a term for reproving a woman.

332 Vincent Ferrini's project is *Nine American Poets*, edited by Robert Cooper in Liverpool, and published as *Artisan*, no. 2 (Spring 1953). Contents by Creeley are the poems "The Crisis," "The Riddle," "The Kind of Act of," and "The Innocence"; prose piece "To define." Raoul Denney (b. 1913) was, at the time of the letter, an associate professor of social sciences at the University of Chicago; he was made the 1939 Yale Younger Poet for his *The Connecticut River and Other Poems*. Creeley remarks on the unfocused miscellany of poets included in the pages of *Origin*, comparing the practice to Louis Untermeyer's mainstream anthology *Modern American Poetry, A Critical Anthology*, in many editions including the "mid-century edition" (New York, 1950).

333 Souster reprints the fifth section (or "montage") from the Werner Heider and Joanna Jalowetz translation, "edited" by Corman for *Origin*, 4, of Gerhardt's "Letter For Creeley And Olson," on pp. 191–92. Creeley will develop his criticism in a 15 July 1952 letter to Olson.

334 Following are Creeley's proposed titles for unpublished prose brought to his attention by Olson in the correspondence; see especially Olson's 15 June 1952 letter above, IV.134 and its note 64, and VI.195 and its note 200.

335 The revised version of "There Are Sounds…," which Olson typed out in his 26 June letter above. Olson had sent an early version of the poem to Creeley in November, 1950; see III.150–53 for Olson's draft and Creeley's comments, and the photograph following p. 81 there.

336 Probably Alfred Korzybski's *Science and Sanity: An Introduction to Non-Aristotelian Systems and General Semantics*. The 3rd edition (Lakeville, Connecticut, 1949) is in Olson's library at the University of Connecticut.

337 Perhaps Corman's "First Farm North," with its dedication to the Creeleys, which had appeared in the Creeley *Origin*, 2, pp. 69–70. The poem was first collected in *The Precisions* (Corona, New York, 1955), pp. [9–10], printed at Divers Press.

338 *Ferrini & Others*, edited anonymously by Vincent Ferrini (Gloucester, Massachusetts, [1953]). Creeley will specify his complaint in a letter to Olson of 15 July 1952.

[339] See Olson's 25 June letter above for his query concerning the line from Creeley's "The Question."

[340] Creeley's example of academic myopia is supplied by Donald C. Dorian, then of Rutgers University, whose close reading of the word "days" in Milton's sonnet "On His Blindness" appears in *The Explicator*, X, no. 3 (December 1951), pp. [4–5].

[341] D. Jon Grossman, a slavish disciple of Pound, was a frequent contributor to the first numbers of *Points*, a bilingual journal which had been in publication since February 1949. Starting with the double number 11/12, in November 1952, Grossman served *Points* as its poetry editor. The young Grossman's borrowing of elder-statesman Pound's high-handed, pedantic essay style did not wear well with the readers of *Points*, however, and he would be asked to resign following number 16 after a flurry of letters to the editors calling for his head. Creeley quotes from Grossman's letter to the editor, published in *Points*, no. 9 (February–April 1951), p. 89, in which he defends his essay on Evelyn Waugh ("Decline And Fall Or A Handfull [sic] of Novels," which had appeared in *Points*, no. 8, pp. 57–73).

[342] Perhaps Robert Duncan's "Africa Revisited," which Olson probably sent in response to Creeley's request for material for the American issue of *Fragmente*. The poem would appear that summer in *Origin*, 6, pp. 80–86 (Olson acknowledges receipt of his copy in October, *Olson & Corman*, p. 291); collected in *A Book of Resemblances* (New Haven, 1966).

[343] Lines 3–5 from Paul Blackburn's "What the Tide Gave," in *Collected Poems*, p. 19.

[344] Blackburn's poem "The Birds" was published in *Origin*, p. 76. See V.59 and note 54 there.

[345] The opening line of Williams' "The End of the Parade," in *Collected Later Poems*, p. 45 and *Collected Poems*, II, 20; a line often cited by Creeley in the correspondence.

[346] Louis Bromfield (1896–1956) Pulitzer Prize–winning author and the gentleman farmer of Malabar Farm, in Ohio.

[347] I.e., Ocracoke, resort island in the Outer Banks chain off the North Carolina shore.

[348] French: "slump, crisis." Olson only hints to Creeley concerning his marital problems, but will dramatically announce in his note of 9 November [1952]: "Con left me some weeks ago...."

[349] *The Decisive Moment: Photographs by Henri Cartier-Bresson* (New York, in collaboration with Editions Verve, Paris, 1952); 126 photographs, and a cover by Matisse.

350 See Creeley's "The New Odyssey," in his letter of 29 June 1952 above.

351 In 1927, perhaps an act as president of his class at Worcester's Classical High School, or as captain of the debating team there?

352 Perhaps from "cethyn," obsolete form of *seethe* (*OED*), meaning "to boil, to stew." Or from the Anglo-Irish "cess," as in the phrase *Bad cess to you!* (meaning "May ill luck befall you")?

353 A collection of examples of fatuity. See note IV. 148. Also, Pound writes, in "A Visiting Card" (*Selected Prose*, ed. Cookson, p. 302), that "Flaubert published his *sottisier*."

354 In the opening of Chapter 7, "And in the Open Air," *The Brothers Karamazov*.

355 In Chapter 7, "The Nightmare," *Kangaroo*, where Richard Somers tells of his own military physical examination, and of an assistant chemist's cruel and humiliating examination of a collier's rectum.

356 Creeley's ideal reading list for the kind of courses on narrative prose that he thought to offer at Black Mountain. Cf. Olson's ideal course description for Beginning Prose, "Black Mountain College Courses of Instruction, 1954," in *OLSON*, 2, p. 39.

357 The vehicle of Olson's metaphor is the uncut fingernails favored by the mandarins, or high officials, of the Chinese Empires. His contemporary reference is to "Ex Tempore," a poem by William Hull, and its line "...I am passion clipped from a mandarin's nail..." (*Golden Goose*, Series III, no. 3, April 1952, p. 118), which Olson read in Creeley's 17 June letter, p. 160 above.

358 Novelist Thomas Mann (1875–1955) was born in Lübeck, Germany. In 1900, he published *Buddenbrooks*, a study of a Lübeck family. Olson is slighting the novels Mann wrote during his long exile in the U.S. during and after World War II. Olson told Pound that his mother's name was Lybeck; see I.51 and note I.49.

359 A familiar Olson citation, which he attributes to Rimbaud; see notes V.66 and IX.65.

360 Keats coins the term "egotistical sublime," in reference to Wordsworth, in his 27 October 1818 letter to Richard Woodhouse. In Keats' famous 27 (?) December 1817 letter to George and Thomas Keats, he defines "*Negative Capability*": "...that is when man is capable of being in uncertainties, Mysteries, doubts, without any irritable reaching after fact & reason...." Olson mentions "negative capability" in "Projective Verse" and "Equal, That Is, to the Real Itself."

361 I.e., Lawrence's essay "We Need One Another," in *Phoenix*, ed. Edward D. McDonald (New York, 1936), pp. 188–95.

362 Frieda Lawrence, wife of Professor Ernest Weekley when Lawrence eloped with her in 1912. And Susette Gontard, the wife of Hölderlin's employer, whom he met and fell in love with in 1796. Her identity as Diotima in the poems was not established until 1921. The name Diotima comes from Plato's *Symposium*, in which she is the priestess of Love. When J. F. Gontard's jealousy forced Hölderlin to leave his Diotima, the poet suffered a nervous breakdown; at the news of her death, in 1802, Hölderlin became schizophrenic.

363 Radio commercial jingle for Gillette razor blades.

364 Olson typed out "Idle Idyll" and "The Leader" for Creeley. "Idle Idyll" was sent to Souster for *Contact*, in Olson's ca. 11 August 1952 letter, but remained unpublished until *A Nation of Nothing But Poetry*, pp. 91–92. Olson sent "The Leader" to Corman in his 12 July 1952 letter; the poem was finally printed in *Archaeologist of Morning*, p. [85], and reprinted in *Collected Poems*, pp. 273–74.

I. Index of Persons Named in the Letters

II. Index of Works by Charles Olson and Robert Creeley Cited in the Text

Printed August 1996 in Santa Barbara
& Ann Arbor for the Black Sparrow Press by
Mackintosh Typography & Edwards Brothers Inc.
Text set in Palatino by Words Worth.
Design by Barbara Martin.
This edition is published in paper wrappers;
there are 250 hardcover trade copies;
100 hardcover copies have been numbered & signed
by Robert Creeley; & 20 copies lettered A to T have been
handbound in boards by Earle Gray & are signed by
Robert Creeley and Richard Blevins.

RICHARD BLEVINS is the editor of *The Collected Poems of George F. Butterick* and volumes 9 & 10 of *Charles Olson & Robert Creeley: The Complete Correspondence*. He studied with Robert Duncan and Edward Dorn as an undergraduate at Kent State University and holds advanced degrees in English literature from the University of Oregon and the University of Pittsburgh. While editor of Zelot Press, he published work by Joel Oppenheimer, Douglas Woolf, Fielding Dawson, Basil King, and others associated with Black Mountain College. He is the author of *Three Sleeps*, a book of poems. Blevins is currently an Associate Professor at the University of Pittsburgh at Greensburg.